# STORY BEHIND THE BOOK COVER

In January 2014, the author was hiking in the Cascade Mountains near Seattle. He was sitting on a moss-covered log to rest when he saw it. Directly in front of him was this contrast between light and dark. It was stunning and beautiful, and he felt compelled to take the picture. As he sat contemplating the scene, lines from two of Robert Frost's poems came to mind. "The woods are lovely, dark, and deep." And then, "Two roads diverged in a wood, and I – I took the one less traveled by, and that has made all the difference."

# OUT OF DARKNESS INTO THE LIGHT

## Learning to See Life from God's Point of View

Jay R. Ashbaucher

Reid Ashbaucher Publications
Toledo, Ohio U.S.A.

Reid Ashbaucher Publications
Toledo, Ohio U.S.A.
https://ra-publications.us

OUT OF DARKNESS INTO THE LIGHT
Learning to See Life from God's Point of View

Third Edition

Copyright © 2014, 2017, 2021, 2024 by Jay R. Ashbaucher
All Rights Reserved.

No part of this publication may be reproduced, stored in a retrieval system, or transmitted in any form or by any means electronic, mechanical, photocopying, recording, or otherwise, without the prior written permission of the author.

The views expressed in this book are solely the authors. No resources noted in this book should be seen as an endorsement of any kind towards the content of this book.

Due to the changeful nature of the Internet, any web site address or link contained in this book may have been modified or deleted since publication and may no longer be functional as published.

Scripture quotations taken from the Holy Bible, New Living Translation, copyright 1996, 2004. Used by permission of Tyndale House Publishers, Inc. Wheaton, Illinois 60189. All rights reserved.

Copyright permission can be obtained from the author through the following website: https://jay-ashbaucher.com

Cover photo by Jay R. Ashbaucher

Library of Congress Control Number: 2021904995
ISBN: 978-1-7350948-4-7 pbk.
ISBN: 978-1-7350948-5-4 eBook

Printed in the United States of America
U.S. Printing History

First Edition: October 2014
Second Edition: November 2017
Third Edition: March 2021

# Table of Contents

Preface of Third Edition .................................................................. vii
Acknowledgments .......................................................................... ix
Introduction ..................................................................................... xi

1. Becoming Open to the Grandest and Most Marvelous Story ............ 15
2. Truth—A Human Dilemma: What to Do with It ................................ 23
3. What Does It Mean to Be Converted? ............................................... 33
4. Can I Know if I Am Converted, Saved, and Going to Heaven? ......... 41
5. The Bible—Your Choice to Trust It or Not ........................................ 49
6. Is Christianity a Religion of Dos And Don'ts? .................................. 63
7. What Is Faith? ..................................................................................... 75
8. Seeing God in the Happenings of Daily Life ..................................... 87
9. You Have a Theology—What Is It? .................................................... 95
10. Does God Send Good People to Hell? ............................................. 105
11. What Is the True Nature of Human Beings? Who Am I? ............... 115
12. Facing and Answering the Problem of Death ................................ 125
13. How Does God Want Us to View the Church? ............................... 133
14. What Prayer Tells Us about Ourselves ........................................... 143
15. The Value of Suffering .................................................................... 153
16. How Christians Need to Think about Sin in Their Lives ............... 161
17. Trusting a Hidden God ................................................................... 171
18. Love Your Enemies—Forgiving Others and Yourself .................... 179
19. What Is Love—The Kind That Makes Good Marriages? ............... 189
20. Finding a Biblical View of Sickness and Healing .......................... 199
21. Have You Discovered the Power of Why? ..................................... 207
22. Stress and the Calming Presence of Our Faith .............................. 217
23. Healing Our Grief ........................................................................... 229
24. Sorting Out the Gods ..................................................................... 239
25. The Problem with Being a Good Person ....................................... 249
26. Humility—The Virtue That Makes Us Great ................................. 263

Discussion Guide ................................................................................ 273
About the Author ............................................................................... 275

# PREFACE OF THIRD EDITION

*Out of Darkness into the Light* came about because I had lost my voice and could no longer teach. For forty-two years, I have been what the Bible calls a "pastor-teacher." That means one of the ways I care about people and love people is to teach God's Word in a way everyone can understand and practice.

I never intended to write a book because I was content to teach those in my local church and in a one-year Bible college. Then, in my later years of teaching, I lost my voice. Through the prayers of friends, God's grace, surgery, and medical treatments, my voice has partially returned. But at the time, this was a disturbing development since talking was such a key aspect of what I did. I could no longer teach publicly nor even converse with people one-on-one, and that was frustrating. I told people in the church I would wake up every morning and say, "Testing, testing," to see if I had a voice.

One morning, as I was reading the Bible, I came across Acts 20:20, in which the apostle Paul said, "I never shrank back from telling you what you needed to hear, either publicly or in your homes." I suddenly received a flash thought: *I can still teach! I can teach people by writing!* So I began writing. I sent writings in letters and emails to people associated with the church. Some began to encourage me to put these teachings into book form. I ignored this for a long time; I never saw myself as an author for I had no training to be a writer. The only thing I ever learned about writing was from a movie about a writer. In the movie *Finding Forrester*, Sean Connery, a writer, said something to the effect that you simply start writing about things in your heart and then go back and write with your head. *All right then*, I thought, *that must be how you do it, write with our heart and then with your head.* I found that I enjoyed writing, and eventually, through a series of providential circumstances and the continued urgings of others, I became convinced to do it. I rewrote the original teachings and added new ones.

Early in my career as a pastor-teacher, I was intrigued by a verse about Jesus that said, "He knew human nature. No one needed to tell him what mankind is really like" (John 2:24–25). I told God, "If I'm going to help people, I need to know what is in people." Little did I know I also needed to learn more of what was in me.

The opportunity to learn what was in people, including myself, came when I was asked to be a fifth-step counselor at a twelve-step chemical dependency center. I learned what was in people; I heard twenty years of men's and women's and teenagers' life stories. I saw their good and bad sides as they shared the results of their fourth step, which was to take a fearless moral inventory of their lives that often revealed the deepest and darkest parts of their inner beings.

I thanked them all for sharing their stories with me. I saw myself in many aspects of their stories, and when I saw how such honesty helped them, I thought that everyone, including Christians, needed to go through that kind of honest exercise to get to know who they were. Everyone has a good side, but these people's dark sides had overrun their good sides, and they struggled to find their way back to the good.

As I listened to their life stories filled with sadness, heartaches, and regrets over what they had lost, I would ask them if they wanted to hear how Jesus could help them with the particular problems they hadn't resolved. These mostly had to do with feelings of guilt. In all those years, only one person expressed no interest.

Learning much about what is in people and much about what is in the Bible has resulted in being able to better help those walking in darkness to come into the light. I trust God will use this book to help others grow in their faith, or if they do not have one, to find a faith.

It's important to see life from God's point of view because we humans can offer no guarantee for a good life and future. We can become so entangled in life's messes that we become confused and cannot see our way out. We want to live in peace and happiness, not constant troubles and defeats. To do so, we need to see our world for what it really is and not hide from its troubles and pain. Many people live in fantasy worlds of their own making in order to cope with their disappointments; they need lives and futures of God's making, not theirs. Seeing God's view is the way things really are; His way leads to a guaranteed good life and future.

# ACKNOWLEDGMENTS

This book is the result of many important mentors in my life. The following are a few.

- My parents, with whom I got my start as a believer in Jesus.
- Christ Jesus, a friend who rescued me from my fears and the corruption of this world and who continually teaches me what life is all about.
- Trinity Evangelical Divinity School, which gave me a solid foundation for my entire ministry as a pastor and impressed on me that I was entrusted by God to share the good news of Christ and His teachings.
- Kenneth Kantzer, one of my seminary professors, who influenced me to respect others, learn from them even though their beliefs might be contrary to mine, and try to understand why they believe the way they do.
- The Western Conference of the Evangelical Church, of which I am proud to be a part, ever inspiring and encouraging us to be innovative in building the church and the kingdom of God.
- My weekly men's group—Harvey, Tim, and Bill—for continuing these many years to be a support system in my life and friends I can count on.
- My son Andrew, a person with keen insight who encouraged me to write a book a long time before I had any thoughts about it.
- My daughter Tami for believing I could do whatever I put my mind to.
- Connie, my understanding, exemplary, insightful, beautiful, and supportive wife without whom I would not have kept maturing in positive ways to be the person I am still becoming today.

# INTRODUCTION

Life is good, but it doesn't stay that way all the time. The kind of world we live in won't let it. Remember the nursery rhyme about Humpty Dumpty? As I recall, it goes like this: "Humpty Dumpty sat on a wall. Humpty Dumpty had a great fall. All the king's horses and all the king's men couldn't put Humpty together again." What I have written in this book has helped me with falls in my life and with being put together again. I also write about the positive side of life—our enjoyments, our hopes for the future, victory over evil, and a new and good world to come.

On the Humpty Dumpty side of life, I have struggled at times with my faith. Is it true? Does it work? Much of what I have written are conclusions that helped me overcome the doubts that try to destroy my confidence in what I believe. The book makes a good reference tool to keep on hand for when I reread chapters such as "Seeing God in the Happenings of Daily Life" or "Stress and the Calming Presence of Our Faith" or whether the Bible can be trusted or the one on sorting out the gods, they strengthen me intellectually and emotionally and reassure me of the truth of what I believe.

I have also struggled to maintain a strong personal faith that can give me steadfastness, direction, and peace in troubled times. I have suffered at times with fears and panic attacks that make me feel my life is falling apart. I have struggled with worries about the future, with sins that create depressing guilt, feelings of inadequacy, and thoughts of not being a good person. I have struggled to accept my own suffering and death.

In wrestling with these issues and wanting to know what God says about them, I wrote chapters that deal with the true nature of human beings, how Christians need to think about sin in their lives, facing death, the value of suffering, and what is faith. As I engage in these topics, I sense light; those chapters strengthen my faith and enable me to overcome the fear of falling off the wall and breaking. We all need a solid center within us that will hold us together and give us a positive outlook no matter what our circumstances.

I often run into people hurting and struggling with issues threatening to make their lives fall apart. They are trapped in their imperfections, environments, and unfortunate circumstances and are trying to find their way out. I met a man in a train station who was on his way to a halfway house to overcome his drug and alcohol problem. I met a man who felt he was a worthless failure because he could not change things about himself that needed changing. He said he had tried Jesus, but it had not worked. I met a woman involved in prostitution who wanted to start a new life. I've met lots of people whose relationships or families were breaking apart, and they were hurting. As I briefly spoke with these people, many of whom I never saw again, I wished I had had the time to help them understand things that had helped me put my life together again. But no one experiences a quick fix; it takes time and learning, and it may seem that our lives cannot be put together again, but they can.

This book is not just for me but also for those like the ones I met, and all who want to overcome the darkness. Our world is full of evil forces that work against us to cause all that is good to fall. Our greatest weapon is faith. The Bible says, "Every child of God defeats this evil world, and we achieve this victory through our faith" (1 John 5:4). Faith in what? Faith in the person who said, "I am the light of the world. If you follow me, you won't have to walk in darkness, because you will have the light that leads to life." Will we believe Jesus? Will we commit to following Jesus? And if so, what does following Him mean and how do we do it? I have written to help individuals answer these questions. My prayer to God is that He will let us see Jesus and help us develop the faith and courage it takes to follow Him.

I desire that people grow in faith, that is, in the truth, life, and ways of God. Developing a mature faith begins with insight, seeing how things are. I visited one of my granddaughters' high school basketball practices; the coach was showing an instructional video to let the girls see how plays were supposed to be run, in hopes they would be able to run them better in practice. *Out of Darkness into the Light* uses the Bible to help us see life as God sees it. Once we see God's view, we can move toward becoming and doing what life is all about.

I realize some do not like to read. They don't have to read this whole book to benefit; they can read whatever topics interest them. Each chapter focuses on one topic in hopes that we can better understand it and work its truth into our thoughts and lives. But the topics dovetail, and the more readers read, especially the Scriptures, the more complete

God's view of the world will become, and the more their faith will be strengthened.

A major goal of this book can be explained using the analogy of a jigsaw puzzle. A jigsaw puzzle consists of a picture that has been cut into pieces. The object is to put the pieces together. At first, the picture seems very confusing; it is hard to know which pieces go where and connect to what. But as we figure out how to put the pieces together, the picture begins to make sense. When all the pieces are in place, the picture is complete and enjoyable.

Life is like that. We try to make sense of it, but pieces are still missing, and life is not the way we want it to be. The various aspects of life I write about are like puzzle pieces that slowly form a whole. As we put the pieces together, we begin to see the larger picture. We keep putting the pieces together until the picture becomes clearer and makes sense. Like the completed picture on the outside of a jigsaw puzzle box, the Bible is God's completed picture, and we often need to look at it to get a better idea of how and where pieces fit. I want to present many pieces of the puzzle of life so readers can put them together to see the truths, life, and ways of God. We will thereby grow into the beautiful pictures God has designed us to be.

This book is good for believers and nonbelievers alike, for people of faith, and for people who are still trying to find a faith. Believers will grow and mature in Christ-centered faith, and those searching for faith will see what that faith involves so they can make informed decisions. I want what I share to help people think. Personally, I need ideas and truths simplified so that they make sense to me. I want this book to make sense to any reader, but also to be deep enough to appeal to those who like more engaging thought. Right living starts with right thinking, and these writings attempt to present right-thinking based on what God says in His book. The Bible is a book that definitely needs to be discovered or rediscovered in today's world. The psalmist believed this: "For you [God] are the fountain of life, the light by which we see" (Psalm 36:9). "Send out your light and your truth; let them guide me" (Psalm 43:3).

I include Scriptures throughout this book to act as checks on my viewpoints; the Bible's view is what counts, not mine. Read the Scriptures to see if you agree that what I write compares favorably with what the Bible says. It is necessary to see life from God's point of view because if there is an eternal God who is a personal being, who is ultimate life and wisdom, there could be no better source of information about life and the world than Him. Learning should be a lifelong pursuit of discovering true things to replace faulty things. Not everyone needs to see life as I do, but we all need to see life as God does. We are lost in the sea of our own limitations and imperfections if we reject what God offers us.

# Chapter 1

## BECOMING OPEN TO THE GRANDEST AND MOST MARVELOUS STORY

Some people don't like metanarratives, but I have yet to meet such a person. I doubt that *metanarrative* has made it into most dictionaries. The prefix *meta* means "that which is beyond us, transcendent, specialized, or higher," while *narrative* of course means "story." Together, they mean a great, all-encompassing, or grand story that is presented to get others to submit to it or be controlled by it. But people don't like being controlled by anything other than their own self-chosen stories and lifestyles and desires. They don't mind living in their own localized stories, but they object to buying into other people's stories just because other people want them to.

Groups that try to convince people their grand stories are the right knowledge and truth for everyone may include scientists, historians, religions, the church, or political ideologies such as Marxism. Some people object to metanarratives because they think such stories might be false. History, for example, cannot be trusted because it likely contains inaccuracies about what really happened. This trend of doubting metanarratives is a reason why some think the church in many parts of the world has been declining in influence. Whether the word *metanarrative* is in people's thinking or not, many people do not trust the church or the latest scientific word on dieting or anything else that tries to convince them they need to believe this or that. What can be said about such objections to metanarratives or grand stories, particularly to Christianity, the church, and its message?

Metanarratives of course can be false. Some consider Christianity a metanarrative, and admittedly, much has been found to be wrong with the church. It has promoted wars, oppressed people, been unscientific in its thinking, and is full of hypocrites who don't live what is preached.

However, Christians do not profess perfection for human beings but perfection for God and Jesus. We say Jesus came to save us from our imperfections and our ugly behaviors, and He promises a new and satisfying life for all who courageously follow Him (Luke 19:8–10; John 10:10).

As a part of the church, I have apologized in other writings for how you may have been hurt by the church, but I hope you are wise enough to reexamine and discover what you may have missed seeing. Christ-followers claim that the Bible is God's unique story and points the way to an abundant and eternal life. Any failure by believers to live the teachings of the Bible does not nullify the validity of what God reports or teaches in His writings. Those truly born of God (John 1:12–13) want of course to live by the Bible as best they can (2 Timothy 3:15-17).

Many people see the Bible as a collection of stories that teach valuable moral lessons but not as a unified story that invites all to participate in its grand adventure. The Bible is a metanarrative; it claims to be God's truth for all people. It begins with an account of how the world came to be, what went wrong, how God revealed Himself along the way, how He includes us in His plan to restore all things, and how the world will end with a re-creation.

The Bible's stories are related to this great theme of God's work and plan for history. Jesus is at the core of making everything good and right. He is the answer to our individual and personal dilemmas and struggles. If there is a true *metanarrative*, and if God as author did speak into human history, God can give us the true perspective about our lives and world. Someone once said, "God has communicated a story to the world that can give meaning to us all." Christians may have wrongly tried to impose beliefs on others, but we cannot impose anything; we can only make the narrative known. All of us are invited to question, examine, learn, and decide whether we want to trust God's story. So what's new? People were rejecting metanarratives in Plato's day.

Plato (ca. 427–347 BC) wrote his allegory of the cave[1] to demonstrate what it would be like for people of his day not to be open to a grand story. In brief, he told of people chained in a cave and able to see only the wall in front of them. Behind them was a source of light, and

---

[1] Plato, *The Republic*, Book VI, "The Allegory of the Cave."

when objects passed in front of the light, their shadows appeared on the wall. Those shadows were the only reality the people knew. One day, one person escaped and discovered that beyond the light was a doorway that led out of the cave and into blinding sunlight. After his eyes adjusted, he saw all kinds of wonderful things, the way the world really was, and he could hardly wait to tell his comrades what he had discovered and what they had been missing. He went back into the cave and tried to convince them of a grand, marvelous world beyond what they knew. They accused him, however, of falsehoods; they refused to listen, choosing to stay with the only reality they knew, their shadow world. Plato was concerned that people of his day were unwilling to be enlightened by wise thinking, and he hoped his allegory would help them see there was something more to be open to.

Jesus came into our world from a realm beyond this one (John 18:36). He attempted to help people see beyond the shadows (John 8:12), but in the end, He was crucified as a common criminal. Like Plato, Jesus wanted people to see there was more to life than they thought. He knew people loved the darkness more than the light and didn't want to see what the light would expose (John 3:18–20).

People don't want to be controlled by a metanarrative, but they don't realize they are being controlled by their own self-imposed limitations. Jesus came to free us and give life, not control life, but most are not open to see how that works (Galatians 5:1). Early followers of Jesus also tried to help people get beyond their shadow worlds and see the marvelous things God had for those who were open, but few bothered to listen and understand (Isaiah 53:1–3; 1 Corinthians 2:7–10).

In his book *The Last Battle*, C. S. Lewis also shared a story about close-minded people wrapped up in their own stories.[2] A group of dwarves lived only to satisfy their own interests, so they discounted a grand story others told them. They later had an opportunity to enter the grand story and discover all it had to offer, but they huddled in their own circle and remained blind to all the good spread before them. They had always been for themselves and remained that way even after their former world ended. When we close ourselves off to other worlds

---

[2] C. S. Lewis, *The Last Battle*, Chapter 13, "How the Dwarves Refused to Be Taken In" (New York: Collier, 1956), 136–48.

because we reject a story we misunderstand or don't like, we may miss the grandest and most marvelous story ever written, one meant for us. I can understand the scientific community limiting itself to the physical universe that is closed to other dimensions of reality because that is all their observational methodology allows. I am thankful for philosophy, metaphysical studies such as theology, and the Bible because they open us to the possibility of other dimensions of reality and living.

I like this statement: "We don't make truth, we find truth." Some would say, "It finds us." If universal truth exists, I would think it worthwhile to spend my life searching for it. Jesus told stories about finding things so grand that they were worth selling everything we have to own them (Matthew 13:44–46). God encouraged straying and lost people with these words: "If you look for me wholeheartedly, you will find me. I will be found by you, says the Lord" (Jeremiah 29:13–14). God encourages all of us to enter His story by inviting us to "Seek the Lord while you can find him. Call on Him now while He is near" (Isaiah 55:6). In tough times, God gives us an option to seek Him, and He will let us find Him (Deuteronomy 4:27–29). Jesus said, "Keep on asking and you will receive what you ask for. Keep on knocking and the door will be opened to you" (Matthew 7:7–8).

Sometimes, we are in no condition to seek God, so He seeks us and comes to find us. If we are in trouble, He may search for us to rescue us (Ezekiel 34:11–12); He may seek us even when we have not been trying to find Him (Romans 10:20). It is fortunate that truth sometimes finds us. Is there a truth that will add eternal good to our lives and change how we view everything? Yes, a universal, legitimate, grand truth. All the signs point to it for those whose minds and eyes are opened.

Kimberly Shumate, a professed witch, told about her long journey leading to her conversion to Christ.[3] One day, she heard that God had a big story He had been telling to the world, that the Bible was a single unit from beginning to end. This verifiable fact helped open her eyes. She wondered, *How could a book written by so many different people over the course of many hundreds of years fit together perfectly as if one amazing storyteller had written the whole thing?* She told how this among other things impacted her. "I

---

[3] Kimberly Shumate, "I Was a Witch," in *Today's Christian Woman Magazine* 24, no. 5 (September/October 2002), 38.

felt my vanity and arrogance melting away with a power stronger than any hex, incantation, or spell I had ever used. Suddenly, the blindfold I'd worn for almost 30 years was stripped away, and instantly I knew what I'd been searching for: Jesus!"

What will become of those who remain outside the story, those who refuse to participate? Jesus was speaking of the universal story when He talked about the days of Noah (Matthew 24:37–44). After Noah proclaimed the story, the people would not enter the story and get on the ark; they perished in the forewarned flood. Although many do not believe this event was historical, Jesus told it as historical fact to say that our opportunity to enter the story was still being offered. Jesus warned that some would refuse to come out of their caves and some would huddle together in their self-made communities, and would miss out when He came again to complete His story. Whether we believe it doesn't change His grand and marvelous story; and our decisions about the story will determine our destiny (Matthew 25:1–13, 7:13–14, 24–27).

Jesus could be likened to the one in Plato's cave who broke his chains and was freed. It happened by way of His resurrection from the dead (Romans 1:4). And now He comes to us as the one who tries to get us to see. He was clearly prophesied in the days of Moses as the grand storyteller (Deuteronomy 18:18–19). This conveyor of the grand story for all times is the key figure from the beginning of time to its end. He is the Alpha and Omega (Revelation 1:7–8, 21:6–8, 22:12–14). He has always been the central figure in history. Prior to His appearance in our world, He was looked for as the coming Savior (Isaiah 53, 62:11–12; Micah 5:2; Zechariah 14:1–9; Luke 1:67–75). Following His appearance in our world, He is still looked for as the coming Savior (Matthew 24:29–31; Acts 1:11; 1 Thessalonians 1:9–10; 2 Thessalonians 1:7–11; 2 Peter 3:3–13). We are continually reminded He is a central figure in our history, for even our calendar has been determined based on His appearance. Christ's story has and is being spread everywhere (Matthew 24:14; Luke 24:44–48; Acts 1:8). Why then is He and His story ignored by so many? Why do people prefer to remain bound in their chains of ignorance, thinking they are free? Jesus gave His answer in John 8:31–47. Furthermore, His creation is visible to all people, so there is no excuse why anyone who wants to know the story cannot discover it, become one of the many stories in it, and benefit from its progression and fulfillment (Romans 1:19–20).

Why would anyone want to become part of God's grand and marvelous story? There are basically two ways to know the answer. First, ask those who have become part of the story what it means to them. Second, listen to your heart that wishes to be free from the troubles, incompleteness, dissatisfactions, addictions, guilt, or brokenness you struggle with and want to overcome. Is that not enough reason? Decide to follow Jesus and experience His story for yourself.

If you are fine with your life as it is and see no need for learning the story, by all means, go your way; Jesus forces no one (Mark 10:17–22; John 6:66–68). But all need to know that the story is for everyone; all, whatever they have done to feel disqualified, are welcome to enter (John 3:16, 6:35–40, 8:1–11). God's ever-present help and wisdom are wonderful benefits, and the story offers the best hope for the future of our world and its people. Everyone knows our world is not self-sustaining and is wearing down (Psalm 102:25–28). We need outside help for continued existence, and God alone can guarantee it.

The earth can be called a biosphere, a collection of systems that sustain its life. During the late 1980s and early 90s, Biosphere 2 was an attempt to duplicate the earth's biosphere to see if one could be built in outer space.[4] Science still uses the biosphere for scientific studies, but the original experiment failed to sustain human life. People attempted to live in it, but they ended up needing help from outside and ultimately had to leave. After the first group left the biosphere, a second group tried to make it work, but it failed again for another reason: the people involved could not get along due to conflicts among them. Is there any system that has all it needs in itself to work, or will we always have something lacking, necessitating looking to an outside source? Materialists say this world consists only of the physical, with no immaterial substance such as mind, soul, or God. They believe life is lived in a closed system. But in light of evidence of the possibility of reality outside our universe, could something more than we know actually exist? If so, does our

---

[4] The Biosphere 2 experiment can be researched in many sources on the Internet; one is "Biosphere 2: A Successful Failure" by Trevor Freeman, October 2008, www.trevorland.com.

existence depend on such a reality? Are these not valid questions to explore?

Christians believe in a sustaining force outside the universe that is personal and can be known (Colossians 1:15–17; John 17:3). God has communicated to us in the person of Jesus Christ and has revealed in the pages of Scripture His grand purpose for creation. However, too often those who have entered, know, and believe the story do poorly at living it. If we as Christ-followers want to have a better influence and be heard by those outside the faith, we need to do better in advertising it with lifestyles of doing good and loving others (Galatians 6:10; Titus 3:14). Todd Hunter emphasized this point in *Giving Church another Chance*; he wrote that we must "engage the practice of Scripture reading in order to make its story visible and present in our bodily living."[5] Commenting on Todd's book, Ed Stetzer, president of LifeWay Research, said, "The church is not a place to go to, simply another meeting, but the way God has chosen to make Himself known to the world."

Some people claim that they never see God or that He never shows up when needed. Actually, He shows up often through the loving actions of His people in whom He lives and through whom He works to meet the needs of individuals and communities. We believers have the opportunity to represent God to our world each day. Jesus said we would be recognized as His followers by how we love (John 13:35). What kind of love did He mean? The answer is in 1 Corinthians 13. It is the kind of love that makes all who receive it be accepted and healed. Divine love is exemplified by Christ, and its symbol is His cross, which tells us true love is sacrificial. To love like this is to give people who are in the spheres of our individual and corporate lives what they need in spite of the cost to ourselves.

People like to think they can create their own worlds closed to the outside; they believe they are safe and secure and have it made. But they fail to see the insurmountable problems in and outside themselves that prevent a peace-filled, much-sought-after, and pain-free world. In our own stories, this world will never be peace-filled and pain-free in spite of our dreams. When we open up to the possibility of a grander scheme than our own, we discover satisfying and unending potential.

---

[5] Todd D. Hunter, *Giving Church Another Chance* (Downers Grove: IVP Books, 2010), 90.

Jesus came from a kingdom outside this world to redeem a world gone awry. Not everyone chooses to believe there is such a kingdom, but to deny it, one would have to show that Jesus did not live, that we do not have His true words, and that He did not rise bodily from the dead. Of course, that is what some people try to prove. They seem satisfied that they have successfully accomplished this even though such attempts fall short in the face of contrary evidence. So be it! (John 12:37). But for those who believe, what a great hope they have.

Individually or collectively, we could never accomplish a world like Jesus offers; we are too imperfect, needy, and lacking in power. That is why we need Jesus. Where we can't, He can and will. We who know the story need to learn it better, and we need to come out of our caves and into the light not just as storytellers but also as those who live this grand and marvelous story so others can see it in operation (Matthew 5:14–16).

## *Chapter 2*

## TRUTH—A HUMAN DILEMMA: WHAT TO DO WITH IT

A world without truth would end in disaster; truth is essential for a good world to exist. Without truth, trust in one another crumbles, and relationships cannot survive. But even though we know truth is important to preserve good relationships, truth is often perceived as dangerous so that deception and lies become truth's alternative. Children and adults can be afraid of punishment for wrongs done and think that lying is the best way out. Truth is dangerous to us when it comes to revealing things about ourselves that could result in the awful pain of people rejecting us. Truth is dangerous to a person accused of a crime when it means a possible prison sentence and loss of freedom. How often do we want to hide the truth for fear of "being found out"? Courtrooms recognize the need to know the truth, the whole truth, and nothing but the truth because it is the only way for fairness and justice to be achieved. Somehow, there is in people a sense of what truth is and that living by the truth is the way life ought to be (Romans 2:14–15), but we can easily fear it and lie and deceive to protect ourselves from hurt. At times, we perceive that truth can be dangerous, so we avoid it.

A TV commercial was produced for a soda drink called "Splode."[6] Three people, one at a time, bungee jumped off a high bridge to grab a can of Splode sitting on a rock below. The first two each grab a can and drink it. The third person opens a can, it explodes, and the person dies. The observers watching the event are shocked. The true message of the

---

[6] The TV commercial titled "Splode" was created by the Alliance Advertising Agency for an anti-smoking campaign (American Legacy Foundation, July 2000).

commercial is revealed: "Only one product actually kills one-third of the people who use it." The word *tobacco* appeared on the screen followed by the word *truth*. In spite of the truth that a third of tobacco users die of it, people ignore the truth and risk shortening their lives. Why? Not because the truth is dangerous to them, but because the truth limits their desires and pleasures. Many would rather take a chance that the truth does not apply to them than accept it and change their lifestyles. The truth limits their freedom, so they avoid it.

We are in a dilemma when it comes to truth; we cannot survive without it, but we cannot survive with it. Truth is difficult to live with because it exposes our personal evils, and so we fear it, we hide from it, and we prefer to live in the shadows of our lives. Truth can potentially destroy us, but at the same time, living without truth can destroy us as well. The only way we could live with truth is if we knew it was safe. Unfortunately, few find it safe, and so for most, truth must be avoided for the two reasons stated above, to protect ourselves from being hurt or to preserve our freedom to live as we want. No wonder the world devises ways to avoid truth. Still, when we practice truth, we recognize its value and goodness, and truth as a virtue is honored among us. Truth—what a dilemma. What do we do with it?

Pilate, Jesus' judge in a trial, felt the dilemma of truth. He believed Jesus was innocent and should have been released, but if he released Him, he would have a public fight on his hands, and for failure to keep the peace would very likely lose his position as governor. When he questioned Jesus, Jesus told him He had come to bear witness to the truth (John 18:37–38). "What is truth?" asked Pilate, as if to say the question of truth could not be known or satisfactorily answered so there was no point in discussing it. Pilate was not interested in Jesus' truth or in making an accurate judgment and a right decision. He was more interested in saving his position as governor. Perhaps Jesus had something valid to say to Pilate about truth, and Pilate would have done well to listen to Him.

What is truth? Here is a commonly accepted definition: Truth is whatever exists, what is factual, the way things really are. Truth is an absolute reality that will not let you down if you entrust your life to it. We live our everyday lives based on this definition. We live by truth in the everyday world. For example, workers rely on the truth of their measuring tools when they build something. Any measuring tool that could not be trusted to be accurate in cutting boards to the right length or sheetrock to fit the plans would result in a poorly constructed house and would be tossed aside. We also live by truth that exists and comes from outside of our world. For example, when God shows up and speaks, we have truth meant for all persons to live by such as love God and your neighbor as yourself (Luke 10:26–37). God provides us with eternal truth that applies to everyone the same. Some do not believe such truth exists, but it does and is present in our world.

We can know truth two ways. One is by believing something that lines up with the facts. If someone says, "I ate pizza for lunch," we believe that person is telling the truth if he or she really did eat pizza for lunch. If someone says, "Jesus was raised bodily from the dead," we believe he or she is telling the truth if Jesus actually did rise from the dead. The facts are the truth, and we come to know the truth when we believe the facts exist. We can examine evidence for the existence of the facts, but at some point, we must choose to believe that the existence of those facts is warranted. Luke, in writing a gospel about Christ, presented the results of his investigation of the facts so we might know the truth about things that were being said (Luke 1:1–4). Of course, to know the truth, we must also believe the person giving us the facts does not lie. God is the ultimate truth-teller; He cannot lie, for it is not in His nature (Numbers 23:19).

A second way to know truth is through what our senses experience. What we see, hear, and touch are ways we recognize truth. John the apostle appealed to these senses when he recommended Jesus to us as the true life of God for all those who believe in Him (1 John 1:1–3). Many think our senses can deceive us so we cannot know the truth through them, but because we can correct our sense perceptions, we can still learn the truth.

I climbed a hill at a camp and looked down at a pond. It was winter. I saw a dam built of dirt at one end of the pond I didn't remember having seen before. I wondered, *When did they do that?* When I came down, I saw there was no dam; my eyes had deceived me. The pond was frozen at one end, and from the hilltop, it looked like a dam. But when I saw it up close, I saw the truth; my senses no longer deceived me.

In the movie *A Beautiful Mind,* a schizophrenic person sees nonexistent people he believes are real. This was disturbing and troubled his life, but he was able to correct his faulty senses in the following way. When a stranger approached him, he would ask a bystander if he saw the person. If the person said yes, he knew the stranger was not just a figment of his mind. Some say we cannot experience truth by what another person says because we perceive words differently and don't understand what they mean. But again, we can correct such misunderstandings by further communication. Sense experiences may sometimes fool us, but they are correctable.

We humans can be our own worst enemies when it comes to recognizing truth. We hinder truth in many ways. Even though there is a measure of truth that we all must live by, we often cannot see it, agree to it, or more important, live by it. Many things prevent people from recognizing the truth, including refusal to look at and accept data (Romans 1:18), being disinterested, being skeptical or unbelieving, being inappropriately biased, being blinded by Satan's deceptions (2 Corinthians 4:4), believing good-sounding but false philosophies or ideas (Romans 1:25), or a prideful "I am right, you are wrong" attitude. We must overcome such hindrances if we are to discover what's true.

One day, truth entered our world as a person. Jesus made the claim, "I am truth" (John 14:6). Jesus was not from this world; He had come from God (1 John 4:14). During His trial, Jesus told Pilate His kingdom was not of this world (John 18:36). Jesus said on another occasion, "You are from below, I am from above. You belong to this world; I do not" (John 8:23). God became human and lived among us (John 1:1, 14). Jesus claimed God's Word was truth (John 17:17). The truth is eternal, the truth can be known, and God's truth is for everyone. We learn truth when we accept Jesus' invitation to follow Him. Many people believe that truth is absolute and can be known. By absolute, I mean what really exists and is the same for everyone whether we believe it or not. But many challenge or reject the idea that truth is something that is absolute and can be known. That is nothing new. People, like Pilate, have always struggled with truth, and they don't like it hanging over them.

People believe that truth is dangerous or that it limits their freedoms, and so they will find ways to ignore it or redefine it.[7] Here are some

---

[7] An excellent book on the subject of truth is Harold Netland, *Dissonant Voices: Religious Pluralism and the Question of Truth* (Rapid City, Eerdmans, 1991).

statements I'm sure most of us have heard at one time or another. To escape from truth, some will say, "There is no truth that is absolute or ultimate that applies to everyone." Of course, there is no way a person can make such a statement unless he or she knows everything there is to know. A truth that applies to everyone might exist outside the realm of that person's knowledge. Furthermore, is their statement that there is no absolute truth a truth that is absolute for those they are talking to? If it is, there is absolute truth. If not, the person must admit to being wrong in their statement. Perhaps the most accurate statement such a person could make about absolute truth is that he or she does not know whether such a truth exists but doesn't believe it does.

Another statement people make to escape truth is, "Truth is relative; it depends on one's situation and so differs for everyone." Agreed, truth does possess relativity, but it is also absolute. Here is an illustration. Two people in the same room could differ in their attitudes about the temperature; one could feel hot while the other could feel cold. The room temperature is relative to each person's bodily make-up. However, if we have a way to measure the temperature, the room could be said to be absolutely seventy degrees, whether you feel hot or cold. Relativity is a part of what truth is, but so is absoluteness. If there were not some things the same for everyone, life would be chaotic. Maybe the reason we have a chaotic world is that the absolute things that need to be seen as truth are not acknowledged as such.

Some actually say, "Everyone determines his or her own truth, and it is wrong for someone else to put his or her truth on me." If they are saying it is wrong for me to put my truth on them, are they telling me I cannot determine my own truth? Are they trying to put their truth on me? I can agree with them that it would be wrong for me to force my truth on them, but what is wrong with saying a certain thing is true and allowing others to make up their minds about it?

Unfortunately, society cannot live by a code that each follows his or her own truth because some truths everyone needs to follow, like stopping for red lights to avoid chaos. What if my truth is that I can steal from you because we should be equal materially? You might not like that, and so your belief we all should be allowed to make our own truths becomes impossible to live by. I understand that people are aware that they have to live by certain moral standards of truth and that their concern is simply to let them choose some truths they want for themselves. Fine, but don't try to deny the possibility of an absolute truth to which everyone is accountable and tell me I am wrong to suggest such a thing. It would be foolish to say there cannot be absolute truth anywhere in the world (Psalm 14:1).

One other statement people make to get around having to admit there is truth we all need to live by is, "Truth is determined by our culture." Culture is always changing, and so truth changes to conform to what a culture accepts as true. If there is a God who puts forth truth that differs from a culture's standards, are we saying cultural truth trumps God's truth? I'm sure not everyone accepts all the "truths" of his or her culture, so where truths in a culture differ, whose truth wins out? Does a truth that is right according to a higher law, for example, God's law, win out? Probably no; the one that wins is the one with the most power to assume control or the one most people agree on.

What about differing cultures? What if one culture decides might makes right and attacks your culture to destroy you? Should we expect every culture to stay within its borders and live by its own ideological truths? Do we force democracy on other nations? Do they force militant rule on ours? Lust for power or revenge often wins out. Our world has grown smaller; what one does affects others. Who decides what culture is to have its way? It seems to come down to whoever has the most power. Yes; cultural standards do change, but does that mean they are right or good?

Tolerance is a modern answer to all this argument over what is truth. We need to tolerate others and give each other freedom to be themselves and decide truth for themselves. Tolerance works as long as no one does anything to me I can't tolerate. I believe in tolerance and acceptance of people who differ with me, but in everyone's life, some things can't be tolerated. Given the corrupted nature of human beings, the newly defined definition of tolerance is unworkable in creating a peaceful life or world.

Truth, when accepted and believed, is very powerful and can lead us out of darkness and into light, out of evil and into goodness, out of turmoil and into peace. God gives people new life through the truth of His Word (James 1:18). The Bible says that truth leads and guides us in the right direction (Psalm 25:5, 43:3; John 14:17, 16:13). God's truth changes us. Jesus said to those who believe in Him, "If you remain faithful to my teachings… you will know the truth, and the truth will set you free" (John 8:31–32). The Bible makes it clear we can know truth. Jesus is the truth, and we are changed through an intimate loving relationship with Him. Jesus says that we are all slaves to sin, but "if the Son sets you free, you are truly free" (John 8:34–36).

I have noticed many ways that the truth of following and knowing Jesus has made me free. I am free to be completely vulnerable to God and know that I am loved and accepted. I am free to be more vulnerable in trying to help others and risking their rejection because of God's love for me. I am free from fear of death because of the truth that in Christ I will never die (John 11:25–26). I am free to accept the sufferings of life, knowing that they are temporary and that something better is coming. I am free to take criticism from others, knowing it can help me be a better person. I am free to enjoy life knowing it is a gift from the Creator. I am free to live right knowing any other way is destructive. I am free from guilt feelings knowing that I am forgiven. I am free from destructive types of selfishness because truth is transforming me. I am free from the danger of false philosophies and untruths that sound good but can lead me astray because I have access to the wisdom and guidance of truth. I am free from negative thinking and lies about myself that can cause me to feel depressed because I know the truth of what God says about me and can counter those negative or depressing thoughts.

Jesus and His truth have made me free in many ways. I have discovered that rather than truth restricting my life and keeping me from doing what I want to do, I am being made into a new self, discovering who I really am and being free by fulfilling my God-given potential. Freedom is not the right to do what I want to do but the power to do what I was made to do. Truth leads to that kind of freedom.

As followers of Christ Jesus in a world that fears the truth and wants to be rid of it, we realize we are at risk of being rejected or even killed by those who hate the truth. It happened to Martin Luther King and many other martyrs of the faith. Jesus warned us of this possibility: "Anyone who rejects you is rejecting me" (Luke 10:16). As Christ-followers, let us pray we will not fear standing for truth but will be able to wisely and boldly proclaim it when the opportunity arises, for in doing so, we have the opportunity of influencing another life for good.

Jesus was put to death by those who refused the truth but He rose from death to live forever. Truth can never be destroyed, and it does not change. Unfortunately, those who ignore it will ultimately be the losers. Living the truth may produce sufferings, but it also produces a willingness to engage in those sufferings because there is a certain hope that truth will live forever, as will its believers and followers (Colossians 1:4–6; 1 Peter 3:13–17). We believers need to be careful how we engage others concerning truth. The Bible says do not quarrel but be considerate and gentle (2 Timothy 2:24–26). Truth is never to be separated from love. Love is not out to destroy people but to help them come to truth by making it safe for them to receive it if they so choose.

What is truth according to the Bible? God is truth (Numbers 23:19; Titus 1:2). Jesus Christ is truth (John 14:6). The Holy Spirit is truth (1 John 5:6; John 14:17, 15:26, 16:13). What God creates is truth; meaning that the universe is real and truths can be discovered through observations of its workings (Romans 1:20). The Bible, being God's Word, is truth (John 17:17; Psalm 119:160). Truth is the message of God's salvation. The most wonderful truth God wants us to know is the good news about Jesus Christ (Ephesians 1:13; Colossians 1:5–6). The church is the pillar and foundation of the truth (1 Timothy 3:15). This does not mean the church always does or says the truth, but when it accurately proclaims and lives the message of Scripture, it is proclaiming the truth of God. The apostle John said he had no greater joy than seeing the children of God following truth (3 John 4). Following truth means having a proper relationship with God the Father, Son, and Holy Spirit (John 4:24). To follow the truth is to rely on, listen to, believe, and obey Jesus.

If God is truth, and the Bible is God's book, then the Bible as the revelation of God is a valid source of truth. God is ultimate reality; He declares what is real. We can gain true knowledge and wisdom from God, who invites all people to turn to Him and be saved, for He is God and there is no other. If we despise His knowledge, He lets us go our way and we are swallowed up by the evils that come due to our neglect of truth (Isaiah 45:18–23; Proverbs 1:22–33).

Jesus offered Pilate the opportunity to enter the world of truth, but Pilate chose not to listen because he had more urgent and self-serving matters, controlling the crowds and managing the trial of Jesus. But who was really on trial? In the end, we are all judged by Jesus and subject to His lordship (Acts 17:30–32; Isaiah 45:23; Philippians

2:9–11). Jesus said to certain people in His day, "You are trying to kill me because I told you the truth" (John 8:40). Today is still the same—Christ is ignored or "crucified." How so? Christ is killed by Darwinian evolutionists and materialists who say Jesus is not the Creator; by humanists who say that we, not Jesus, are the masters of our fate; by religionists who say they are the way and Christ is only one way among many. Philosophers, scientists, educators, governments, psychologists, and social programmers say they have the wisdom, knowledge, and answers, while Christ and His followers are ignorant and out of touch with modern times and progress.

Christians are accused of not living in the real world. The voices of the people say, "Don't tell us about truth; we will decide what is good and right for us." If Jesus is truth, then the persons who seek God and who come into an intimate relationship with Him are the blessed ones who are living in the real world, whereas those without Him are living in an unreal world full of delusion and ultimate disappointment. Any hopes or dreams not based on truth will vanish like an evaporating mist. Truth is a human dilemma. What do we do with it? Jesus asked, "Since I am telling you the truth, why don't you believe me?" (John 8:46). How would you answer this question? If you were in a face-to-face discussion with Jesus, what would you tell Jesus is the truth?

*Chapter 3*

## WHAT DOES IT MEAN TO BE CONVERTED?

The idea of conversion is well known in our American culture. Kids play with toy transformers where trucks or planes are changed into bionic figures and vice versa. We have converters that allow old TVs to receive digital signals. Jewelers can convert rings into necklaces. Conversion is changing one thing into another. In the Bible, its basic meaning is to turn away from something and to turn to something. Jesus had His own unique terminology for being converted. To one person, He said, "I tell you the truth, unless you are born again you cannot see the kingdom of God" (John 3:3). To others, He said, "New wine is stored in new wineskins" (Matthew 9:17). To a woman, He said that by asking Him, He would give her living water so she would never thirst again (John 4:10–14). Jesus is love and wants to give her the love she has been looking for. He wants to convert the unloved to the loved.

We can ask many questions about the kind of conversion Jesus was talking about. Is it active or passive—meaning, is it something we do, or is it something done to us, or both? Is conversion an instant, one-time act, or is it a process happening over time, or both? Why are some people not converted? Why do people need to be converted? We are converted from what to what? How does a person become converted? Answers to these questions help us understand the meaning of conversion in the Bible. All through the Bible, in many ways, God tries to persuade people to turn to Him. Why? Here are some of God's reasons.

First, God loves the world and wants people to turn to Him because all people need what God has to offer (John 3:16). God offers life, for there is no life apart from God (Genesis 2:7; Psalm 36:9). Following the introduction of death into the world, and because there is a sense in which we died, Jesus came to restore to us God's kind of life (John 10:10;

11:25–26). God's life is the true and ultimate source of all that is good, right, beautiful, peaceful, and loving. God offers us an opportunity to turn to Him because His home is the place we truly belong (John 14:1–3; Revelation 21:3–7). In *Loving Wisdom*, Paul Copan made an interesting observation from the study of nature.

> Arctic terns annually travel 11,000 miles from the Arctic to the Antarctic regions and back again—often to the very same nests. Monarch butterflies follow their homing devices, migrating each year to their nesting grounds in California or Mexico. Whether we realize it or not, we humans have a homing device for God. Though people may not care about God but instead fill their lives with secular substitutes, this doesn't mean that God's presence isn't their proper home, that His family isn't their true family.[8]

St. Augustine, an early theologian of the church, is credited with this statement: "Thou hast made us for thyself, O Lord, and our hearts are restless until they find their rest in thee" (Matthew 11:28). The Bible agrees in Hebrews 4:11: "So let us do our best to enter that rest." To be restored to our true home, God wants to provide us with what we really need—life from above. Like the father and the prodigal son, it doesn't matter who you are, or what you have done, or how long you have been away, he loves you and wants you to come home. Jesus loves you and like a good shepherd who finds the sheep that is lost, he will pick you up and carry you home (Luke 15:11-31; 1-7).

Second, God wants people to turn to Him because evil is real and destroys us and our world. Due to evil in our personal lives and in the world, we often find ourselves experiencing wreckage and heartache. Evil is ever causing damage, ruining lives and relationships. Jesus said all are slaves to evil within (John 8:34; Mark 7:20–23). Even all creation is in slavery to death and decay (Romans 8:21). History has endless stories of nations overrun by other nations causing suffering and killing. War may not occur in free lands, but life-threatening crimes occur every day, and unloving behavior tears families apart. Though we try to run from evil and deny its presence, it follows us everywhere, and we

---

[8] Paul Copan, *Loving Wisdom* (St. Louis: Chalice Press, 2007), 16.

cannot escape it. But God can free us from evil's power and its inevitable undoing of our lives (John 8:31–36; Hebrews 2:14–15; 1 John 4:14).

A third reason God wants people to turn to Him is because people fail us. A secure personal life and world do not come by trusting in failed human abilities or promises, but in God, whose abilities and promises never fail. We all need the hope of a world filled with righteousness, peace, love, and joy instead of evil, and only God promises such a world (2 Peter 3:13; Romans 14:17). Jesus instructed His followers to pray, "May your kingdom come soon. May your will be done on earth, as it is in heaven" (Matthew 6:10). His kingdom has come and is here now, and its future aspect will surely come, and due to His faithfulness, His promises will not fail (Psalm 100:5; 1 Corinthians 1:9; 1 Thessalonians 5:23–24).

One more reason for God wanting people to turn to Him is because no person can live the kind of perfect life required in God's holy kingdom (Matthew 5:48; Romans 3:10, 23). To live in God's kingdom, we need righteousness that only God can give us (Romans 4:5). People need to become new creatures fit for life in God's kingdom; they would otherwise spoil it just as they spoiled this world. We cannot enter God's kingdom without change (Ezekiel 36:25–27; 1 Corinthians 15:50–53; 2 Corinthians 5:17).

Jesus made a clear and astounding statement when He said, "Unless you turn from your sins… you will never get into the kingdom of heaven" (Matthew 18:3). Jesus told us what is necessary for entering God's kingdom: we must turn. By this statement, Jesus also implied that people who thought they were in with God may not be. Jesus told a story about a man who went to a wedding party improperly clothed and was thus out of character with what was acceptable. He apparently thought he was good enough the way he was, but he did not truly belong, and so he was cast out (Matthew 22:11–13). Many people have a lot of goodness in them, and this makes it easy for them to believe they are okay the way they are and that their lives are safe. But Jesus put a stipulation on entering His kingdom. It is not about our being good enough, it is about procuring a needed change, and that cannot happen without a conversion. Because God loves and cares for all people, and is not willing that any perish, Jesus came into our world to help us see what is needed (Ezekiel 18:32; 2 Peter 3:9; John 3:16).

What makes us think about turning to God to receive new life? It may be that our lives are falling apart and we need something to help us get it together. It may be a word someone said that sticks with us and bothers us until we must act on it. It may be a concerned parent or Christian friend saying, "You need God in your life" or a book, or a crisis, or an illness, or a fear of not being with loved ones in heaven, or a financial reversal, or relationship problems, or a fear of death and perhaps God's judgment. There are many reasons for coming to God, but the basic need for doing so is that we experience problems because we are not right with God, we rebel against His way of salvation, and we need forgiveness (Matthew 1:21, 9:2–6; Luke 7:47–50, 24:45–47; John 8:23–24).

We think conversion is our choice, and it is, but it is also God's miracle without which we could not be converted. It is easy to think that becoming converted means just deciding to turn our lives around by trying something different like changing religions or adopting a new set of morals. Conversion in Christianity is not solely a decision to turn from a former way of living to try Christianity. Deciding to change and trying to live the change does not make us Christian. Conversion is a decision on our part to make a change in our lives; but it is also a supernatural action by God that actually changes us, not just something we can choose to try for a while. Someone once said in a prayer to God, "Convert me that I may be converted." Conversion relies on a miracle, God's life born in us. We must allow God to do His work in us. Consider the saying, "People do not need to turn over a new leaf; they need new lives." God can give us that new life by giving us the indwelling gift of His Spirit (John 7:37–39; Acts 2:38–39; Romans 8:9).

How does a person become converted? The biblical story of Cornelius in Acts 10 provides a model. Seeing people who have been changed by God gives us hope that the same can become true of us. Before Christian conversion takes place, there is normally an event or problem that gets a person thinking about a need for change. This is followed by a period of hearing about God or Christ Jesus and learning what He is requiring of us. We can conjecture that Cornelius, a Roman and possibly a worshipper of many gods, must have become dissatisfied about something in life that made him seek for an answer not available through his religion or his own reasoning. Something in the Jewish religion must have appealed to him, so he turned to Judaism. He converted to a religion, but his conversion to God had not yet happened.

Acts 10 reports that Cornelius was a good man who did many wonderful deeds to benefit the people he now "hung around" with. People tend to think bad people need converting and good people don't. This account of Cornelius shows us that even very good people need to be converted. Being a good man was not enough for Cornelius to enter God's kingdom. He needed something more. God arranged, by a series of circumstances, to have him hear and receive what he needed to be truly converted. God sent the apostle Peter to Cornelius' home to share the good news of God's forgiveness and glorious kingdom. Cornelius believed the message and trusted his life to Jesus, and the Holy Spirit came into him, enabling superhuman change to take place.

The circumstances of conversion may differ from person to person, but most often conversion is the same for everyone. God opens our eyes to see our need. We learn about Christ Jesus and hear God's message of grace and forgiveness. By the help of God's acts of mercy, we trust and obey the message, and the Spirit of God transforms us into new creatures (John 5:24; Ephesians 1:13–14). "The old life is gone; a new life has begun!" (2 Corinthians 5:17).

How does God convert us? We are turned from what we were to a new creation by the Holy Spirit when we repent and believe (Mark 1:15; 1 Corinthians 6:9-11). The Bible refers to this as "a baptism of the Spirit" (Acts 2:38; 1 Corinthians 12:13). His divine person and energy flow into us, and we are empowered to be changed. It is a mystery, but this Spirit baptism does not suddenly turn us into perfect people; it changes our hearts toward God in such a way that we want to learn, love, serve, and do His will (Acts 2:42–47). When we are converted, we know our life has turned in a new direction. We have a new heart as described in Ezekiel 36:26–27 and Deuteronomy 30:6.

We can think of conversion as an instantaneous happening when we turn to God, but it also involves an ongoing process of what we could call "mini conversions" or turnings. A word used in the Bible for this process is *transformation* (Romans 12:2). The Greek word is *metamorphosis*, which we use to describe a caterpillar changing into a butterfly. Conversion begins with a Spirit-led decision; the Spirit of God inhabits us, but then, God's Spirit leads us in a day-by-day divine transformation of our lives (2 Corinthians 4:16). The initial and primary conversion involves changing our heart so we find ourselves committed to loving God and His ways. Once this initial conversion takes place, there follows the process of continuing to be converted. For example, people may be converted from bad habits to good habits, from misunderstandings to "Now I get it!" from lies to truth, from not knowing themselves to knowing themselves better, from selfishness to giving, from unhappiness to contentment, from loneliness to belonging, from aloneness to community, and so forth. People can make changes like those just mentioned apart from a Christian perspective and experience, but ultimate change cannot happen apart from Christianity. An example of changes people cannot make without God includes freedom from guilt to forgiveness and peace with God and change from physical and spiritual death to new bodies and eternal life in God's kingdom.

God is interested in fully restoring us to His image. This process will not be completed until we emerge from our cocoons, until we emerge from our graves and come out with new bodies no longer tainted with evil and death (1 Corinthians 15:42). According to the Bible, these bodies will be like Jesus' transfigured and resurrected body (Philippians 3:20–21), and we will live in a newly created heaven and earth. This is our ultimate conversion and destiny. Remember Jesus' words, "Unless you turn from your sins you will not enter the kingdom of heaven." For now, believers are still in the cocoon where they are transforming day by day. Conversion generates new thinking and behaviors, and a new lifestyle develops (Luke 3:7–14; Acts 26:20); we are an ongoing work of God which He will complete (Philippians 1:6, 2:12–13).

Many people say Christianity is their religion but have not had true conversions. They think they are Christ-followers when in fact they are Christian in name only. They may think being brought up in a church makes them Christian, or they may be deceived by initial heightened spiritual experiences or decisions. But their incomplete conversion will eventually show itself. They might abort the faith, fall away from the church, or never mature in their faith (1 Timothy 1:19; Hebrews 6:4–6; 2 John 9).

Even longtime believers could go the other way, demonstrating that their conversion process was shallow. Or if they are truly Christians, only God knows. If there are no signs of growth, there is no reason to believe their profession, nor can they enjoy the assurance that they belong to Christ (1 John 2:3–6).

Considering examples of people who turned away from the Christian faith may help some avoid pitfalls that could lead to their downfall (2

Peter 3:17). Charles Darwin was one person who, by his own admission, went away from Christianity. At one time, he was a professing believer with a conviction that the Bible was the true Word of God. A series of events caused him to move away from the faith. Darwin wrote, "Disbelief crept over me at a very slow rate, but at last was complete. The rate was so slow that I felt no distress and have never since doubted even for a single second that my conclusion was correct."[9] Here are some of the things Darwin said happened in his life to turn him away from the faith. People laughed at him for believing the Bible as God's moral truth. He came to believe that the stories in the Old Testament such as the tower of Babel and the flood were not historical events. The more he studied nature and the fixed laws of the universe, the more he came to believe miracles could not happen. He believed God created the universe and left it, never intervening in it, so he rejected the idea that the Bible was a revelation from God. The writers of the New Testament gospels differed in many important details, which caused him to believe their writings were not accurate. His young daughter's death drove him further from God.

His wife tried to get him to read John 13–17 to help him be converted so they would be in heaven together, but he declined to listen to her.[10] Here are Darwin's words according to one of his personal letters: "I am sorry to have to inform you that I do not believe in the Bible as a divine revelation, and therefore not in Jesus Christ as the Son of God."[11]

Darwin was a gentleman who cared about his family and never spoke against anyone's religion, but for all we know, he was never converted due to these events, thoughts, and disbeliefs he acquired at

---

[9] *The Autobiography of Charles Darwin*, Nora Barlow, Ed. (London: Collins Clear-Type Press, 1958), 85–87 (Charles Darwin's statements about religion in his life).

[10] Emma (Darwin, Emma) to Darwin, C.R., 21–22 November 1838. (wants Charles to read John 13–17). A large collection of Darwin letters is held at the University of Cambridge, and this one is accessible at *www. darwinproject.ac.uk/entry-441*.

[11] Darwin, C. R. to McDermott, F. A., 24 November 1880 (I no longer Believe Bible nor Jesus is God' Son). A large collection of Darwin letters is held at the University of Cambridge, and this one is accessible at *www. darwinproject.ac.uk/entry-12851*.

various times throughout his life. We offer no final judgment on his life, for people can change and only God knows anyone's ultimate destiny. Besides, our main concern needs to be that *we* do not fall away.

We are all at different places in our life journeys. Some never choose to pursue turning to God while others are not yet ready to take that step. They may not be willing to give up something to follow Christ; maybe they think it would make them weird or cut fun out of their lives. Some may think they have strayed too far from God and He cannot forgive them. Maybe they have a false idea of Christianity from Christians who are not yet what God is turning them into, or from a church that has disappointed them, or from wrong assumptions about Christianity. God, however, loves everyone and continues trying to persuade them to receive the miracle of new birth He promises those who "seek, knock, and ask" (Luke 11:9–13). Unfortunately, those who put it off may reach a point of no return (Proverbs 29:1). But Jesus will save those ready to open their hearts to Him.

One final thought about conversion: some may not know exactly when their conversion took place. As Jesus said, "The wind blows wherever it wants. Just as you can hear the wind but can't tell where it comes from or where it is going, so you can't explain how people are born of the Spirit" (John 3:8). The important thing to know is not when it happened but that it happened and that you know you are trusting God and depending on Him for what you need, that God is your loving Father and you are His child. Do you hear the sound of the wind?

## Chapter 4

## CAN I KNOW IF I AM CONVERTED, SAVED, AND GOING TO HEAVEN?

Many years ago, a friend with whom I shared the gospel of Christ was interested in being saved. He asked me how that could happen, so I suggested he get alone with God, open the door of his life, pray, tell God what he needed God to do for him, and ask Jesus to come into his life and save him. About a week later, he told me that he had done what I had suggested but that nothing had happened. I asked, "What did you expect to happen?" He said he thought there would be some kind of lightning from the sky, some kind of feeling that God had saved him. I responded that we were not saved by some kind of feeling or bolt of lightning but by our faith in what Christ did for us and by faith in His promise to live in us if we ask Him.

When I asked him if he had sincerely invited Christ to come into his life and save him, he said yes. I said, "Then Christ must have done what He said He would do—He came into your life. Jesus said He would be in those who believed in Him. Do you believe He did what He promised?" (John 17:20, 23).

The last I heard, he was still persevering and growing in the faith. But how would my friend know if he was truly converted and if Christ really had come into him and was saving him? There may be an immediate knowing by faith, but from a human perspective, the longer-term answer is that such confirmation comes about when a transformation takes place in the believer's life. On the question of how we can tell a true believer from a false believer, Jesus said, "You can identify them by their fruit, that is, by the way they act" (Matthew 7:15–23). Some profess to know God, but the way they live shows that they deny Him (Titus 1:16). Faith is recognized by how it is lived (James 2:14–18).

Can we know that our conversion is real and that we are going to be in heaven someday? Some people think that this is not for us to know, that we have to wait and hope we make it. We should avoid two extremes in our quest for certainty about our salvation. One extreme is that due to our desire for 100 percent certainty, we could become so worried and fearful that we have no peace or rest in our souls. The other extreme is that we are not worried and fearful enough and could miss heaven altogether (Hebrews 2:1, 4:1). There is a reason for concern that some may miss heaven. Jesus said that when He appears, many will say to Him, "Lord, Lord," indicating that they believe they personally know Him and are glad He has come. But Jesus will say, "I never knew you. Get away from me, you who break God's laws" (Matthew 7:21–23).

Have you ever struggled with doubts about God or your salvation? I have. I have thought, *Is all this Jesus stuff true? Does prayer work, or do things happen the same whether or not we pray?* Doubts can be good when they cause us to struggle so we develop a more solid faith, and they can be bad when they cause us to go the other way. Those who are teetering should not give up the faith too easily without taking the time and making effort to search for answers to their doubts.

A variety of things cause doubt, including books that criticize the Bible or people who stir us to question our faith. They might say, "Religion is only a man-made crutch for the weak" or "The Bible is full of errors and cannot be trusted as reliable." Such comments can cause us to entertain doubts, particularly when we are uncertain of the facts. Did Christ really live and die and rise again and guarantee new life, or is all that stuff only a fairy tale? What if Christianity is not true (1 Corinthians 15:17)?

Others may doubt because they see the awful things they have done in their lives, or keep doing, and have a hard time believing God could forgive them: *What if I find out God hasn't forgiven me? What if I'm fooling myself?* Others doubt because God doesn't answer their prayers or because bad things happen and God doesn't seem to care. *Is He really there?* If we have doubts, how do we get past them?

The apostle Paul challenged us with an intriguing statement: "Examine yourselves to see if your faith is genuine. Test yourselves. Surely you know that Jesus Christ is among you; if not, you have failed the test of genuine faith" (2 Corinthians 13:5). Faith means turning your life over to Christ because you know you cannot save yourself.

Are you convinced that only by Him can you be saved (John 14:6; Acts 4:12)?

When we say "turning your life over to Christ," we do not mean simply believing with our minds that He is the Savior but actually putting ourselves in His care and trusting Him to make us right with God and take us to heaven. Imagine standing on the shore of a lake believing a boat can take you across. You know the boat is real because you can see it, but you won't get across the lake until you trust your life to the boat by actually getting into it and letting it take you. Getting into the boat corresponds to committing your life to Jesus and letting Him take you where you cannot take yourself. Trusting in another person is not always easy because others may have violated your trust with abuse or failed promises. You must overcome your inability to trust.

We seek to examine ourselves by asking, "Do I have a faith that trusts Jesus to be in me? How do I know that He is?" I am indebted to R. Gene Reynolds who in his book *Assurance* pointed out that the apostle John in his first of three letters presented vital signs of God's life in us.[12] He likened these signs of spiritual life to our physical vital signs. Just as we check for signs of physical life by checking our pulse, blood pressure, respiration, and temperature, we check our spiritual life by looking at the signs of life described in John's letter. Reynolds wrote that he anxiously sought for freedom from his doubts until he found peace through the Apostle John's letter. I don't remember his exact discussion of these Scriptures, but his discovery enabled him to overcome his nagging doubts and put his mind and heart at ease.

When we see such signs in our lives, we can gain confidence and assurance that Christ is dwelling in us, making us right with God, and convincing us, we have entered his kingdom. The apostle Paul not only posed the challenge for us to examine our faith to see if Christ was among or in us, but in another place he told us, "It is no longer I who live, but Christ lives in me. So I live in this earthly body by trusting in the Son of God, who loved me and gave himself for me" (Galatians 2:20). So we ask ourselves, *If Jesus is truly dwelling in me by faith, what life am I now experiencing?*

---

[12] R. Gene Reynolds, *Assurance, You Can Know You're a Christian* (Carol Stream: Tyndale House, 1982).

We turn to the first letter of the apostle John. He has written to us who believe in the name of the son of God, so that we may know that we have eternal life (1 John 5:13). What does he say that indicates we are truly converted, saved, and going to heaven? Let us be clear before beginning. These are signs of life, not efforts to earn life. These are behaviors we find ourselves doing because Christ has given us new life and new hearts through our conversion. It is possible that a person who is not a true believer could duplicate some of these signs, but are that person's actions and motives self-oriented rather than Christ-oriented? Are they out of a sense of duty to earn God's acceptance? True believers will not be perfect in living these signs of life. True believers will sometimes find themselves struggling with mixed motives, imperfect love for Christ, and self-interest. But in spite of imperfections, we believe God will continue to refine us (Philippians 1:6). The following are biblical signs God's spiritual life is in us because Jesus, by His Spirit, is in us (Romans 8:9). Let us examine ourselves in light of them.

First, if Christ is in us, we will have a lifestyle of willing, voluntary, and loving obedience to God (1 John 2:3–6). A true believer possessing God's Spirit has a new heart that wants to live in harmony with God's will. His will is known to us by what He has revealed in Scripture, by His Spirit-communicated promptings to our conscience, and especially by Jesus' teachings in the Bible.

We professing believers can examine our lives to see if loving obedience to God is how we want to live and how we have been living. This does not mean we will be able to obey 100 percent of the time (1 John 2:1). At times, we may disobey, but we should recognize that and seek to correct it (1 John 1:8–9). It may seem like a contradiction to read John's words that say a true believer does not or cannot sin (1 John 3:6–9 compared to 1 John 1:8–2:2). This is not saying that a Christian never sins but that our new spiritual nature will not permit us to keep doing the wrong things we used to do. If we are walking in fellowship with God, we will not continue to habitually practice the same sins that have been plaguing our lives. Instead, we will want to please God and work to overcome sins in our lives. I have messed up many times in my Christian life, but the Spirit "bugs" me until I make those things right by continuing to let the Spirit guide my life (Galatians 5:16).

The Bible's teachings tell us we must take sin as a serious offense against God; we cannot flippantly say that it is okay to keep doing something wrong because God will forgive us. When I do wrong, no matter how many times I may repeat the same sin, I must sincerely be remorseful, repentant, willing to receive forgiveness, make any needed restitution, and plan to not repeat it. The key questions are, As I look at my overall life, do I see a willing, heartfelt desire and effort to obey the Lord? Can I think of times when I have demonstrated by my choices a desire to live a pure, holy life before God? What are my motives for obeying the Lord? Do I please God because He loves me in spite of my struggle with sin, or do I please God to earn acceptance?

Another way we know that Christ is in us is by our love for other believers (1 John 3:14). Because some people think of church as dry Sunday morning meetings and judgmental attitudes, they misunderstand what the Lord's church is all about. Admittedly, the church is sometimes to be blamed for people's withdrawal, but when people withdraw, they may have a hard time convincing others they are part of God's family (1 John 2:19). While it is true that many people for various and often-good reasons have a hard time with churches, the church as defined in the Bible is where God's people come together. The Bible commands us to love one another (1 John 4:7). Paul commended the members of one church by writing, "Your faith is flourishing and your love for one another is growing" (2 Thessalonians 1:3). How is it possible for this to happen if there is little or no contact with God's family? Our love for other Christians may be lacking at times, and there often seem to be certain individuals who are troublesome, but on the whole, many loving, nonjudgmental relationships exist in the church.

The biblical command to be involved with each other is an area in which Christ's followers can improve. Excuses that they are not "people persons" don't carry valid weight for choosing to be loners. Understandably, some cannot get to church for geographical or personal reasons, but they still can find ways to bless other believers. Christ's community is all over the earth. A true believer can go anywhere in the world, meet another believer, and experience a heartfelt bond. Whenever we are with other believers, no matter where it is, we sense our oneness. Our love makes us willing to lay down our lives for each other (1 John 3:16) and to help meet our fellow believers' needs (1 John 3:17).

So do we have Christian friends? Do we sense a special love between us due to our belonging to God? Are we helping our fellow believers in their times of need? Do we encourage each other in our faith? How do I see myself loving others in Christ's church?

The Holy Spirit, given us at conversion, enables us to know that God's life abides in us (1 John 3:24; Acts 2:38–39; 1 Corinthians 12:13). Satan accuses us of not being accepted followers of Jesus; he wants to convince us Jesus could not be in us; why would He want sinful people like us? Revelation 12:10–11 tells us how we can overcome Satan's lies and accusations. We overcome by the blood of the Lamb and the word of our testimony, the testimony of our faith in Jesus to save us, and the knowledge that even death can no longer destroy us (Hebrews 2:14–15; John 11:25–26; 1 Corinthians 15:55–57).

It works like this in my life: Satan accuses me by putting thoughts in my mind of being too sinful for God to accept. He also makes these accusations about me to God, much like his conversations with God about Job (Job 1–2). When Satan's voice in my head says I am not worthy of God, I agree with him and answer, "I know I'm a sinner not worthy of God, but Jesus died to pay for my sins, and I believe Him. My sins are forgiven, and God accepts me because of what Jesus did on my behalf." In effect, I know I have died with Christ on the cross, I see I cannot save my own life, but I trust Jesus to give me His life. Satan can have no argument with that. The matter is settled. This is how I rid myself of those accusations. The Holy Spirit reminds us of the truth of God's life in us when we need it (John 16:13).

At times, I become keenly aware of my failures to live in ways that please God. I come into the presence of God with a hurting heart, needing to hear His confirmation that He loves me still. I yearningly ask God, "Do you love me? Am I your child?" I desperately listen in the quiet of that moment and hear God's loving, gentle voice say, "Yes, I love you. You belong to me" (1 John 3:1). Even now, when I recall times of doubt and God's response, tears well up in my eyes. I do not doubt it was God's voice; His Spirit bears witness with my Spirit that I am His child (Romans 8:16).

Let us not forget the Bible was written by the Spirit of God (2 Timothy 3:16; 2 Peter 1:20–21). When the words of the Bible penetrate our hearts, it is God's Spirit talking to our spirits. That is why it's so important for each of us as believers to know the Bible. It is the voice of God. When we recall the things God says to us in His Word, we will find ourselves believing what God says—that Christ abides in us, God loves us, He will never forsake us, we possess the life of Christ, and so forth. That is not my voice speaking, it is God's.

Is there a deep sense in you that you are trusting Jesus, not yourself or anything you can do, to save you (2 Corinthians 13:5)? Is God's Spirit through His Word and in your heart giving you that certainty of a personal, secure relationship with Jesus?

Here are a number of other ways presented in John's letter that show that Christ abides in us. If Christ abides in us, we will have the love of God the Father in us and will not love the ungodly ways of the world (1 John 2:15–17). We will confess that Jesus has bodily come from God (1 John 4:2–3). We will accept the apostles' writings as the way to know truth and thus avoid being deceived (1 John 4:6). We will have a genuine interest in and determination to learn and grow from the Bible's teachings. Also, we will confess that Jesus is our Lord and Savior (1 John 4:14–15).

How do we publicly confess Jesus to be a priority in our lives? Through our public baptism, by avoiding foul language, by praying before meals, and by telling people we believe in Jesus. I once asked an elderly man, a faithful churchgoer who was deaf, why he came since he could not hear anything. "I just want people to know whose side I'm on" was his response. He was confessing Jesus as Lord.

Another way we know Jesus abides in us is that we believe in the love God has for us (1 John 4:16). To know deep in our souls that God loves us and that nothing can separate us from His love is the greatest stabilizing element we can have. Knowing by experience God's love can keep us sane and encouraged in times of trouble (Romans 8:35–39).

If Christ abides in us, we will be confident that on the Day of Judgment, we will not have to fear God's punishment (1 John 4:17–18, 2:28). Do we have any fear of God's future judgment? Do we deeply feel His love, forgiveness, and acceptance?

Perseverance is another way we can know that our faith is real and that Christ lives in us. We live in an evil world in which bad things happen to us. If we can work through disappointments or feelings that God doesn't care and has abandoned us or questions about why God let this or that happen and continue to believe God is with us and is good, then our persistent faith is proof," or evidence that God is in us (1 Peter 1:6–9).

It may take a while for all these signs of life to take hold and grow in us before they reveal to ourselves and others our faith and life in Christ. And we will experience ups and downs and sometimes feel we are not making progress. But as we stay with it, we can look back and see our lives have changed. Jesus is working His life in us, and the ultimate change is yet to come.

What part do emotions play in our conversions? Emotions vary from person to person depending on personalities, life experiences, and circumstances surrounding conversion. Think of two people in danger of drowning; one is able to tread water while the other struggles to stay afloat. When they are rescued, the struggling one feels much deeper gratitude and emotion because that person's struggle and agony was greater. Jesus said, "I tell you, her sins—and they are many—have been forgiven, so she has shown me much love. But a person who is forgiven little shows only a little love" (Luke 7:47). The miracle of being converted can feel different to different people, but feeling or lack thereof does not determine the reality of the conversion. It is a person's faith and resulting godly lifestyle that determines the reality of conversion. Our assurance comes from faith in Christ and His acts to save us and from seeing evidence in our lives that our faith and conversion are genuine (James 2:18–24).

Some theologies teach that once a person is saved, he or she will never lose eternal life. Supposing this to be true, people can lose assurance or confidence in their salvation. If they claim an experience of believing in Christ and salvation but do not experience the ever-growing signs of a Spirit-filled life described in the Bible, there is little reason for them to be assured of their conversion and going to heaven. They need to be concerned they may not be saved and take steps to make their salvation sure in their minds and hearts (2 Peter 1:3–11). If we are genuinely converted by God's grace through faith so that the divine nature of Christ Jesus truly lives in us, the signs defined in John's letter will become and be seen to be a part of our lives. Physical vital signs such as pulse and breathing are not things we have to do; they occur because we are alive. When we have Jesus' life in us, the signs are just there. We may have to nurture them, help them along if they are faltering, but they are there.

## *Chapter 5*

# THE BIBLE—YOUR CHOICE TO TRUST IT OR NOT

The Bible is said to be a revelation from God to man. In this scientific-minded world, the Bible is often rejected by those who cannot believe God actually spoke to people and wanted them to put His message in a book. Some skeptics believe those who wrote the Bible made it up. Such skepticism is understandable when you consider the number of religions that claim messages from God. If you study comparative religions, you discover that because their messages are contradictory, it is easy to dismiss all of them as not true. Some believe the miracle stories in the Bible are far-fetched ways to persuade people to believe in God. Miracles are not taken literally because divine revelation and miracles aren't thought to be possible. This is because, in a scientific world, natural causes tend to explain everything that happens without the need of God to make them happen. Therefore, many with scientific backgrounds and materialistic views aren't likely to believe the Bible. Actually, the Bible is probably not read in any depth by most people, including many who believe in it. Most in our technological, communication-crazed, and fast-moving world are too busy to delve into it. Some do not read it is because they think it's an ancient, outdated, and irrelevant book. Many consider those who take the Bible seriously to be uneducated, ignorant, old school, or not up with modern times and cultural changes.

In spite of the fact that the Bible gets a bad rap in the world and is widely ignored, it must be important to many people because it is still a worldwide top seller that has been translated into more languages than any other book. The Bible does not go away; its existence continues to raise significant questions worth thinking about. Is it uniquely different from other books? Did those who wrote it really hear from God? Is there a

God whom the Bible says created the universe, cares about people, and can intervene in our world with miracles? What if those who wrote the Bible and witnessed its events are telling the truth about what they heard and saw (1 John 1:1–3)? Is there any good reason at all that such could be the case? What are the consequences of believing it or not? Should we so easily dismiss the Bible without giving it serious consideration? Is there any reason to embrace it? I have no great arguments to convince uninterested people to embrace the Bible, but I can share a few simple reasons why I embrace it. Perhaps something I present may provide for you a bit of new or previously unknown information that will help serve as another opportunity for you and others to decide whether you will trust it or not.

What is the Bible? The Bible is God's written communication. God gave information to many writers in a variety of ways over periods of time to tell us what He wants us to know that otherwise would not be known (Hebrews 1:1–2). Having recognized these writers were messengers of God (Exodus 17:14, 24:4; Jeremiah 30:1–2; Luke 24:27, 44–45; John 20:30–31; 2 Peter 3:15–16), God's people gradually collected their writings and put them into what we know as the Old and New Testaments. The Bible is God's story of His acts in history. It tells us that God created the world, that His creation became corrupted by evil, that God cares about us, and that He intends to restore all things through Jesus Christ. It tells us that we can become new creations in Christ and establish good relationships with God and each other, that the world will end, and that God will eliminate all evil and create a new universe for His people to enjoy forever. Persecuted people have longed to have a copy of this book, some have died to preserve it, and many have discovered it answers their deepest questions about life's meaning and purpose and helps guide them daily.

Is the Bible a source of unchanging truth worth entrusting our lives to? I have faced my own doubts and skepticism, have searched for answers, have come to certain understandings, and will share with you what I came to believe about it and why. This is an important issue for me because life has very few certainties that serve as an anchor for the soul. Life's storms can twist us around until we are not certain who we are, what life is about, or where we should be headed. Things go wrong, and deceptions and confusion can easily sway our minds. We need a compass we can count on to always guide us. Many self-help books and well-meaning professionals and friends offer advice; they can give us encouragement and helpful words when we are troubled and hurting. That's good, but we need a reality that can provide us with reliable, unshakeable ground to stand on and true knowledge that everything will ultimately be all right. Only an all-knowing, all-powerful God can provide such a hope. The Bible tells us that it is better to trust God than to trust human wisdom that lacks godly input (Psalm 118:8; Jeremiah 17:5, 7). At some point, we must decide whether to accept the Bible as our anchor to reality. After all, if the Bible is God speaking, there really is no higher authority than that. Jesus said that God's Word is truth (John 17:17). Jesus lived and died trusting it.

Based on accepted principles of textual and historical analyses that find the biblical records trustworthy historical documents, I have chosen to accept what Jesus believes about the Bible and what the Bible says about itself.[13] God has spoken; holy men wrote as they were inspired by God's Spirit; and they wrote what God wanted them to say (2 Timothy 3:16; 2 Peter 1:20–21). When Paul said to Timothy the Bible was inspired, he was saying the Holy Spirit influenced the authors to write what God wanted written.

Though the Bible was written by human personalities using their own styles of writing, it is not like any other book. It claims to be God's Word; the authors of the Old Testament said their words came from God (Jeremiah 23:1–2, 25:1). Moses said he received his information from God (Deuteronomy 6:1) as did the other prophets. On numerous pages of the Old Testament, we find words like, "God said…" or "the word of the Lord came…", or "the Lord has spoken this message…" (1 Samuel 3:10–11; 2 Samuel 12:11; Isaiah 7:3–4; Ezekiel 6:1–3; Amos 3:1, 13; Haggai 2:20; and many others). A study of the gospels reveals that Jesus accepted the Old Testament as God's Word, historically accurate and telling the truth (Matthew 12:38-42; 19:4-5; 22:29; Luke 24:44-47). Concerning New Testament writings, Jesus promised that the apostles would have the Holy Spirit to remind them of His words (John 14:25–26). He also promised the Spirit of God would guide them into all truth (John 16:13). When the author of John's gospel tells us

---

[13] John Warwick Montgomery, "History & Christianity," chapter 2, *The New Testament Documents* (Downers Grove: InterVarsity Press, 1965), 25–40.

the reason for his writing (John 20:30–31), should we not conclude that what he wrote was the work of the Holy Spirit, whom Jesus said would inform His apostles? An interesting comment made in 2 Peter is that the apostle Paul's letters were considered to be on the same level as the rest of the Scriptures (2 Peter 3:15–16). Because the Bible is God-ordained, He tells us no one should add or take away from its content (Deuteronomy 4:2; Revelation 22:18–19; Proverbs 30:5–6).

Many religious writings claim to have come from God; for example, Islam has the Koran, and the Church of Jesus Christ of Latter Day Saints has the Book of Mormon. What are we to think of these and others? God gave His people three ways to test whether a message was from God. First, if the message defined God and His ways different from the way God revealed Himself in the Bible, even if there are miraculous signs accompanying their message, it was false and not to be followed. (Deuteronomy 13:1–5). Second, when the message contained predictions about things that are going to happen, those events must happen (Deuteronomy 18:21–22). Third, miracles were a part of what God did to verify His words as true (Exodus 4:1–9; John 2:18–22; Acts 2:22; Hebrews 2:3–4). If other writings claim to be from God but fail any of these tests, we should be suspicious of accepting them as from God.

A fourth can be added: if any other writing presents a message about how to be saved that differs from the one proclaimed by Paul, that word is to be rejected (Galatians 1:6–9). I respect other people, their religions, their writings, and truth claims, and I acknowledge that each has truths that can benefit us. But based on enormous and exclusive differences, I reject the belief that all religions are basically the same. Those differences include how each religion explains life and the world as we know it and the answers given to humanity's important questions such as where we come from, who we are, where we are going, and how we get there. Although similarities exist, a study comparing the religions would reveal wide differences.

How the Bible came to be written is a mystery. Many years ago, while visiting a person, I found out that he was into spirit writing. He heard from spirits and wrote what their voices said to him. Being with that person and talking to him at great length convinced me this was a demonic activity. I was in the room while he consulted the spirits to ask them if I was telling the truth. He wrote their answer which said he was not to believe me. This experience showed me that it is possible for a person to write down information through the influence of supernatural beings.

People have haggled over the issue of whether the Bible's writers wrote word for word what God dictated to them, or if God revealed truth to them that they accurately expressed in their own words. Is it necessary to have to explain exactly how the Bible was written to believe God did it in a way that resulted in His intended truth for all to know? People have also argued over whether the Bible is factually accurate, and if not, if God's truth was still present. There are also questions about the translation of the Bible from the original Hebrew and Greek into other languages; one question being, do we lose the truth of the Bible when we use different words to relate to people from differing language groups? But is it not true that in our use of language, statements can be made in a variety of ways without losing the intended meaning? I appreciate the difficulty of these and other issues. Regarding translations, Bible believers do not claim that every translation or paraphrase is inspired and inerrant as are the original writings of the Bible. Good translators, however, make it a point to be as accurate as they can in maintaining the true meaning of the original languages. If anyone has a question as to the accuracy of a biblical translation, we have accurate copies of the original manuscripts in Hebrew and Greek that can serve as checks.

I make a point to read how the translations I use came about because I want to trust those translators and be as sure as I can of the accuracy of their work. In spite of these questions, I sometimes think, *Why would God go to all the trouble of having His book written but not preserve its accuracy for future generations?* I have made the decision to trust the Bible as God's Word and rely on it as the guide for my daily living and future well-being. I do not fathom God giving me a Bible that would lead me astray from the truths He wants me to know.

I do have questions about some things I read in the Bible; some are answered and some aren't. I keep those unanswered questions in the back of my mind, thinking that one day the answers may come, but these unanswered questions do not keep me from believing in the truth of the Bible. Mark Twain was credited with saying, "It ain't those parts of the Bible that I can't understand that bother me, it's the parts that I do understand." I do not need to understand everything before I can benefit from its message of salvation and practice its teachings for right living.

Following are some of the discoveries that have helped me work through my doubts and questions and accept without hesitation the Bible as God's Word. First of all, I am convinced that the Bible as copied over time has been accurately passed on to us. I talked with a man on an airplane who said he did not believe the Bible because, being full of copying errors, it had been changed over time and is not the Bible that was originally written.

Is the Bible full of copying errors? When theologians say the Bible is inerrant, they mean that in the original writings there were no errors. However, we possess only handwritten copies of the Bible as our original sources, and copyists have made thousands of errors over the years. This is what causes some to question whether the Bible handed down from the originals is accurate or whether the Bible has been changed so that we no longer have the Bible as it was originally written. The sole purpose of one field of study is to determine what the originals said using the thousands of hand-copied New Testament documents in existence.[14] I learned from reading the results of these studies that nearly all discrepancies are simple, fixable errors such as spelling mistakes or omitted words. Other copying errors, less than 1 percent, may be more difficult to decipher, and although some scholars would claim these alter a few of the Bible's teachings, actual evidence seems to indicate that none of them affects any major truth of Scripture. This is because if one text is questionable, the teaching still appears clearly in another text. I no longer question whether we have an accurately preserved text.

Second, I believe the Bible is God's Word because of its fulfilled prophecies. How are these to be explained if there is not a God who has a plan and the power to make His words happen as He says they will? I have considered the beliefs of some that the writers of the Bible wrote prophecy after the events happened, but there are too many predictions of future events that do not fit that possibility. Other religious books have made predictions, but they do not have a perfect track record as

---

[14] Bruce Manning Metzger, *The Text of the New Testament* (Oxford University Press, 1968). Another excellent source on this subject is J. Harold Greenlee, *Introduction to New Testament Textual Criticism* (Grand Rapids: Eerdman's, 1964).

does the Bible. For example, hundreds of years before Christ's birth, it was prophesied He would be born in Bethlehem, and He was (Micah 5:2; Matthew 2:4–6; Luke 24:27, 44–45). How do we know this is a reference to Jesus' birthplace? Apparently, Scripture-minded Jewish persons took this to be a reference to their coming Messiah. Also, could not Jesus Himself have taught it to His disciples during the time on earth between His resurrection and ascension? Knowing the character of Jesus, would He lie or be mistaken about such a thing?

Third, it helps to confirm God's Word as true when archaeological discoveries often verify the Bible's factual content by showing that people and places named in the Bible existed. Bible critics have at times said something in the Bible could not be true only to have an archaeological discovery prove them wrong. The Smithsonian Institute, I am told, approves the Bible as a valid guide to possible archaeological dig sites. It is impressive to read about the amazing Bible-related discoveries recorded in many archaeology books.

Fourth, I believe the Bible is God's Word because I have seen that it is an accurate description of the way people in the world, including me, really are. We are people gone astray and in need of life changes. By hearing and responding to the Bible's good news, many have experienced new and changed lives. The Bible proves itself to be God's instrument to change people (Romans 10:17; 1:16). I became a believer in Christ Jesus because others shared the words of the Bible with me, I believed them, and God used His Word to miraculously change my life. As the Bible promises, "You have been born again, but not to a life that will quickly end. Your new life will last forever because it comes from the eternal, living word of God" (1 Peter 1:23).

How many people who were saved by Christ Jesus have entered into God's kingdom because they heard the message of the Bible (Ephesians 1:13–14)? Most of them is what I would wager. And how many believers in Christ are helped daily to overcome guilt, lies, negative thoughts, grief, or fears because they use the Bible as "the sword of the Spirit" to ward off "the fiery arrows of the devil" who tries to get us to fall into destructive patterns (Ephesians 6:16–17)? Believing the Bible has turned my life around, and the lives of countless others. The Bible's promise of a new birth is a miracle of God, His power at work (John 1:12–13; 2 Corinthians 5:17). Those who have experienced this miracle know they have come alive in Christ, and they can see it in others (1 John 5:12).

Fifth, I believe the Bible is God's Word because Jesus is qualified to know. If Jesus came from God (John 8:42) and was Himself God, (John 1:1–2, 14), and spoke the words of God (John 8:26), this is good reason to accept what He said about the Scriptures being God's Word (Luke 24:44–45). His quotes of the Bible were made with the understanding that it was God's Word and was to be believed and obeyed (Matthew 12:38–41). Jesus referred to David as speaking by the Spirit (Matthew 22:43; 2 Samuel 23:1–2). I don't think Jesus had the original copies of the Old Testament when He quoted from them. The Jewish scribes had an amazing system of making sure all their copies were accurate. He must have believed that they had been accurately copied throughout a lengthy history. Archeological discoveries of Old Testament texts appear to verify this.

The greatest reason I embrace the Bible is because, without the Bible, the world would know virtually nothing about Jesus Christ. The Bible is the only substantial record we have of His existence and life on earth. The Bible reveals the person of Jesus Christ, the one of whom it says, "In these final days, he has spoken to us through his Son" (Hebrews 1:1–3).

A high school graduate wanted a car for college, and his father promised him one. But when the son left for college, all the father gave him was a Bible and the encouragement to read it, for it would give him life and guidance for living. The son thanked him and promised he would read it. All the way through college, he wondered why his dad had not kept his promise of a car. He asked his dad about the car, and his dad replied, "If you had opened your Bible, you would have found a check to cover it." This story illustrates a reason to open the Bible—not for a check, but to discover the person of Jesus Christ. Jesus said that the Scriptures testify about Him and that Moses wrote about Him (John 5:39, 46). If Jesus is all the Bible claims Him to be, nothing in the world is worth having more than Him.

Why would the Creator of the universe bother to provide us with a written document? Because God wanted a relationship with those He created, and chooses what He deems to be the best way to communicate with us. He could choose to appear to everyone in person to let us know about Himself, His Son, and His teachings. I am sure many would like Him to do that, but when He did that in Christ, Christ was not too well-received (John 1:10–11). Perhaps that is not the best way to do it. He appeared directly to His people in Moses' day, but apparently, they were not able to bear it, so they asked that in the future, God speak to them through human means (Exodus 20:18–19). It is certainly possible that unholy people cannot survive being in the immediate personal presence of a holy God.

Another way God could communicate with us would be to reveal Himself to a few trusted people and have them pass on to others by word of mouth what He said. This is what He has done, but what would likely happen to His message after the original messengers died and all we had was an oral tradition from generation to generation? It is not a stretch of our imagination to believe that the message would be forgotten in its original form or that its true message would be changed and thus be lost to future generations. The Bible is a way for God to preserve His message throughout the history of the earth. I know for myself that because of important things I want my children and grandchildren to know when I am gone, I plan to leave a written record for them, and hopefully, it will be passed to all my future generations. I am glad God left a written record of His acts in history, because through that book, by faith in its truths, many others and I have come to know about God and Jesus, and we have been enabled to know Him personally as a redeemer and friend.

Following are other problems I wrestled with to keep faith in the Bible. Five are listed below, but rather than expound on these issues that other books cover in great detail, I will simply ask a few questions that when answered with information that is available for you to discover can point toward sensible solutions. One issue I wrestled with involves problems raised by critics, those who say the Gospels do not contain Jesus' words and deeds but only what church leaders wanted the Gospels to say to promote their purposes. In other words, the Bible's writers made up what they wanted people to believe. But here are my questions: Why can't the Gospels be firsthand accounts accurately passed down by honest eyewitnesses (Luke 1:1-4; 1 John 1:1–2; 2 Peter 1:16)? Why can't God's Holy Spirit make sure His words and deeds were remembered and recorded (John 14:26)? These are strong possibilities.

Second, many point to what they see as contradictions or inaccuracies in the Bible. For example, the Bible is not true because the gospel writers differ in the number of women who went to the tomb and the number of angels who were at the tomb during the resurrection event (Matthew 28:1; John 20:1; Mark 16:5; Luke 24:4). Could not each writer have had his own purpose for writing that did not necessitate sharing the same facts? Or might it be that a reason they did not all agree is because all the facts were not available to each of them the same? Perhaps it would be quite possible to explain discrepancies if all the facts were known.

Kenneth Kantzer, one of my seminary professors, told of a person who received a report that the mother of his friend had been hit by a car and killed instantly. Another report said the mother had been hit by a bus. The reports seemed contradictory until the facts became known. She had been first hit by a bus, and a car picked her up and was rushing her to the hospital when they were hit by another car. Both reports were true, even though each person reporting the facts did not know all the facts.

Books have been written that identify hundreds of supposed contradictions in the Bible, and they give plausible answers that make sense. I am not suggesting every explanation is correct, but the point is that reasonable explanations could remove these supposed problems. People can choose not to believe the Bible by making these issues insurmountable problems; often, they are not willing to hear any explanations or discuss solutions. Some people don't want to believe, are not open to consider other ideas, and will use any excuse to justify their unbelief. I do not negate that they may have good reasons for not believing, but I question their unwillingness to consider possible solutions.

Third, some claim that miracles are not possible, that they were primitive ways for uninformed people to explain life's mysteries. It's accepted today that modern science and the philosophy of naturalism can explain all events in the universe scientifically and naturally, so there is no need for "otherworldly" explanations. But why can't the universe be open to divine intervention instead of being closed to divine intervening possibilities? Similar miracles happen in the world today that millions of people testify to, so why could they not have happened in Bible times?[15] Certainly, if there is a God as the Bible portrays, He can enter our world as He wishes.

Fourth, some say no one can really claim that the Bible's truths are the same for everyone because everyone reads the Bible according to his

---

[15] Craig S. Keener, *Miracles: The Credibility of the New Testament Accounts* (Grand Rapids: Baker Academic, 2011).

or her own subjective views and interpretations. But why can't there be one interpretation intended by the author of Scripture so that if we set aside our ideas as much as possible and objectively seek to understand the message intended, we are more likely to see it? After all, if I write a letter to someone, I don't intend that those who read it can take it to mean whatever they imagine. I expect them to understand it as I intended. We need to read the Bible to discover what God intended in His message; most of it is not hard to figure out. We are generally capable of understanding what others tell us; should we not give proper effort to try to learn what God intends? There are rules we use to understand any piece of literature. Aren't such rules useful to help us interpret the Bible?

Must people always understand the Bible as God intended it? I think that is the proper goal, but I have no problem if God wants to use His Word to speak to people in unusual ways. Here is what I mean. An acquaintance told me that a fellow worker once reprimanded him for a simple oversight. He suddenly felt a surge of anger and wanted to punch the man. Immediately, a King James Version Bible verse came into his mind, "Lay hands suddenly on no man," and he resisted giving in to the temptation to become wrathful. I laughed, and I was sure he couldn't understand what I was laughing about. That is not how the verse was meant to be applied. The verse is found in 1 Timothy 5:22 and typically has been understood to refer to laying hands on the head of a person to ordain that person to some ministry in the church. Timothy was not to put a person into a ministry before that person had been determined to be reliable and qualified. The application of that verse to my friend's situation was totally out of context. But so what? The Spirit of God used it to keep my friend from giving in to his anger. People can make the Bible mean anything they want it to mean to justify their actions or beliefs, but I am not one for using verses out of context. However, in this case, I thought, *So what?* I think God also enjoyed it and was pleased the man wanted to be the kind of person who cared to do right.

Finally, ethical issues can be a huge problem; they have bothered me. Many are so bothered that they are tempted to not want to believe in God or the Bible. For example, sensitive persons may ask, "How can a loving God command His people to go to war and kill men, women, and children?" or "How can a loving God allow evil to keep going?" It seems that God lets innocent people die and evil people thrive, which is difficult to accept. The Old Testament father of our faith, Abraham, dealt with the issue of God destroying innocent people (Genesis 18:20–33). Habakkuk, an Old Testament prophet, wrestled with the issue of God allowing the wicked to get away with evil (Habakkuk 1:13). Here are questions that I have asked and answered for myself. Does the judge of all the earth do right in all He does? If God is good, loving, and just, can we trust He never commits wrong in any of His actions? Is it possible we cannot understand His goodness, love, and justice due to our finite minds? Would not a further and more complete study of the circumstances surrounding these ethical issues answer some of our objections? I am thankful for people who have concerned themselves with these issues and have written about them, for example, *Is God a Moral Monster?* by Paul Copan.[16] When we come to problems that make it hard for us to believe the Bible, we can let the problem stand unchallenged, say there is no answer, and let it eat away at us until we give up faith in God and the Bible. Or, we can believe there is an answer to our questions or doubts and do some serious searching to bolster our confidence in God and in the trustworthiness of the Bible. I take the approach that there must be a valid answer to my questions, and I will not so easily accept criticisms, problems, or possible misconceptions that turn me from God and the Bible. Many try to discredit the Bible, and will readily accept any proposed problem without examining things further. By having looked further into these issues, I have decided that the Bible can be trusted, so I choose to keep building my life on the Christ it reveals and on its teachings. Although it is not my motive for trusting the Bible, I would hate to be on the wrong side if it proved to be true (Hebrews 2:1–3). Also, I realize that believing the Bible is not what makes it true; real things are true whether we believe them or not, and I believe the Bible to be in the "real and true" category.

I use the Bible in a variety of ways, and there are also ways I do not use the Bible. One way I use the Bible is to read and study it to get a sense of who God is and to give God an opportunity to speak to me. The Bible is the voice of God that communicates His goodness for my life. I also need frequent reminders to keep me on God's path (2 Peter 3:1–2; Psalm

---

[16] Paul Copan, *Is God a Moral Monster? Making Sense of the Old Testament God* (Baker Books, 2011).

119:105; 2 Timothy 2:14). I use the Bible as a counselor to learn who God says I am and to give me direction for right living (Psalm 73:23–25). I use the Bible for comfort and encouragement when I am hurting (Psalm 119:50, 82). I use the Bible to meditate and get deeper insights and to draw intellectually and emotionally closer to God (Psalm 119:97–100). I use the Bible to teach others and myself so we can have a better understanding of what it means (James 3:1; Hebrews 5:12; Deuteronomy 6:6–7; Ephesians 6:4). I trust the Spirit to bring certain Scriptures that I have previously learned into my mind to change a negative thought (Philippians 4:8), to ward off temptations (Luke 4:3–4), or to give me hope and joy in times of sorrow (1 Thessalonians 4:13–18).

I do not use the Bible in certain ways. I do not use the Bible to promote myself as one who knows more than others. I will continue to learn and correct any wrong views pointed out to me. Nor do I use it to unquestionably support my personal biases instead of trying to be open to what the text is really saying. I want to say what the Bible says, not use it to confirm what I say. Finally, I try not to use it to manipulate people through guilt or fear. It is the Holy Spirit's job to speak to each person's life and needs.

The Bible is as trustworthy today as it was in Moses' day when he recorded and passed on God's words as follows: "You must commit yourself wholeheartedly to these commandments that I am giving you today. Repeat them again and again to your children" (Deuteronomy 6:6–7). The Bible is as trustworthy today as it was in Joshua's day when he wrote, "Study this Book of Instruction continually. Meditate on it day and night so you will be sure to obey everything written in it. Only then will you prosper and succeed in all you do" (Joshua 1:8). The Bible is as trustworthy today as it was in David's day when he benefitted from it.

> Oh, how I love your instructions! I think about them all day long. Your commands make me wiser than my enemies, for they are my constant guide. Yes, I have more insight than my teachers… I am even wiser than my elders. (Psalm 119:97–100)

The Bible is as trustworthy today as it was in Isaiah's day. "It is the same with my word. I send it out, and it always produces fruit. It will accomplish all I want it to, and it will prosper everywhere I send it" (Isaiah 55:11). The Bible is as trustworthy today as it was for Jesus, who used it to defeat temptations from His enemy: "People do not live by bread alone, but by every word that comes from the mouth of God" (Matthew 4:4, quoting from the Old Testament). The Bible is as trustworthy today as it was in Paul's day when he said to a young man named Timothy, "You have been taught the holy Scriptures from childhood, and they have given you the wisdom to receive the salvation that comes by trusting in Christ Jesus" (2 Timothy 3:15).

The Bible is to be used today as it has always been used, to promote God's warnings, to declare His salvation, to enable us to know and love the triune God, and to teach godly living. I very much prefer not to live in the prison of a closed universe; one that the scientific world in agreement with the Bible has discovered is dying (Isaiah 51:6). I would rather know that there is something existing and real outside our universe that will satisfy my longings. I enjoy this life and this world and those I love too much to want to see everything end, and me with it. If what the Bible says about Jesus is true, then a personal being outside our material world sustains it, cares about it, and promises a never-ending future.

The Bible is physical evidence I can examine to see if it offers concrete and probable cause to trust it. I choose to complement my faith with adequate reasoning because I do not want to put faith in something unwarranted and false. For me, the Bible has enough evidence to warrant taking it as a trustworthy and divinely given book. If we agree that the evidence for its truth is enough to warrant our trust, the certainty it conveys to us is that the universe is open and there is something beyond that is worth discovering. As others have discovered, the Bible is a true and ongoing story that invites us to enter its story, become part of it, and experience its amazing adventures in this age and in the age to come. The Bible: your choice to trust it or not.

## *Chapter 6*

# IS CHRISTIANITY A RELIGION OF DOS AND DON'TS?

I was mildly jolted one day by a comment from a friend whom I viewed as a strong Christian: "I get tired of trying to be a good Christian and trying to live a good life." Apparently, my friend did not fully understand what a relationship with Jesus was all about. Even though Jesus promotes right living, the Bible says that God's "commandments are not burdensome" (1 John 5:3). I wonder how many feel overwhelming pressure to be good and to be constantly under the weight of having to obey all the rules and commands of the Bible and the church. How many at times feel bad because they are not living up to what they believe God requires of them? Some may avoid church for this reason; some may hesitate to become Christians because of what they believe God will require of them, or because they think they cannot live up to the standards or even want to. Outsiders and maybe some Christians often see Christianity as a religion of dos and don'ts, with people judging them or God condemning them if they fail to obey the prescribed religious rules. Those who think these ways misunderstand what Christianity is about, but here are two reasons people are justified in feeling and thinking these kinds of thoughts.

First, the Bible does give many rules, including the Ten Commandments (Exodus 20:1–17). God says in the Bible that those who obey Him shall live and those who don't shall suffer loss or die (Numbers 15:32–36; Deuteronomy 5:31–33; 1 Kings 9:4–7; Ezekiel 18:18–20). God told Adam and Eve that if they disobeyed His command, they would die (Genesis 2:16–17). God put to death a number of persons who disobeyed His commands (Leviticus 10:1–2; Joshua 7:20–26; Acts 5:1–11). Jesus said we are to be perfect as God is perfect (Matthew 5:48). The Old and New Testaments tell us to be holy because God is holy (Leviticus 19:2; 1 Peter 1:15–16). The Bible says that we will be judged on the basis of our deeds and that our destiny will be determined on judgment day (Matthew 25:41–46; Romans 2:1–11; 2 Corinthians 5:9–10; Revelation 20:11–15). The Bible is clear: obey and live or disobey and die (Proverbs 19:16).

Second, people are justified in believing that Christianity is a religion of dos and don'ts because the church preaches that we are to obey the teachings of the Bible. Unfortunately, the way the church preaches this often makes people feel guilty and ashamed for not living up to God's standards. Someone told me how the elders of his church would stand around the town's movie theater to see if church members attended, and they were reprimanded if they did. Twice in my ministry as a pastor-teacher, I was told I should make people feel guilty to motivate them to live better. People can be put under pressure and made to feel second-class for failing to live right. No wonder people feel that Christianity is a bunch of rules. Thus, for the two reasons stated above, it is easy for people to conclude Christianity is a religion of dos and don'ts.

It is easy to be confused about the Bible's teaching on this subject and be involved in something called legalism. Legalism is defined as strict, literal conformity to religious laws in an effort to earn the favor of God or others. Problems result from this approach to the Christian faith. Some may become discouraged and drop away from Christianity because they become tired of trying to live up to standards they can't meet. Another problem results when people tend to judge one another on performance, and those who judge think that they are right or better than others. Self-righteousness and hypocrisy are problems because there is a tendency to reject persons who need love and acceptance (Luke 18:9-14). As a consequence, those who need acceptance but fear judgment will hide their true identity so others will think well of them. This discourages honest and open sharing needed to help each other get healthier and more mature in our walk with God (James 5:16). Christians can also self-righteously have nothing to do with those outside the faith whom they judge as sinful. But this judging is clearly forbidden by the apostle Paul (1 Corinthians 5:9–10).

Is Christianity a religion of dos and don'ts? The Bible is divided into two parts: the Old Testament and the New. The Old Testament contains what is called the Law of Moses, or simply the Law (2 Chronicles 34:14). The New Testament contains the gospel, which means the good news about Jesus Christ (Mark 1:1). These are two testaments—that is, two covenants or agreements God made with His people. In the Old Testament, His people were primarily the nation of Israel (Deuteronomy 5:1–3; 6:1–7). In the New Testament, His people are the church (1 Peter 2:9–12). In each covenant, God sets the terms for His people. Concerning the Old Covenant, the agreement was that God would provide laws for good and right living, and in return, His people would agree to obey these laws because God had rescued them from slavery and was thus worthy of their loving obedience (Exodus 19:4–8). God created a people for Himself and wanted them to live by His laws as a witness of the true God who differed from the false gods of surrounding nations. Concerning the New Covenant, God provided a Savior, Jesus Christ, and on the basis of what Christ did through His life, death, and resurrection, God offers to graciously forgive people for their disobedience to His laws and to put a new, divine dimension of life in them (Luke 24:46–49; Hebrews 10:16–18). His people agree to these terms and are to live by faith (Galatians 2:19–20).

But the new way does not mean that God's laws are bad or that there are no laws to live by. In fact, even those outside Israel and the church are responsible to God for how they live. All people have a moral conscience and are judged by whether they obey it (Romans 1:18–32, 2:12–16). No one escapes rule-keeping as is implied in the biblical statement, "You will always harvest what you plant" (Galatians 6:7).

There is something about the Old and New Testament covenants God made with His people that can be confusing. They are alike in some ways but not alike in others. Here are two ways in which the Old and New covenants are alike. In both, God's people were to practice God's laws and moral teachings with a heart of love for God (Deuteronomy 6:5–6; John 14:21). Also, both testaments contain a message about Christ that all are encouraged to believe (Galatians 3:8–9; John 8:56; Hebrews 11:13). Believing God's word and obeying it are alike in both testaments, so it seems the Christian faith does have dos and don'ts. But the Old and New Testaments are also not alike and when we understand the difference between these covenants of Law and gospel, we can see how Christianity is not a religion of dos and don'ts. Thus, followers of Jesus have a faith of dos and don'ts, and they do not have a faith of dos and don'ts. I warned you it can be confusing. How can both be true?

Consider the difference between the Law and the gospel. The Law, based on God's character of righteousness, demands perfect obedience. Justice must be done whenever it is violated. The only mercy provided was a temporary built-in sacrificial system (Leviticus 16:15–18), but that did not remove sin and make us perfect (Hebrews 10:1–5). The Law can never give us a right standing with God because we cannot keep it, and so God's just and fair punishment is always upon us; we can never escape its curse and condemnation (Galatians 3:10; Romans 1:18; Ephesians 5:6; John 3:36). Even failing in one law while keeping the others is enough to condemn us (James 2:10–11).

On the other hand, the gospel does not demand law-keeping and perfect obedience for us to be right with God. Recognizing we are not capable of obeying the Law, the gospel is an offer of mercy and forgiveness granted us through faith (Galatians 2:16; Romans 4:4–5). The gospel can give us a right standing with God because Jesus Christ, by dying on the cross, has received God's punishment in our place; Jesus provided the perfect sacrifice for us (Isaiah 53:4–6; 1 Peter 2:24). God can be merciful and declare us to be right with Him based on our repentance and faith in what Christ Jesus did for us (Romans 3:21–26, 4:5). Those who trust Christ Jesus to be their Savior escape condemnation (Romans 8:1).

In summary, the Law is do or die; the gospel is living by faith (Galatians 3:11–12). The Law destroys right standing with God because we can't keep it; the gospel provides right standing with God because God's justice is satisfied by Christ, whose life and death have provided for our forgiveness (1 John 1:9, 2:1–2).

If the Law could never make us right with God, why did He give it to us? Besides being God's way for His people to live and so distinguish them from others (Deuteronomy 28:9-10), there are two primary reasons for the Law. One is to show people their sinfulness by giving them a standard by which to measure themselves (Romans 3:19–20; Galatians 3:19). And once we see that the Law does not work as a way for becoming right with God a second purpose for the law kicks in; it makes us seek another way of becoming right with God (Romans 3:20–26). That way is through the gospel of Christ. The Law was never meant to be a way by which we could be saved or made right with God; it was meant to reveal our sinfulness and show us our need for a Savior. The Bible makes the point that God gave the gospel before He gave the Law and therefore the gospel is God's better way to live (Galatians 3:6–9).

There is a huge difference between obeying the Law and obeying the gospel. It is like the difference between having to do something you don't want to do and wanting to do something because you love doing it. We must obey God's Law because if we don't there are consequences we do not want to experience. Even if we want to obey God's Law because we love God (Psalm 119:97, 129, 137) we find we fail at it, and that is disheartening and leads to judgment and death (Psalm 32:1-4; 51:1-4). By being under pressure to live by the Law, it is easy to think the Bible is full of dos and don'ts in a negative sense and we can get weary of having to try to keep them. But the gospel is based on grace and love. We feel we want to obey the gospel because it is motivated by the love of God for us and our love for Him. Experiencing God's love motivates people to receive the dos and don'ts in a positive sense and want to keep them (Psalm 51:10-12). Your relationship with God determines if you obey God's rules grudgingly or willingly.

Can you see what is meant by Christianity being a religion of dos and don'ts and not being a religion of dos and don'ts? The moral laws of God seem effortless to obey if we are given a heart of love that wants to obey them (Matthew 11:30; Romans 5:5). The motivation of love born in us by faith in Christ Jesus makes all the difference in how we view the dos and don'ts of the Bible. In Jesus' day, there was a rule about how to treat guests in your home. A man and a woman treated Jesus differently. Jesus made a point about this by saying that love determines how you will practice the rule about receiving a guest (Luke 7:47). We do not all love and obey God the same. Varying degrees of experiencing God's love is why some will be better at wanting to obey God. Love is the ultimate mover, and the Christian's task is to seek to experience God's love more deeply. Thankfully, God promised to give His people a heart to be able to love Him, a heart inclined to respond rightly to His teachings and commands (Jeremiah 31:31–34; Ezekiel 36:25–27; Romans 5:5).

Jesus and John the apostle said that if we love God, we will keep His Commandments (John 14:21–24; 1 John 2:5). When we love God, we more readily want to keep His Commandments. But sometimes, we obey with an unwilling spirit, and even though doing the right thing without liking it is still an act of love, we can conclude that we are not allowing

His love to be fully experienced. The problem is not God or the command, but our hearts. We lack or resist God's love.

Though I am a follower of Christ, at times, I battle against doing what God asks me to do (Galatians 5:16–17). With gentle reminders, God never lets me off the hook. I know what He wants me to do is the right thing. For example, He has asked me to confess to some people how I had wronged them and to ask their forgiveness. I eventually did it but with fear of rejection and not wanting to humble myself due to pride. He also has asked me to help needy persons who were seeking handouts. I did so but with feelings of resentment for being interrupted in my schedule or anger at them for not having their lives together.

These experiences made me realize I didn't love God or others as He would want or I would have felt freer to happily obey Him. These were tests of my own heart to show me where I stood. But these thoughts of wanting a greater heart of love made me realize I have already received the desire to have a heart like His, a heart that wants to love others as He loves me (1 John 4:19). As I grow in His love, following His commands will not be a duty or burden but a loving response from my heart. Undoubtedly, future things God will ask me to do will reveal how I am doing in becoming more like Jesus. If I am in His love and His love is in me, I will do His will naturally, like breathing. As we go through life, if we are engaged in spiritual formation, growth toward this ideal of love should happen.

How does disobeying the Law differ from disobeying the gospel? When I disobey the Law, I am guilty, feel like a failure, and fear God's punishment and consequences. I keep trying to do better at pleasing God, but it's never good enough. When I disobey the Law, I can easily give up and think God is a mean ogre for requiring from me things I can only fail at. Before his conversion, Martin Luther felt this way about God and could never have peace because of God's judgment constantly hanging over him. But when he came to the truth, he found peace.[17]

Disobeying the gospel is an entirely different experience. I feel sorrow over disappointing God. I tell Him that I want to overcome the wrongs in my life and ask for His help. I try to figure out why I messed up and what I can do to overcome it. I thank Him that I am forgiven through what Christ Jesus did for me. I carry no ongoing

---

[17] James Kittleson, *Luther the Reformer* (Minneapolis: Augsburg, 1986), 79.

guilt and feel free from judgment or condemnation (Romans 8:1). As I experience more deeply God's faithful forgiveness and love for me, I am increasingly motivated to love, serve, and obey Him. His patient, gentle reminders of my wrongdoing never seem harsh or demeaning. His acceptance is felt always, maybe His disappointment at times, but always acceptance. He does not give up on me.

To summarize, in the Law scenario, disobeying the dos and don'ts results in guilt, discouragement, and feelings of failure and condemnation. I feel I can never be acceptable to God. But in the gospel, or "good news" scenario, although disobeying the dos and don'ts may result in feelings of guilt, there is instant forgiveness, no ongoing guilt, and a sense that I am still loved.

How could we answer my friend who thought being a Christian was too hard with too many rules to obey? Perhaps we could ask questions whereby he could make his own determination of changes needed in his thinking and life. It could be asked, Are you looking at God's commands as duties you must perform or as welcome guides to living that make your life more secure, healthy, and mature? Is your personal relationship with God one of genuine love and friendship, or is it an authoritarian relationship in which you see God as demanding and unbending? Do you have a deep, heartfelt appreciation for what God did for you on the cross, or do you take Him for granted with little feeling toward what He has done for you? Do you welcome God's teaching in your life, or do you resent it? Like the psalmist, do you really love God's laws, seeing them as great guidelines and benefits for your life (Psalm 119:97–100)? Are you obeying as one who thinks he must keep the letter of the Law or as one who understands what it means to be freed from the Law, having within God's Spirit of new life (Romans 7:6; 2 Corinthians 3:6)? Do you have an understanding of the difference between the old and new covenant, and are you alive to the new? Are you trying to do it on your own, or do you ask God's help daily? Are you relying on your own power to obey, or are you relying on the help of God's Spirit (Galatians 3:2–3)? Do you feel God loves you, even when you disobey Him?

A new commandment, which is not new, is having a changed heart, being willing and able to live by God's rules without fear if we fail, and without external pressure to have to perform them in order to be loved (1 John 2:7–8).

Although it was never meant to be, the Law for many has come to mean a way of achieving heaven. A man came to Jesus with the impression that keeping the Law was something He could do to get to heaven (Matthew 19:16–22). Jesus wanted to point out to people who tried to save themselves by keeping God's Commandments that this could not be done. By giving him a direction he could not or would not take, Jesus showed this man there was always something of God's commands we are unable or unwilling to do, so no one is good enough to live in the realm of a perfect God. Just as we cannot stare into bright sunlight for long, we are unable to exist in the presence of a holy God without being made holy.

Many people have the impression that going to heaven is a matter of how moral and nice they are compared to others or of how their good deeds outweigh their bad. There is not a person on earth who is capable of submitting to God and doing His will in all He requires (Ecclesiastes 7:20). If we think we can get to heaven by keeping God's rules, Jesus could always challenge us with something we do not or are unwilling to do. The issue is not whether we are nice most of the time or whether our good deeds outweigh our bad. The real issue is whether our hearts are with God or not. Do we love God because Christ has rescued us from sin and death? Do we adore and follow Him because He has loved us and is an excellent model of how to love (1 John 4:19)? Have we received Christ's Spirit of love? Are we moved by it to do God's will? Those who think they are right with God have only to read the Bible to see if they are in compliance with what He tells them to be or do. Certainly, there are many of His commands that would require us to say, "I am not obeying your commands, nor have I wanted to."

Jesus wants us to see that the Law is never a way to get to heaven (Titus 3:4–7). We resist God's will at too many points to qualify for heaven. But having come to eternal life by way of faith does not mean there is no rule-keeping to be done. We are to live by the law of Christ's love, loving God and one another, and even our enemies (Matthew 5:38–48). Faith without works is dead (James 2:14–26). We are freed to live by the moral principles of the Bible (1 Peter 2:16; Galatians 5:1, 13–18). Being saved under the New Testament means that through God's special enablement, by mysteriously putting a new motivation in us, we can be internally motivated to do God's will compelled by love, not external pressure.

Under the gospel, does it matter if I do wrong since God will forgive me? Some believe that since God is forgiving, they can do what they want, simply confess it, and gain forgiveness. They know they are doing wrong but keep doing it. I have been there. But the apostle Paul would say that it definitely does matter (Romans 6:1–2, 12–18). Those who have received God's lovingkindness, grace, and forgiveness will not want to keep doing wrong things. They will feel God's displeasure when they keep doing wrong and will want to avoid it because it is destructive to their lives and relationships and dishonors God who loves them and whom they love. Why would anyone want to go back to doing things that weren't good for him or her or for his or her family? Sometimes we slip and fall. We are not perfect. But those times are to be forsaken, and we should try to overcome, so our falls become fewer and fewer. Help is available from each other and is one reason for a close relationship with other believers (Hebrews 3:13, 10:24–25). God knows our heart and forgives, but He will discipline Christians who continue doing wrong and will attempt to correct them because He loves them and His reputation is at stake. He wants all to represent Him well to the world as ambassadors so others will seek His salvation and healing (Romans 6:15–18, 13:13–14; Hebrews 12:4–12; 1 Peter 2:9).

Jesus said, "All who love me will do what I say" (John 14:23). How does Jesus mean for us to understand this? People sometimes manipulate others by saying, "If you really loved me, you would do this or that for me." Is Jesus saying, "Prove your love for me by obeying my words"? We hear that from boyfriends or girlfriends, from parents, or from husband or wife, and we feel trapped because we know we should love them and so we give in to their demands to prove that we do love them. This is a sick and unhealthy relationship based on selfishness and manipulation to get another to meet our wants or neediness. Jesus is not playing that game. He is not trying to guilt us into doing what He wants. He is simply making a statement about love. Genuine love will act to please the one we love, not to prove our love, but because that is what love does. Love gives of itself to meet another's need or to please another. The key to getting others to love us is not to make them feel guilty by demanding proof of their love but by building loving relationships where they grow to love us back. Jesus is saying, "If you loved me, doing what I say would be a natural result of that love." Obedience does prove that you love someone, but it is not an act to try to earn others' love. Jesus is making a plea for us to grow into a loving relationship with Him. Grow to love Jesus and you will learn to freely and gladly follow Him and His direction for your life.

How can you build a loving relationship with Jesus? First, realize all Jesus has done to love you, and then receive His love by believing He loves you and not doubting it. Of course, this is not easy because we know or feel we don't deserve it. Also, for some it seems hard to receive gifts; we don't want to feel indebted, so we refuse gifts or try to pay back those who give to us.

Sometimes, we suspect that the giver wants something in return, so we ask, "What's the catch?" My wife took a gift of food to a man to thank him for the good work he was doing at his job. His response was one of suspicion and a look of bewilderment—a "Why are you doing this?" attitude. When she said it was simply a thank you and she shared her appreciation for what he was doing, he was able to receive it with gratitude because there was no expectation in return. It was a loving gesture to encourage the person to keep up the good work. Relationships in which you feel you have to pay others back for something or that make you feel suspicious that others want something from you are not loving relationships.

Conditional relationships require something from the other in order for those relationships to work. For example, I will loan you this item but I expect it back. Or, I will love you but I expect you to remain faithful to me. Or, I will take you out to eat if you will type this report for me. These are not necessarily bad relationships. I think we might call conditional relationships ones that are often necessary and helpful to promote getting along with people so that we remain on each other's good side. They can make things run smoothly between people and can hold us accountable for being or doing what we should. Love may or may not be involved in a conditional relationship. Some people will not accept Jesus' invitation to follow Him because they think He wants only to control their lives or that they will be expected to follow His rules and standards. They see Christianity as a religion, a set of morals and ethics that must be followed. Christianity is only a religion if keeping rules or following certain procedures is necessary to be accepted by God. But Jesus calls us to a relationship of love, one that keeps on loving even when we fail to perform. Grace is what makes Christianity differ from what the world calls religion.

How should we respond to Jesus' statement, "All who love me will do what I say"? Are we to feel guilty when we fail to do what Jesus says? It would be easy for us to feel that way. We who follow Jesus as our Lord, do not always do what we know is His will. But Jesus does not want us to do what He says out of guilt or duty to prove our love for Him. He knows that we cannot be perfect and that we will fail to do all He asks of us. His love for us is such that when we fail Him, He does not keep a record of our wrongs or count our wrongs against us, but He keeps forgiving and encouraging us by loving us and wanting us to love Him. If we keep receiving His love and forgiveness and if we stay in love with Him, keeping His word will happen more frequently, voluntarily, and joyfully (Jude 20-21). Yes, in a sense, following Jesus involves dos and don'ts. But in another sense, following Jesus is not like living by do's and don'ts. It all depends on whether we live our lives in a relationship with Jesus based on conditions for acceptance or based on love that has already accepted us, based on law, or based on faith in His good news.

## *Chapter 7*

# WHAT IS FAITH?

God told His people to cross the Jordan River into the Promised Land. How would they get across? God said that as soon as they stepped into the river, He would part the waters (Joshua 1:10–11, 3:12–16). It was an act of faith to step out, believing that God would do what He said. In a case like this, faith believes what God says, and that if I act, God's promised results will happen.

I once mentioned to someone that faith grows. He disagreed. He said that everyone has all the faith he or she needs and either the person uses it or not. I was willing to concede he had a point worth thinking about, but now, I'm not sure what to think. Rather than argue a point that I don't know enough about, I'd rather simply say what I mean by "faith grows." There are times when we cannot bring ourselves to believe something, but later we are able to believe it. For example, I may think I have faith that when I die I will go to heaven, but when I am actually faced with death, I find that I am fearful and not so sure—doubts creep in.

The story is told about a great tightrope walker who stretched his rope across a deep chasm. He walked across, and then he asked the crowd if they believed he could carry a person across. They all cheered that he could do it. "Who among you believers will volunteer to let me take him or her across?" No one volunteered. Did they have faith in him but decided not to use it? Or did they find that their faith in him was not strong enough to trust him? Did their faith need to grow, or did they need to grow so they would be willing or able to use their faith? Maybe both.

When I say faith grows, I mean that at times we cannot trust, but as we grow, we find we can trust, and we do. Whether faith grows or whether the person grows is not worth debating. All I know is that faith is tied to us, and at some point, we cannot bring ourselves to believe but later we can. I may say, "Their faith grew," and others may argue, "No, the person grew." Does Jesus' statement in Matthew 17:19-20 or Luke 17:5-6 have any bearing on this question? Think what you will, but somehow, we need to be able to exercise our faith in areas where previously we could not. Leaving this issue behind us, let's move on to some things we can say about faith that can help us understand what faith involves and how we can grow, whether it is in our faith or in our ability to exercise it.

We are created beings, and therefore, we are finite. This means we are not God, and we do not know everything. Because of our limited power and knowledge, we cannot be 100 percent sure of most things. For example, you cannot be 100 percent sure you will reach your destination in a car or plane. You cannot be 100 percent sure surgery will accomplish the health objectives you hope for. You cannot be 100 percent sure that what you teach your children is getting through to them. We simply do not know enough to be 100 percent sure, but in spite of uncertainty, we still go ahead and act on what we know. Faith is that natural part of our finite humanity that enables us to act on something even though we may not be sure of the outcome. If we required absolute certainty before doing what we needed to do every day, we would not get much done. Everyone has faith. It is interesting that some people live on less than 100 percent certainty for most of life, but when it comes to the Christian faith, they want 100 percent proof before they will believe.

Faith is an act of exercising the mind. Faith involves objectivity which means faith always has an object. It believes in something. Faith is saying yes to what we believe in whether it is visible, like Jesus and His resurrection, or invisible, like God, or a statement such as "God is love." Our minds weigh objective evidence for the existence and truth of these things and decide to believe them or not. Faith is not necessarily a blind leap into the unknown but has reasons, whether good or bad, for what is believed. We don't blindly jump into an airplane; we have reasons that tell us it is trustworthy enough to get us to our destination. Faith involves reasoning, an exercise of the mind.

Faith is an act of exercising the human spirit. Faith involves subjectivity, meaning that faith is a person's total commitment to its object. For example, I will commit myself to this airplane and get on. Faith is reliance or dependency on the character, ability, strength, or truth of someone or something. It is an inner disposition of trust that places confidence in someone, something, or a statement. Faith is transferring control of your life to the object you trust. Once, when I was late picking up my wife at the train station, someone asked her if she needed a ride. "No thank you," she replied. "My husband will be here." Even though I was not there when expected, she had faith in what I promised her and in me—that I would show up. She had committed her well-being to me.

These two aspects of faith are involved in Christianity: the mind involving objectivity, and the spirit involving commitment. The Bible says that faith involves information to be believed and a person to be trusted, turning over the control of our lives to divine truth and a divine person. John 14:10–11 discusses both aspects of faith. Jesus asked others to subjectively believe Him or believe the objective evidence of what He said. Faith involves objective and subjective acts.

Faith never acts without an object; we believe in something rather than nothing. The problem is that there are two kinds of objects to believe in: the good or the evil, the true or the false. God represents all truth, meaning what is real and good; Satan represents what is evil and false (John 8:44). Therefore, when we are presented with something to believe, we need to determine if it is good or evil, true or false. If the object is true, our faith in what it promises will be rewarded, but if the object is false, our faith will eventually be disappointed. We must always investigate the objects of our faith to determine if they are worth believing.

What we believe in terms of religion will lead to life or death. People say all religion is good, but this is not so. Though there may be truth in all religions, they can be based on falsehoods and thus fail to deliver what they promise. If I take a wrong pill by mistake, my faith in it may be okay, but it will not do what it was supposed to do. The object I believe in must be real and true for it to deliver what is expected. It is possible for Christians to have a wrong idea of what the Bible teaches and end up disappointed because something believed did not prove true. For example, I could believe God will always make my life better and remove my suffering and problems, but that will not happen because God never promised that. Our faith has not failed, but the object of our faith failed because it was not true. Is the object of our faith true and worth putting our faith in? That's the issue. The apostle Paul said about one of the objects of our faith, "If Christ has not been raised, then your faith is useless" (1 Corinthians 15:17). What we believe must be true or real for it to produce what is promised and expected.

Hebrews 11:1 tells us, "Faith is the confidence that what we hope for will actually happen; it gives us assurance about things we cannot see." Faith places confidence in the following: that God exists, that He has spoken and can be understood, and that He will reward all who trust Him. Faith for these Hebrews 11 people was more than a wish; it produced in them the assurance and the conviction that an unseen God and His yet unfulfilled promises were sure things. According to this verse, faith results in a knowledge that is certain. God is the most trustworthy object of faith in existence, and faith that accepts God and His word as trustworthy dispels any confusion and doubt. Hebrews 11:6 says no one can please God without faith. God wants us to believe Him, and faith gives us victory over the world of uncertainty and evil (1 John 5:4).

God wants us to have a strong, unwavering faith. In terms of our ability to commit to something, faith can be weak, and it can fail or get stronger. If we claim to have faith in something but experience fear, doubt, worry, depression, or panic, as much as we claim faith or are trying to have faith, our faith needs strengthening, or else it has been directed to the wrong object. If, for example, we have faith in the true meaning of Christ's death, God promises forgiveness for our wrongs, which means freedom from condemnation and possession of the gift of eternal life (Romans 5:1, 8:1). But doubts will weaken our faith if we are thinking, "The guilt of my wrongs is overwhelming within me, and I have a hard time believing God can forgive me." A strong faith will not doubt but believe God's promise of forgiveness in Christ. As a result, there will be peace with God and peace of mind and heart within oneself.

Weak faith is due to a lack of confidence in what God has done and said. Doubts can be indicators that reveal the condition of our faith or lack thereof. But doubts can help strengthen our faith by challenging us to work through our issues. Working through the issues may mean reviewing and agreeing with the facts in the case, working on our character defects that prevent our ability to believe, or asking God to help our faith. Someone once said to Jesus, "I do believe, but help me overcome my unbelief" (Mark 9:24). This man wanted to wholeheartedly believe but needed help. Jesus answered his prayer and helped him be able to believe.

I once was battling an ongoing health issue. "God, where are you? Why are you not helping me?" I asked. Doubt that God cared about me arose because I did not see God helping me. I thought I was strong enough spiritually to keep believing God was with me, but I started doubting Him, and that bothered me. One night, tired of my mental battle with unbelief, I pleaded with God to speak something to me about my condition and show He cared. I desperately needed to hear from Him, so I asked, "Why can't I get past these nagging doubts and have faith that you are with me and helping me?" I suddenly heard this thought: "You think you are spiritually strong enough to fight off your doubts, but you cannot win this battle when you do not see the truth about yourself. The truth is that you are trusting in your own faith to overcome this, but in reality you are a doubter." It was a gentle and loving "voice" of reprimand. I instantly became humble and agreed with God's assessment of my life. I did not have as strong a faith as I thought. I did my best to repent by saying, "God, you are right. I am trying to believe, or as some would say, 'to have faith in my ability to have faith,' but I am a doubter. I do not want to be those things. Help me overcome them." I immediately felt peace and joy and thanked God for His honesty and for opening my eyes, to be honest with myself. I then relied on His forgiveness and asked His help to be changed.

We are not free to trust Christ more fully if we are putting our faith in our own perceived strength instead of in Christ and what He can do. Admitting my weakness, I got myself out of the way so Christ could do something. As a result, my faith is stronger because it is truly in Him, not in myself.

Peter is an example of a faith in danger of failing and in need of strengthening. Peter believed he would take a stand for Jesus and even die for Him, but Jesus challenged his belief by saying Peter would deny Him three times. He was trusting in his own ability to be strong when in truth he was weak. Jesus told Peter that Satan wanted to destroy his faith. But, Jesus said, "I have pleaded in prayer for you, Simon, that your faith should not fail" (Luke 22:31–34).

How could Peter's faith have failed? He could have been so down on himself over his failure to stand up for Jesus that he decided he didn't have what it took to be a loyal follower. He could have concluded Jesus was upset with him and didn't want him. Or his faith could have failed because, like me, his faith was in his ability to stand instead of in Christ's ability to help him stand. By not seeing the truth about himself and believing the lies he was telling himself, Peter shrunk from following Jesus.

Lies we tell ourselves or Satan's lies can cause us to fall away from the truth. Would Peter believe Jesus still loved and wanted him? Would Peter believe Jesus needed to be his strength instead of trusting his own strength? Jesus prayed that Peter's faith would not fail. Part of faith not failing is putting it on the right object, which is, as some have phrased it, "I can't, but He can." I frequently need to put faith in an object that can come through for me, and it is not I.

When Peter was walking on water but took his eyes off Jesus, he began to sink. He cried out for Jesus to save him, and Jesus did (Matthew 14:28–33). He learned that when his focus was not on Jesus, his faith failed because it was focused on the wrong object, but when it was on Jesus, he was saved. He has it reconfirmed that Jesus was capable of saving him and was a trustworthy person to believe in. Jesus asked, "Why did you doubt me?" Peter could have answered, "Jesus, I doubted because my circumstances seemed overwhelming to me and I focused on them instead of you." He could have answered, "Jesus, I doubted because I lacked confidence in how reliable you are." This latter answer may not have been totally true of Peter; after all, he did get out of the boat and walk on water. But many do lack confidence in God and need their faith to be strengthened by increasing true knowledge concerning the object of their faith.

Because we struggle with faith, the question occurred to me, "Do we have free will to exercise faith? There is a sense in which we do not. For example, some will not get on an airplane because of fear it will crash. Some have an unwillingness or inability to trust anyone because too often others have abused them or lied to them. People can have deep-seated prejudices and emotions from past experiences that are entrenched deep within them, and these pre-conditioned factors can prevent them from exercising faith. Factors inhibiting the exercise of our faith include fears, doubts, skepticism, unwillingness, a need for more knowledge, and rebellion, among others. Are people free to believe, or do these hindrances prevent their faith from acting? Do people have to deal with certain factors before they are willing or able to exercise their faith? We are not free to exercise faith when we are limited by factors that prevent it. A good question to ask ourselves is, "What keeps me from having faith?"

How can we acquire or build stronger faith? It is good for us to develop a firm root system so we don't fall away from faith in times of testing (Luke 8:13). Here are four actions we can take that will help us acquire or strengthen our faith. First, Romans 10:17 tells us, "So faith comes from hearing, that is, hearing the Good News about Christ." The apostle John said that his eyewitness accounts of Jesus' life, death, and resurrection were written so we might believe and thus gain eternal life (John 20:30–31). This tells us that faith can happen through hearing or reading God's Word concerning Christ Jesus. I once shared the message of God's salvation with a woman and asked her if she had ever accepted Jesus and believed He would save her. She said yes. I was surprised because I knew from her life story that she was not a believer, so I asked, "When did you believe?" She said, "Just now as you were explaining it to me." There seems to be a power in God's word, a force that enables faith in us. Hebrews 11 and Romans 4 have particularly helped me better understand faith and strengthen my faith. Knowing what the Bible says about God and His promises, helps clarify the object of my faith.

A second way we can strengthen our faith is to be part of loving relationships in the church. When we hear the struggles and faith stories of those with whom we fellowship or when we hear the teaching of God's Word through sermons and classes, we are encouraged to believe and keep believing (1 Thessalonians 5:11).

A third way to strengthen our faith is to study "apologetics," a study of the defenses of the faith. When we have more evidence and good, logical arguments for the truth and reality of what we believe, this will strengthen our faith.

Fourth, the writer of Hebrews said that Jesus "initiates and perfects our faith" (Hebrews 12:2). That being the case, prayer to Jesus to help our unbelief is a great way to strengthen our faith. Keeping our eyes on Him will keep us focused on the one person who will never forsake us.

Here are two ways to see if our faith in God is real. One is when we see that our faith is not dead (James 2:14–26). Dead faith means we say we believe in God but our lifestyle does not back it up. Faith in God requires a visible living out of that faith. What actions show that a person has faith? Loving others, endeavoring to know the Bible, obeying God's revealed will, doing good deeds motivated by love for God, and drawing near to God through a prayerful life are among them. Seeing things like these in our lives convinces us of the reality of our faith.

A second way to see if our faith is genuine is to notice how we respond under trials and suffering. The Bible says, "The Lord tests the heart" (Proverbs 17:3). One way He does this is by allowing tragedies and sufferings to come our way (Isaiah 45:7). If we have learned to trust God, we will come to have joy in such situations and grow through them (James 1:2–4). God may sometimes test our faith by not telling us what to do in a situation but by letting us make our own decisions. The decisions we make tells us whether we have God's interests in mind.

It is important to understand that faith is not a manipulative tool we can use to get what we want from God. Some believers take God at His word, which is good, but they become demanding. For example, "God, you promised to bless me with health, now I claim it." Then if it does not happen, they may feel something is wrong with their faith. It may not be a faith problem as much as a misconstruing of what God says. The Bible clearly tells us in the case of Jesus' temptation that we are not to test God by putting Him in a position that He has to do what we want (Matthew 4:5–7). Faith simply believes what God says and waits for the fulfillment in His time and way. Sometimes, what we want does not happen because God is more concerned about changing us. Sometimes, God may give us what we want but we come to see it was not such a good thing after all.

Theologians make a distinction between "common faith" and "saving faith." Common faith is what people exercise in everyday living while saving faith requires people to have a special gift of faith from God to be saved from sin and receive eternal life. This distinction is important because it is believed that people are so spiritually dead to God they cannot respond to His message by natural, human reason and faith (Ephesians 2:1). What is being said is that we are free to exercise faith in everyday life but not when it comes to matters involving God's salvation. Whether we can believe God's message of good news without God granting us faith depends on how we answer certain questions: How far have we fallen away from God? What is our faith potential given our sinful condition?

I simply want to raise the question of whether according to the Bible it's possible for common faith to be adequate for receiving salvation. This became a question for me when I talked with a man who said he didn't believe in Christ because God had not given him the gift of faith. He admired believers who had the faith they were saved, and he wished he had the same kind of faith they had. "God has never given it to me," he said as he was expressing concern about his ultimate destiny. By believing he needed to get faith from God, he did not think he could exercise any natural faith he might have had. He could only wait for God to save him, and he could not bring himself to put his "common faith" in God's offer of salvation. I believe he is right in light of Jesus' words that "no one can come to me unless the Father who sent me draws them to me" (John 6:44). It seems that no one can come to Jesus if there has not been previous input from God the Father. But I wonder if he was wrong to expect God to give him the faith he needed. Could it be that he didn't need faith from God but simply special help to overcome the blockages preventing his common faith from accepting the good news of salvation? What if the facts regarding salvation were no different from the facts of everyday life? After all, the facts were public, historical events for all to see. Is common faith enough to believe salvation facts just as it is enough to believe secular facts?

Continuing with this thought, there is a sense in which faith is necessary for us to be saved, but faith is not what saves us. We are saved by God's grace through faith (Ephesians 2:8). Is a part of God's saving grace not to give us "saving faith" but grace to draw us to Jesus in a way that enables us to believe with the faith we already possess? The words *to draw* literally mean to drag, like a fishnet, or someone out of a building. Figuratively they mean to pull on a man's inner life, to compel, to influence the will. Some people may want to believe but are unable or unwilling to believe; either way, they can't without additional help. But what is that special help? Is it the Holy Spirit's conviction of our need for Jesus and the Spirit's work to open our hearts to understand God's gift of salvation? Those are a part of it. I'm sure there are many helps God gives, but what ultimately draws people to Jesus is the conviction of their need coupled with the message of Christ's death and resurrection. That there is drawing power in the message of the cross seems clear in the Scriptures (John 12:32; Romans 10:13–17; Luke 24:32; Acts 26:16–23). Though theological positions differ on this subject, they all claim to be based on Scripture. The truth must be in the discovery of what the Bible actually teaches, which may or may not be the same as our personal theological views.

One morning, following my reading of John 12–16, I wrote this prayer as an expression of my faith.

"Father in heaven, thank you for your marvelously created world and the wonderful life you have given us to enjoy. But all is not good. We live in a world of our own making in which there is so much trouble, evil, sorrow, and heartache. Yet your promise is, that everything we go through in this life cannot defeat us because you have overcome it all and you provide a safe place for those who believe in and follow Jesus. He is my Savior. He is my Lord.

"I have put my faith in Him and in your promise you will let nothing in this life happen to me or my family that is not for our good. For trials in life that have come my way, I have looked to you for help, and I have grown in my faith by learning to trust you in the midst of them, and you have been so gracious and faithful to grant me your peace at times when I was feeling tormented by fears and worries. You enabled me to endure.

"I am sorry for those times I doubted you, but yet you did not abandon me. I hear you saying that I am your child and you love me, and I believe it. I am so grateful that you have given me the righteousness of Jesus, and because of my faith in what He did for me, I know I am welcome to come into your presence in good times and bad. I feel overwhelmed at your acceptance of me for I know I am sinful and often fail to please you. I feel so selfish because I so often do only what I want to do, but hopefully, much of what I do is what you want me to do.

"Thank you that you have made a way to forgive me and I can live without fear of your condemnation but have the hope of eternal life in your heavenly kingdom. Lord, I know that a day may come when my faith falters not because I doubt you but because I may lose the capacity to stay coherent in my thinking. I thank you that you remain faithful to me and will bring me finally to the true home you have prepared for me. It gives me great joy and peace to know this, and I rest in your loving grace.

"Thank you for all the trials in life that you have allowed me to experience so my faith could get stronger as I struggled to keep believing or to submit to doing things your way. Thank you for not testing me to the point that I would fail to believe in you. I thank you for the encouragement I get from your handling of Peter's life, that when his faith temporarily failed, you prayed for him, he made it through, and he was strengthened to do your will.

"I have no one else in the world to trust who can promise the wonderful life and glorious future you are bringing about for me. Help me to remain in you always. And may this faith I have be contagious to those around me, especially to my family and those who know me best that they may also continually put their faith in you. I want them to recognize Jesus' love and the meaning of His death for them so they may be with me, you, and all your saints, both now, and forever in your present and future kingdom. Thank you that we who believe can look forward to enjoying a love-filled, face-to-face relationship with Jesus. Amen."

As an exercise for fun, can you pick out the objects of my faith in this prayer—the things I believe with my mind and the statements that show my inner commitment to God? Faith is an exercise of the mind to believe an object and an exercise of the spirit to commit oneself to the object believed.

## Chapter 8

## SEEING GOD IN THE HAPPENINGS OF DAILY LIFE

I remember hearing about a Russian astronaut who returned to earth and remarked that he had not seen God. That is not surprising, for the Bible tells us no one has seen nor can see God (John 1:18, 6:46; 1 Timothy 6:16; 1 John 4:12). When Moses asked God if he could see His glory, God said no one could see His face and live. He said He would reveal His goodness and allow Moses to see His back but not His face (Exodus 33:18–23). It's not clear to me what this means, but it does seem clear that what we can see of God is His effects. We cannot see wind, but we can see and feel what it does.

Jacob claimed to have seen God, but what he saw was a "man" who wrestled with him whom he acknowledged was God in human form (Genesis 32:24–30). God sometimes appeared in human form and addressed people in that way (Genesis 18:1–3). Some call such appearances "anthropomorphisms." Although the Bible declares no one can see God, it is clear that God can be understood to exist and to care about us by His visible works and by becoming visible in various forms (Deuteronomy 10:21; Psalm 98:1–3; Hebrews 1:1–2; John 14:10–11). Jesus said that to have seen Him was to have seen the Father (John 14:8–11). Since God is an unseen spirit (John 4:24), Jesus showed us through His words and actions what the Father is like.

Natural theology tries to discover if we can learn anything about God from the study of nature. I consider nature to include not only the heavens and the earth but also the events of our daily lives. Nature's objects and events do not reveal God directly but indirectly (Romans 1:20). This means we can understand things about God from observing the material world and from observing things happening in our lives that seem unexplainable without extraordinary influence. For example, from observing how the universe works with such design and life and intricacy (Psalm 19:1–2), we may conclude that something we call God exists as an intelligent and powerful mind. We could also conclude that God exists from observing unusual circumstances in our lives that point to God's existence and care for us (Matthew 11:2–6; Acts 11:1–18). I was visiting with a man who needed money. He said he had walked out of his motel room and asked a passerby if he wanted to buy a computer, a new one he had recently purchased. "Yes," said the man without hesitation; he paid him cash then and there. The seller concluded the hand of God had provided what he needed at that time in his life. God works through people. Studies of nature, including events that happen to us, do not tell us as much about God as the Bible does, but the study of nature and life's mysterious events let us know this someone we call God is at work in the world and in our lives.

This fact that God exists and cares about us can be seen through circumstances in our lives that some call coincidence or chance happenings. Many supposed chance happenings occurred in the biblical book of Esther, in which the name of God is never mentioned, but it is clear that a caring mind was behind the things that happen. Read it and see if you do not get the impression that some amazing coincidental things happened. Were they chance happenings, or was God clearly at work? One example in Esther was when a Jew named Mordecai overheard a plot to kill the king and revealed it; his name was recorded in a history book as one who had saved the king's life.

Much later, a trusted servant of the king named Haman grew to hate Mordecai, built a gallows, and planned to hang him the next day. He was on his way to ask the king's permission. Was it by chance that the king had been unable to sleep the night before, read about Mordecai's good deed of saving his life, and wondered if he had been rewarded? Before Haman could ask the king for permission to hang Mordecai, the king asked Haman what he would do for a man the king wanted to honor. Thinking that he was the one the king wanted to honor, Haman made a suggestion the king accepted. Much to Haman's displeasure, the king had Haman honor Mordecai by parading him through the city.

Esther, who had become queen by a series of unusual circumstances, was in a position to speak for Mordecai and revealed Haman's wicked schemes. Haman was hanged on the gallows he had built for Mordecai (Esther 5:14–7:10). Would we call these events chance happenings or God's guiding hand at work through people and events? The possibility of

God at work is quite real when we know from Scripture that God at times makes input directly into people's minds and hearts to help determine their decisions and actions (Proverbs 21:1; Ezra 1:1–3, 6:22; Acts 13:2–3). It may seem scary to think God can control people's minds, but it isn't; it's comforting to believe God does all things only for good (Hosea 14:9). Sometimes I wonder, *Does God override our so-called free will, or is it that God's will and our will somehow work simultaneously?*

Like the events in Esther, we wonder about many events in our lives and experience a sense of awe, or "wow." When we marvel at such happenings, the thought crosses our minds of a possible supernatural power at work. Some might even say things like, "Somebody upstairs was watching out for me." Following are a few personal stories that, for me, have created this sense of wonder. I have experienced so many of these wonderful happenings that though they seem small and insignificant, I have concluded they are not coincidence or chance but the effects of God at work, and thus, evidence for His existence and His care for us. Perhaps you have many such stories of your own.

When a family visiting us from hundreds of miles away left to return home, their car broke down a few blocks away. As it turned out, the battery was dead due to a failed alternator. Since repair shops were closed that day, this meant disappointment and frustration at having to leave the car, transfer all their stuff including baby seats to a borrowed vehicle, pay for fixing the car, and have someone bring the repaired car to them. But that is not the whole story. They had tried numerous times to get a noise in one of their front wheels fixed. Mechanics had replaced many parts, but it kept getting worse. The shop that fixed their car (it needed an alternator) discovered that the bearings in that noisy wheel were badly ground down; the family could have suffered a major accident, possibly resulting in serious injuries. Was it a chance happening that the alternator had quit working at this time, or was it God's way of protecting them from a life-threatening accident? Instead of writing this off to a chance inconvenience, is wonder and thanksgiving to God in order?

When I was a child, I was sitting on my bicycle under a large oak tree in front of my house. Our dog was barking, wanting out of the screened-in porch. I ignored his barking until finally, it bothered me enough to open the door. As soon as I touched the door handle, I heard a loud crash. I turned around to see that a huge tree branch had broken off and had fallen on my bike, crushing it to the ground. Was this a coincidence—or the hand of God?

One day, my daughter and I had a garage sale to make some money for a mission trip to South America. When the sale was over, I sat in the driveway and counted the money: $199.50. I remarked to God that all we needed was fifty cents to make it an even $200. At that moment, a little boy showed up, looked around at all the stuff, and asked what he could buy. I asked, "How much do you have?" He said, "Fifty cents." I said, "For fifty cents, you can buy anything you want." Was such timing happenchance or God's hand to show He cares even about the minutest things in our lives?

Once, as a postgraduate student, I was asked to preach at a small church. I had only five dollars when the offering plate came around. Being a financially strapped student, I struggled about whether to give up all I had, but I did. As I was leaving, I felt someone slip something into my suit coat pocket that turned out to be a five-dollar bill. Apparently, God wanted me to learn that He was looking out for my best interests and that I should not fear giving up things for Him.

When I was a young child, my mother took the car and left for a few minutes to get my dad from the bus stop at the corner. He usually walked home, but it was storming. Suddenly, there was a loud clap of thunder and flashes of lightning. I was scared and wanted someone to be there with me. I did not know what to do, so I climbed a chair, picked up the phone, and randomly dialed some numbers. I had no idea how to make a phone call, but someone answered. I blurted out that I was scared. As the nice lady was comforting me, I said, "Oh… it's okay now. My mom's home," and I hung up. Years later, I marveled that I had no idea of how to make a call and that I had nonetheless gotten someone on the line. Coincidence? Chance? Or God was with me?

One afternoon, I was driving home, moving pretty fast on a lightly traveled road. I wanted to get through a traffic light before the light changed. As I approached the green light, a thought in my head said, "Stop!" I did. Just then, a car whizzed past right in front of me; the driver had run the red light. Was it intuition or God's voice?

One day during my senior year in college, I was busy studying when the thought came to me that I should not pursue the teaching career I was pursuing but that I should be in the church. From where had that thought come? For two weeks, the thought lingered until I finally concluded God must have been speaking to me about becoming a minister. I knew nothing about how to proceed, but a friend gave me information on how to contact seminaries. After researching twenty schools that I could possibly attend to be trained for such a calling, I selected one. I had never been to the school and had not seen pictures, but because I loved being out-of-doors and enjoyed nature's beauty, I mentioned to God that it would be nice if it was in a wooded area with a pond. When I got there, the school buildings were located along wooded pathways, and there was a huge pond in the center of the campus. To me, this beautiful setting was not a chance happening but a confirmation I was in the place God wanted me to be.

I was engaged to Connie; we were going to get married after college, but I had to tell her I was changing careers. I thought it proper to give her an opportunity to back out if she didn't want to be married to a minister. When I mentioned I had something to tell her, she said, "I know. You're going to be a minister."

"How did you know?" I asked.

She said, "I used to think someday I'd be married to a minister."

A further happening occurred as I was in my last year of seminary, I began to doubt whether this was what I should be doing. I thought maybe I should have been a schoolteacher after all. Part-time jobs for students always appeared on the school bulletin board, and one day as I was struggling with these doubts, I saw a job for a teacher's assistant at a local high school. I took the job, and through it, I realized I had lost my passion for school teaching. God allowed this experience to remove all doubt from my mind and confirm I was going in His direction for my life. These and other personal life events were confirmation that God existed, cared for, and was guiding my life.

The Bible has many similar examples of God at work through people and life's circumstances. Two kings banded together and went to war. God said that King Ahab would die in battle. Knowing this, Ahab disguised himself so the enemy would not recognize him. He thought he was safe, but a random arrow from an enemy soldier shot at no one in particular just happened to strike him in a place his armor did not protect, and he died (1 Kings 22:29–34).

Another example involves Abraham's servant who was sent to find a wife for Abraham's son, Isaac. The servant prayed God would show him the right girl; he hoped that if he asked the right person for a drink, she would offer one for his camels also. He asked a girl who came to the well for a drink, and she did exactly what he had prayed for. This "chance" happening and other events helped confirm in his mind she was God's choice for Isaac (Genesis 24:10–21).

Turning now to observations of the heavens and the earth: can God be seen? Scientists realize that for life to exist on earth, certain conditions must be in place, including liquid water, an oxygen-nitrogen-carbon atmosphere, an iron core to maintain a magnetic field, and a moon of the right proportions to stabilize the earth's axis. It also required a sun just the right distance from the earth so we didn't overheat or freeze, and many more factors that all had to work together for life to exist on earth.

Many scientists tell us that all this came about by chance. But when we examine our world, it looks made. In our everyday lives, we know that things that look made have a Maker, so why do we presume that a universe reflecting order and intelligence happened by chance? Scientist Robert Jastrow, a professed agnostic and materialist and author of *God and the Astronomers,* said in an interview that he could not believe this material world happened by chance, that there must be something other than this material world, but he had no explanation. He said he would like to believe in a God, but his materialist and scientific methodology did not allow that.[18] The Bible says, "In the beginning God created the heavens and the earth" (Genesis 1:1). It also says we can clearly see some of God's attributes through what has been made (Romans 1:20). Is it chance that caused our universe to come together, or is a Creator God the best explanation? By what God created, we can conclude that the Maker possesses mind, purpose, wisdom, power, good, order, and cares for us.

Some say there is a lot of evil in nature. How could a good God create that? Who says God created evil? Could it be that the corruption of nature resulted in a curse on earth due to humanity's choice to allow evil

---

[18] Astronomer Robert Jastrow discussed his views on the origin of the universe in the DVD "The Privileged Planet" produced my Illustra Media; the interview is in the special features section "Questions and Answers."

into the world (Genesis 3:17–18)? The Bible says the earth is waiting to be released from its slavery to corruption (Romans 8:19–22).

We can interpret natural and circumstantial events as chance, coincidence, destiny, or fate; they do not have to lead us to believe in God. But if everything happens by chance, what hope does that leave for humanity? We struggle with our problems, are often fearful of terrible outcomes, and rely on our human resources to make our lives safe. We have some control, but there is no guarantee the future will be good.

However, belief in the God who has revealed Himself in writing, through nature, through Jesus, and through mysterious happenings in daily life gives hope that can cause our hearts to soar at wonderful possibilities awaiting us. This certain, God-promised hope gives us something to look forward to and for me trumps any unknowable future that results from the belief we should do our best and leave everything else to chance.

In a *Lord of the Rings* movie, the ring bearer grew tired and wished his problems had never happened and that the ring had not come to him. But because of the circumstances involving the finding of the ring, he was told he was meant to have it.[19] What was implied was that there was a force for good behind these events, and this gave hope that things would work out because a greater intelligence was in charge. Such hope gave the burdened ring bearer encouragement to keep going.

I know there are many believers and unbelievers alike who have been terribly hurt by cruel and devastating circumstances and events. They have been unable or unwilling to see God in the daily happenings of their lives. Life's events can be very painful and can cause anger and depression. Adverse happenings can cause us to believe that a good and loving God is not there for us. Such feelings are certainly understandable, and I offer no explanation or rebuttal to those who feel let down. I empathize with their sorrow because I have had and will have plenty of my own sorrows to deal with. All I can say is that we must all choose how we look at life, and we must all live with our choices (Joshua 24:15).

---

[19] *The Lord of the Rings*, "The Fellowship of the Ring," produced by New Line Home Entertainment.

But think about it—in the brokenness of my life, could there be a God able to restore it to peace and wholeness if I am willing to trust Him and have the eyes to see Him as my helper (1 Peter 1:3–9)? There are certainly stories in your life that can give you confidence God cares about you and is with you. Seeing God involved in your present or past life can be a sign of hope for you in dark times, that He will fulfill His promises and that things will turn out for good (Romans 8:28; Joshua 21:45). God is at work in our lives more than we know (John 5:17; Proverbs 16:9). Trust Him, rest from your struggles and doubts, learn, and be at peace in the midst of your circumstances (Proverbs 3:5–6).

## *Chapter 9*

## YOU HAVE A THEOLOGY—WHAT IS IT?

What do you believe about God and His miracles (Jonah 1:17, 2:10)? What do you believe about God allowing evil and suffering and giving orders to kill seemingly "innocent" people (Deuteronomy 2:31, 34)? What do you believe about Jesus and Christianity being the only true religion (John 14:6; Acts 4:12)? What do you believe about Christ's church (Matthew 16:18)? What do you believe about how God wants us to live, and why (Psalm 86:11)? What do you believe about how God communicates with us (Hebrews 1:1–2; 2 Timothy 3:16)? What do you believe about God's laws and God's grace (Deuteronomy 30:15–18; Ephesians 2:8)? What do you believe about heaven and God committing people to hell (Matthew 10:28; Luke 12:4–5)?

What do you believe about God's idea of sin and its consequences (John 8:24)? What do you believe about God's judgment (Romans 14:10)? What do you believe about what it means that humanity was created in God's image (Genesis 1:27)? What do you believe about God's purpose for us (1 Peter 2:9)? What do you believe about God's salvation—who, what, why (Philippians 3:20–21)? What do you believe about prayer and prayer's effect on God (Luke 18:1)?

What do you believe about how God wants us to relate to believers or nonbelievers (John 13:34–35; Galatians 6:10)? What do you believe about God creating the universe (Genesis 1:1)? What do you believe about the kingdom of God (Matthew 6:10)? What do you believe about what God is going to make happen in the future (Isaiah 13:9, 11–13; 2 Peter 3:13)? Why do you believe the things you believe about God? Why does that matter (John 8:24; 11:26)? Which of the above must be agreed upon by all and why? You have a theology; what is it?

What is meant by theology? *Theos* is a Greek word for God, and theology is basically the study of God and what is believed about Him, including related topics. For Christians, the Bible is the primary source of true knowledge about God—His person, behaviors, and various doctrines or teachings having to do with Him. Systematic theology is the arrangement of information from the Bible in categories or subjects. Studying the Bible and formulating what you believe about God and His revealed truths can be called "doing" theology. Over time, people can increase their knowledge about God and His truths, often changing various beliefs as they learn more. Many people's theologies probably do not come as a direct study of God's Word but from other sources.

Where does our theology come from? How do we arrive at our particular theological views? Many gather information about God from life's experiences, but in general, we learn theology from our families and our faith communities. Our parents may have told us Bible stories, and at church, we hear sermons or are involved in Bible classes taught by volunteer teachers or paid staff. Parents and teachers teach from books or articles written by people who have attended Bible school or seminary and have certain views about what the Bible teaches.

Those Bible schools or seminaries formed their theologies based on respected scholars in the past such as John Calvin, Martin Luther, John Wesley, St. Augustine, and many others. Many schools and churches are associated with certain theological backgrounds, and so that is what they believe and teach.

We tend to believe what we have been taught from the perspective of our upbringing. When we get older, we may gain additional theological views from the Bible, books, movies, experiences, or friends. Those who did not grow up in a church or in a believing family most likely derived their theological views from bits and pieces they read, heard, or saw in movies or from mystical experiences. From where did you get your theology? From where do you get it now?

Even though the Bible is the best place to derive our theology, it's also where problems develop. People can differ in their understanding of what the Bible says or receive misinformation, so we have many varying theologies among believers. For example, people have different eschatologies, that is, what the Bible says about future things. Some believe there will be a thousand-year reign of Christ on earth at the end of our history. Others believe there will be no millennium on earth at the end of history. Both views rely on their understanding of what the Bible teaches.

Another example concerns how a person is saved, that is, how a person is made right with God. Some have a theology that says God saves us by His determination in which we have no initial choice, while others say we choose salvation by the free will God gave us. These opposing theologies have been referred to as Calvinism and Arminianism. Believers continue this centuries-old debate over this issue of God's sovereignty versus man's free will.

Another area of widespread difference concerns baptism. Some believe in baptizing infants too young to have their own faith, while others say baptism is for believers only. Some say baptism saves the person, while others say baptism is a statement by those who have been saved. There are many other differing theologies based on one's understanding of the Bible that often cause unwholesome divisions between Christian brothers and sisters (1 Corinthians 1:10–11).

Why do we humans tend to take a strong stand on one side of an issue without seriously considering what the other side is saying? Is it because we tend to believe our theology is the right one? Is it because we think we have studied the issue fully and therefore our opponents must be wrong? Are our minds so made up that we cannot bother with hearing another side because we are convinced that the issue is settled? It is easy to have the attitude, "I know I am right, so you must be wrong." Being right may at times be true but certainly not always.

I think nearly every theology has some points that do not fit well with everything the Bible appears to say. It is as if some with a particular theology are trying to force contrary Scriptures into an agreement with their views. I have discovered that other theologies have some valid biblical truths that are missing in my own theology. We see things from different points of view, and we all have blind spots. Maybe God allows various people to see differently so we can learn from each other and fit missing pieces together to achieve a truer picture of the whole.

We may not agree with every point of someone's theology, but certainly, there are parts we could use to build our own theologies by bringing us closer to truth. Maybe we do not want to consider other views because we find it hard to accept something that would require us to change our views. But negating one truth in favor of another would cause us to miss something that could keep us in proper focus or balance.

Long ago I heard a statement from a college science professor that I have never forgotten. He was explaining the behavior of light and how light sometimes behaves like a stream of particles and at other times like a continuous wave. It would seem that it should be one or the other but not both. Here is his concluding comment about particle versus wave action in light: "The truth lies simultaneously at both ends." His statement stuck with me and has served as a guide to keep my life and ideas in proper perspective and balance. It helps me consider that I should hear other sides to issues so I don't miss anything necessary for a truer and proper view of the whole.

An example of the truth at both ends is that Jesus is fully human and fully God. How can He be both? But He is. The Bible can also be said to be both a human and a divine book. Theology has produced an array of many-sided discussions and has engendered much dispute. I try to be open to other people's views because the more we see all sides, the nearer we can come to better understanding God's revealed truths. This is particularly valuable if misunderstanding leads to "misliving."

Because of my observations, I have decided I need to do theology differently. I must not simply accept what has been handed down to me and try to reinforce the rightness of it in my own mind to the exclusion of something else. Like the Bereans, I need to be open to consider what each theology has to offer and to evaluate if it agrees with what the Bible seems to say (Acts 17:10–11).

When I read Scripture to do theology, I usually ask the Holy Spirit to help me understand the truth of His Word. I believe God's Spirit can give us insight, and if we don't understand something but ask and listen, He will sometimes give an answer (1 John 2:27). Also, I don't negate other theologies, but I try and learn from them something I may not know about the Bible's teachings. I read many viewpoints on various subjects and try to assimilate what is biblically true about that particular view. I like to read what others say because there is wisdom in a multitude of counselors (Proverbs 15:22). For that reason, I respect the traditional views written by scholars throughout the many centuries of church history.

I also try to be aware of my own biases and tell myself it is okay to believe something I disagree with if the Bible seems to say it; what the Bible says is what I need to accept. If I have unanswered questions, I put my questions on hold until I get further information; it is okay to not have all the answers. I remind myself that sometimes mystery is involved and I need to accept some things as true without having to reconcile them in my mind. What is reasonable to God may not be to us if it is beyond the boundaries of human understanding (Isaiah 55:8).

In doing theology, I like to consult "experts" in language, if I think it will help me to more accurately understand a Bible word or phrase. I also realize that the Bible was written for people living in differing contexts with particular needs God wanted to address, and those contexts may no longer exist today. At the same time, those seemingly out of date contexts may contain underlying truths that pertain to every culture in every age. Sometimes, people live in contexts in which personal issues at different times in their lives need to be addressed by seemingly contradictory truths of the Bible. Seemingly opposite truths are true in their proper context. In such cases, the principle "the truth lies simultaneously at both ends" makes sense.

Our theology is important because it provides content about God and His plans for our lives and for the future of His world. It is the basis for any hope we have for how things will turn out in the future, whether in our personal lives or in God's great scheme of things. It provides wisdom on which we base our decisions for handling various situations we deal with. It provides the content of the beliefs we are to pass on to our children. Theology is much more than religious knowledge; it is what needs to be lived out. Knowing God's Word is one matter; knowing Him personally in a loving and helpful relationship is another.

If our theology is only about knowing things, it can lead to arrogant pride—thinking we know more or are more important than others (1 Corinthians 4:6, 8:1). It can also lead to meaningless discussions and arguments in which we try to convince others of some truth or that we are right and they are wrong and in need of correction (1 Timothy 1:6). Not knowledge alone, but also loving relationships need to be the ultimate outcome of our theology (1 Corinthians 13:1–3, 16:14; Ephesians 3:17–18, 5:2; Colossians 3:14; 1 Timothy 1:5; 1 John 4:7; Jude 1:21). Though theology has an intellectual side, God wants not only to give us the right knowledge but also to reform us into Christlike people (Romans 8:29; 1 Corinthians 15:49; Philippians 3:21). Our theology is important as a guide to right living.

In one way, doing theology properly is very difficult because it is all about discovering the truth of God and in so doing discovering the truth about ourselves; admitting the truth about ourselves can make us want to hide from it (Genesis 3:8–10; John 3:19–20, 5:40). One of the ways we hide is to major in theology as an academic study to build up our knowledge about God and the Bible rather than letting God's truth tell us who we are and how to live. Managing our lives and doing the will of God by obeying what He wants is very difficult because of our weaknesses, denials, and fears. It takes strength and courage to face the truth. Do not get me wrong—knowledge of what God has revealed is necessary and helpful for guiding right thinking, but knowledge without submission to the life-giving function of theology shortchanges one of the greatest reasons for doing theology.

When we think of theology, the word *doctrine*, which means teaching, comes to mind. The Bible tells us there is such a thing as sound doctrine, wholesome teaching (Titus 2:1). This biblical concept of sound doctrine does not mean knowing what God says about various topics in the Bible; it has a narrower focus. Throughout the Bible, sound doctrine primarily has to do with God presenting His will to us and giving us the option of believing and doing it or not (Deuteronomy 1:1–8, 6:4–9; Jeremiah 18:1–3; Matthew 22:36–39, 28:19–20, 7:24–27).

In the New Testament, sound doctrine is the message of salvation, which includes the facts involving Jesus Christ and is about following His teachings to live a moral and holy life in the power of His Spirit. Anything contrary to the gospel of Christ and the message of salvation, or contrary to living according to the teachings of Jesus, opposes sound doctrine and needs to be refuted (Romans 16:17–19; Galatians 1:6-9; 1 Timothy 1:3–11; 2 Timothy 2:16–19; Titus 3:9–11). Holding to sound doctrine does not mean dividing the church over matters such as God's sovereignty versus free will or arguing for or against particular views of the end times, baptism, healings, spiritual gifts, what day we worship, or how God created the universe. It has to do with God presenting His will for how we are to relate to Him and to one another so we live in faith, hope, and love (1 Corinthians 13:13; 1 Thessalonians 1:3, 5:8).

How shall we handle differences with each other over our theology? According to Acts 15, some issues are worth debating to correct wrong theologies, with the church resolving conflict by coming to one mind on the issue. According to Romans 14, some issues are not worth debating, and we should respect each other's theological differences while maintaining loving unity in Christ. At one time, I participated in a Bible discussion group with believers and unbelievers, and everyone freely shared their views. To believers in the group, some of the views were clearly unchristian or unbiblical, but we all respected each other and listened to each other without saying, "You are wrong" or correcting anyone. We heard the different statements each other made about the biblical subjects. The amazing thing was that as we kept meeting and thinking about things that were shared, the Holy Spirit eventually brought us to the place where our views began to line up with what He wanted us to know. Important areas of agreement happened because God is very good at helping us recognize truth from error in what persons say to each other (1 John 2:27). It is okay to firmly believe what you understand the Bible to say and to allow others under certain circumstances to believe what they understand because God accepts our differences (Luke 9:49–50; Romans 14:5, 17–23).

Our unity in Christ's body does not depend on everyone agreeing at every point of theology. Rather, we can unite in the important things such as believing the Bible is God's Word to us, that Jesus is our Lord and Savior, that holy living in obedience to Christ's teachings is to be our lifestyle, and that we are to work together to accomplish good and meet people's needs. Many things the Bible teaches are helpful, good, and interesting, even important, but our knowledge is likely to be incomplete, and we are always learning more and hopefully changing our views as more information becomes available.

How wonderful if our nonessential differences in doctrine could be overridden by relationships of love (John 13:34–35, 17:25–26). What should we die for, our "right doctrines" or maintaining faith in Christ and the truth of His gospel? Jesus died for people, not for particular ideas or right doctrines. Can there be unity in diversity? Yes, but only in Christ (John 17:20–22). He unifies in the midst of diversity (Colossians 1:17). There is likely to be some truth in all the diverse parts, but we do not find it by clinging to our part and refusing to consider the truth of other parts.

Here is one further thought on getting along in spite of differing beliefs. A principle in 1 Corinthians 8 teaches us to not destroy the faith of a person we feel does not have the knowledge we do and who believes something differing from our belief. I'm not suggesting that God's truth is unimportant and that we should not contend for the truth; I'm suggesting that right attitudes toward fellow believers with different beliefs are important. We need to see where others are coming from before doing something to offend or cause them to lose a measure of what they believe especially if it would disrupt their walks with Christ. Before we act contrarily, perhaps it would help to first learn the motives and reasons behind their theology. There is a difference between wanting or needing to be right and wanting to live for Jesus and obey God's Word from a pure conscience.

If people believe the things they do at this point in their walks with Christ, even though we believe their knowledge may be wrong or incomplete, we must be careful how we approach them rather than to inappropriately or insensitively try to convince them of our understanding of the truth. There are some wise considerations in Scripture to take into account when dealing with our differences with Christian brothers and sisters. In certain situations, it is okay to take others aside and explain the truth to them if they have correct but incomplete knowledge of God's Word. This will increase their understanding (Acts 18:24–26).

Here is some of the wisdom in the Bible that helps us know better how to approach or not approach people. "Avoiding a fight is a mark of honor, only fools insist on quarreling" (Proverbs 20:3). "Spouting off before listening to the facts is both shameful and foolish" (Proverbs 18:13). "The tongue of the wise makes knowledge appealing" (Proverbs 15:2). "Not many of you should become teachers in the church, for we who teach will be judged more strictly" (James 3:1).

You have heard, "A little knowledge can be dangerous." How sure are we that we know what we're talking about? Controversy reminds us that there are more sides to issues than we see. Sorting out the many seemingly contradictory themes in the Bible and in life is not easy, so we should make allowances for differences if we are seekers after the whole truth concerning any issue. The important thing to consider is this: Are we and those we differ with theologically living for Jesus and desiring to serve Him? Are we obeying His Word to the best of our ability? Do we love one another as Jesus would want so as to give the world around us the impression we are one in Him (John 13:34–35)? If someone and I have the same faith in Christ for the forgiveness of sins and the same desire to live to please Him, differences in theology can be instructive points, not points of contention that must be resolved for us to have peace and unity. If making an issue of a particular theological belief would cause a brother or sister in Christ to become upset and confused and would negatively influence his or her faith and good conscience, why pursue the need to be right on matters of theology that may not ultimately matter? Romans 14 provides some good advice on this issue of accepting differing opinions or beliefs. Think about the meaning of statements such as, "You should each be fully convinced" (Romans 14:5) or "You may believe there's nothing wrong with what you are doing, but keep it between yourself and God. Blessed are those who don't feel guilty for doing something they have decided is right" (Romans 14:22). Perhaps the main question we should ask about another's beliefs is not whether what he or she believes is right or wrong but if it leads to Christlike or sinful behavior. We all have convictions before God. If God accepts us anyway, who are we to say another is unacceptable because of a different theological understanding?

You have a theology. What is it? Let each of us simply resolve, with careful thought, to be working toward a greater understanding of our theology (2 Peter 1:4–8, 3:18). Our theology needs to inform how we live, so let us grow in our understanding of God, how we can better know Him and experience His love, and how each truth we learn from Scripture can help us see life from God's perspective so we can live in wise and healthy ways. Let us keep the goal of theology in mind: it is not primarily to make us smart as much as it is to enable us to live godly lives before God, our families, and a world in need of seeing God at work (1 Timothy 1:5–7).

## *Chapter 10*

## DOES GOD SEND GOOD PEOPLE TO HELL?

During my college years, I attended a weekly Bible study group in my dorm. A member of the group said he was upset with the Bible's teaching about hell because, although his father was not a Christian, he thought very highly of his father and could not believe God would send him to hell. Even though I believe in God and in hell, this question has bothered me off and on my whole life. Does God send good people to hell? Some say that God does not send anyone to hell, that people send themselves there. What follows is my attempt to make sense of the issue while being true to the Bible and hopefully answer my friend's and others' concerns.

The question of whether good people are in hell makes us ask, what is a good person? People generally think a good person is someone who conforms to their societies' laws and customs. They mostly do what is fitting and proper because they possess and practice good-natured virtues such as loyalty, honesty, compassion, politeness, caring, and so forth. Good people don't kill, steal, rape, or lie. In the religious realm, good people respect and live by the laws and customs of their God. In the secular realm, good people respect and live by the laws and customs of their societies. Bad people are those who do not abide by the accepted societal laws and customs. They do not exhibit good social virtues as do the law-abiding citizens who exhibit caring personalities and beneficial good deeds. In general, good people are caring and nice to others and contribute to the well-being of society, and bad people cause trouble for society. Of course, people say that even the bad have a lot of good in them. I agree; it's in there somewhere.

Humanly speaking, being a good person is a relative term—good compared to what? Obviously, some consider themselves good when they compare themselves to bad people, but even the best good people are not good all the time. That means they are good somewhere on a scale of, say, one to ten. If they are above a six or seven, even a nine, they consider themselves to be good persons. But what if we calculate goodness on God's scale? What if God tells us to be perfect as He is perfect (Matthew 5:48)? Our standard for goodness no longer fits. No one is good to the degree that God is good. Even our best deeds at times are likely to be tainted by some form of evil if only self-centeredness (Isaiah 64:6; Psalm 14:1–3; Romans 7:19, 21). If God requires perfect goodness in order to enter His kingdom, where does that leave us? No one is perfect, so there would have to be another way apart from our goodness to enter God's kingdom. Thankfully, there is.

Some say humans are basically good; others say they are basically evil. Which is it? Perhaps the confusion is because our nature includes both (2 Chronicles 19:2–3). The Bible seems to say we are a mixture of good and evil (Genesis 3:22). It says we were created good, but evil entered the world and marred our goodness. Sven Wahlroos, a clinical psychologist, wrote, "All of us have a good or kind and a bad or evil part of our personality and we do not readily admit the presence of the latter."[20] He certainly sees both sides in people but observes that people see themselves as good because they ignore their dark sides.

When we observe the world around us, what do we see? We observe that some people have good hearts and are nice. We can attribute much that is good to their environments and the loving, moral families in which they grew up. But there are always some raised in good homes who turn out evil and others reared in bad homes who turn out good. Does something other than environment help determine our good or evil natures? Perhaps whether we are basically good or bad is caused by something that is in us at birth. Or maybe it has to do with how each person responds to his or her environment. Are basically good people those who don't like what they see in their environments and choose to make their lives different?

We notice also that there are degrees of good and evil. Some good people are nicer than other good people, and some evil people are more wicked than others. So are we basically good or basically evil? It doesn't matter really if evil is in everyone to some degree; any person with a mixture of good and evil is unlike God, who cannot allow any degree of

---

[20] Sven Wahlroos, *Family Communication* (New York: Macmillan, 1974), 69.

evil in His realm. Therefore, any evil at all must be rejected by an evil-free God who requires an evil-free kingdom. (Leviticus 19:1–8).

In terms of God's salvation, both good and bad people need to be saved (Matthew 22:8–10). This helps explain the difference between Christians. Some who become Christians have been relatively good people while others have not been so nice (1 Corinthians 6:9–11). Becoming a Christian does not normally, overnight, change a person from being nasty into being a nice person. This is because some who become Christians have more baggage perhaps from their upbringing or habit patterns, and it may take longer to be rid of the rough edges so that they become nicer. The fact that there are bad people who become Christians also explains why many non-Christians appear so much nicer than Christians do. Others, already good people when they become Christians, may not have so much to overcome.

There are then varying degrees of niceness among Christians, though all Christians ought to be making progress toward Godlikeness (2 Peter 3:18; 2 Corinthians 3:18). All Christians are at different stages of development. I have heard good people say things such as, "Before I became a Christian I was pretty good, but after becoming a Christian, I have gotten a lot worse." What they are experiencing is a relationship with God they did not have before. They have gotten closer to God, and when that happens, their imperfections show up more. It is like bringing something that we do not see clearly into the bright light of the sun, and now we can see it for what it is. God is perfection, and to draw close to Him reveals our imperfections, so we appear worse than we were previously. God accepts us that way in Christ but wants us to see the areas of our lives that need continued repentance and work so we can become better people, people with a holy character like His.

When it comes to whom God saves, being good or bad has little to do with it. Since both good and bad people are saved, we cannot say all good people go to heaven and all bad people go to hell. Something besides our goodness or badness determines our destiny. According to the Bible, all people whether good or bad have a bad side that needs transforming (Romans 3:23, 12:2). What is important to our ultimate destination is whether persons recognize not only their goodness but also their badness. It is because of the bad side of us that we need someone to help make it possible for us to somehow be acceptable to God (Romans 5:6–11).

For us to become acceptable to God means repenting of our wrongs and receiving forgiveness, being declared righteous by God (Romans 4:3–5), coming to be on God's side, and accepting Him as the rightful leader of our lives. Whether they are good or bad, those who do not agree to God's terms are lost to God and His kingdom because our goodness is not enough to enable a person to fit into heaven. The evil part of the person must be dealt with, and the person must come to be on God's side.

People who do not admit to their evils are deceived about their goodness (1 John 1:8; Jeremiah 17:9–10). They also do not realize what God can permit or not permit in His kingdom (Matthew 5:20; John 3:3; Hebrews 12:14; Revelation 21:6–8, 27; 22:14–15). If good people are confronted with the fact of being sinners but deny it and refuse to submit to Jesus as Savior, they condemn themselves no matter how good they are (John 3:17–20). They do so by showing they are against God as demonstrated by not believing what He says and by not submitting to His terms (John 6:28–29). How can people, no matter how good, be a part of a world that is under God's rule if they do not accept His rule? They would not fit in.

All of us, no matter how good we are, seem to have the capacity to violate our consciences and fail at doing what we know we should (Romans 7:19). Therefore, unless the evil part of a good person's nature is taken care of, there can be no admittance into heaven lest heaven is like earth, a mixture of good and evil—with evil never eliminated. And we see what kind of a world evil has made this one.

It seems that no matter how we try to have a good world on earth, it comes to be increasingly corrupt. How could those opposed to Christ make good citizens in a kingdom of righteousness where He rules? Would it not make sense to have an alternative place for people to live who do not have a heart to follow Christ's government? Jesus said that any kingdom, town, or family divided against itself would not survive. Jesus said, "Anyone who isn't with me opposes me, and anyone who isn't working with me is actually working against me" (Matthew 12:25–30). He makes plain that there are those for and against Him. My understanding is that hell is reserved for those who will forever reject

His truth and Lordship, those who have chosen to walk away from Christ and from whatever light God gives them (Romans 1:18–21).

The question for all good people is this: Will they accept God's assessment of them as sinners and submit to His way of salvation (1 John 1:8–10), or will they try to save themselves their way, appealing to their own goodness? To refuse God's truth and terms of salvation is to prove oneself to not be on God's side but actually to be His enemy (James 4:4). Being good or nice doesn't save anybody; it's what is done with Jesus that makes the difference (John 3:36; 1 John 5:12). The real issue is not whether a person is nice or not or whether good deeds outweigh bad; the issue is whether the person's heart is with God, whether the person will receive the love of God and do God's will (Matthew 7:21; Mark 3:31–35).

How can people live under God's rule in heaven when they will not submit to His truth and authority on earth? You may be a very good, caring person, but the question is, who really is the ruler of your life—you or God? That's the issue God is concerned with. We have the same concerns whenever we hire people to work for us—we want a resume and references to determine if they will fit with what we are all about or if they will be contrary to our purposes. I was once rejected by a church group because the people there said I did not fit with their goals. In the Bible, there were "good" people who wanted to know how they could get into heaven. Jesus tested them by giving directions to follow to see whether their hearts and values were with Him, or not. Many were willing to follow Him until it required something they did not like or want to do (John 6:59–60, 66–69; Luke 18:18–24). Those who consider themselves to be good, need to read God's instructions in the Bible and determine if they are willing to comply with them. If they are not, are they really on God's side?

A man named Cornelius was a very good person (Acts 10:1–2, 22). But to have eternal life, he needed to trust Christ Jesus to save him. Even though he was a very good man and well respected in the community, he knew he was not good as God is good; he knew he needed God's solution for eternal life (Acts 10–11). The question is will we allow God to transform us so we have hearts enabling us to live in oneness with Him (Ezekiel 36:26–27; Matthew 18:3)?

Hell is a very touchy subject as it should be. Some people cannot believe in a God who would commit people to hell. To loving and sensitive people, hell is unthinkable. Who among us would send our loved ones there? Even if they commit wrongs against us, we still love them. Nevertheless, I am convinced there is a hell for one basic reason: Jesus, the ultimate picture of love, claimed it to be so. As God and a teacher from God, He ought to know, and He warned about hell numerous times (Matthew 8:10–12, 10:28, 13:47–50; 23:33). Yes, according to Jesus, hell exists, but I would not wish it on anyone, and neither does He nor God His Father. God is very plain in His prophetic message: "I take no pleasure in the death of wicked people. I only want them to turn from their wicked ways so they can live" (Ezekiel 33:11; 2 Peter 3:9).

One objection to hell is this: How can God punish for eternity crimes that may not deserve such severity? Infinite punishment for finite crimes does not seem to fit the mold of true justice. But what if the punishment for specific crimes was not the ultimate reason some will be in hell? Is it possible that Christ Jesus, by His death on the cross, has paid for all the sins of the world (John 1:29; 2 Corinthians 5:14–15, 19; 1 John 2:2) except one (Matthew 12:30–32)? Isn't the basis for assigning people to hell their refusal to repent of their wrongs and their rejection of Jesus Christ, whom God sent to save them (John 3:16)? Maybe the reason for a hell is not so much a place of punishment for the sins of people as it is a place for all who refuse to line up with God's essentials for receiving life (Mark 1:15). The righteous and the wicked alike will face judgment for their deeds and receive their due (Acts 17:30–31; Revelation 20:11–13). In that sense, we could see hell as punishment for our wrongdoing, but our bad deeds are not the primary basis for sending someone to hell; such deeds are the product of a deeper issue, the rejection of God's Son and His truth and authority in our lives. Such a rejection is really a sign of rebellion, and if God knows rebels will forever rebel, why wouldn't He send them elsewhere?

Consider also this possibility. If God judges everyone justly for their deeds, will there be degrees of places in hell according to one's deeds? Hell possibly has degrees of existence and will not be the same for everyone (Luke 12:45–48). Some think that after being in hell for a time, a person will cease to exist. I don't agree, but you can believe that if you want. Others think a person will serve a time of appropriate punishment and then go to heaven and get a second chance. I don't see these things in the Bible, but these thoughts are not for us but for God to decide.

We have a place in our world for those who refuse to walk by the guidelines of our society. We tolerate prisons; we lock people away for crimes, some even for life. And some, we say, deserve the death penalty. Maybe these people did mostly good in their lives but now have this one bad deed. Why not let people who are mostly good run free among us? Isn't that the most loving thing to do? No.

We say that the loving thing is to provide a safe society for people. Yes, after they pay for their crimes, we release criminals, but records show that most end up back in prison, and some recommit the same crime, even murder. Most people would likely agree that it would be nice if we did not need prisons. It would be wonderful if we did not have to protect our families from robbers, killers, child abusers, or rapists. Christ died for all, but that doesn't mean all choose to walk Christ's way. So what do you do with people who do not want to follow the rules that make for a safe society? Allow them to make it unsafe?

It could be argued that good though not perfect people abide by the rules, but do they do so as long as there is no opportunity to do otherwise? Are people good only as long as outer controls restrict them? There is an interesting Scripture about an age of peace when Christ will rule the world. One day, when an opportunity presented itself, there was a rebellion by people who banded together against Christ and were banished from Christ's kingdom (Revelation 20:1–3, 7–10). People like this obviously do not belong there, as they are looking for something else. Is it possible that some will continue to be against Christ and choose to never repent of their wayward lives, never coming to terms with Christ? If a person in prison shows reform and no longer poses a threat to society, we allow for parole, but we keep others locked up because they continue to be threats to the well-being of society. Does God know that some will forever be a threat to His society and so must have an alternative place for them?

What if a person never chooses to be with you but always against you? What will you ask of such a person? We experience this to some degree in divorce situations. One person no longer wants to live with another. Do we insist on forcing them to stay together against their will? Two people who do not want to walk together are allowed to separate. Consider also the familiar story of the Prodigal Son (Luke 15:11–32); this happens in many people's experiences. Some children do not want to be with their parents but want to live elsewhere for whatever reasons. In the story, the son discovered that life was difficult and destructive away from his father and so returned. In his case, he chose to return to the father. The father never stopped loving his son, but he did not force his return. The son had to realize where life was to be found—with his father. But if the son refuses to return to his father's loving presence, the father respects his son's right to choose a separate life though he does so with grief. Although God tries to influence people to return to Him, hell results from persons choosing their own destination. God loves people and respects their choices enough to allow them to remain separate. Even if God knows it's not in their best interest, they will have it no other way. What if there are people who refuse God's standards, and for them, there is no remedy (2 Chronicles 36:16; Proverbs 29:1)? What more can God do than what He has done? He keeps on loving people and invites them to return to Him. He has sent His Son, Christ Jesus, to pave the way home. But some will not accept God's invitation, and He will not violate their choice to remain separate.

No one can judge whether another is bound for hell; only God can make that determination. Given His perfect nature as a just God, God will not make a mistake but will do the right and fair thing for everyone (Psalm 9:7–8; 2 Thessalonians 1:5–9). And there will be no arguments against His judgment, for all being judged will know He is right (Genesis 18:25). They will have only themselves to blame. We have a good side to our personalities, but our bad side needs to be taken care of so we are fit for God, one another, and heaven (Isaiah 53:4–6).

The Greek word translated "hell" in the New Testament is *gehenna*. According to the *Zondervan Pictorial Encyclopedia of the Bible*, it refers to a place mentioned in the Bible called in Hebrew Ge-Hinnom or Ben-Hinnom. It was a valley south of Jerusalem known as a place where children were sacrificed in a fire to the heathen god Moloch (2 Chronicles 28:1–3, 33:1–6, 2 Kings 23:10). This abominable practice continued and was even practiced by God's people until Jeremiah announced that the name of the place would be changed to the Valley of Slaughter. God was going to slaughter them and throw them in this valley as punishment for their evil violations of God's holiness (Jeremiah 7:30–33, 19:4–7). It became a death-filled destination for multitudes of people. As history progressed, some came to think this valley was a place of fiery punishment where the ungodly would be thrown. Whether Jesus used the word *gehenna* to refer to a place of eternal torment is doubted by some. They say he was referring to the valley as a place where bodies would be thrown when Jerusalem was destroyed in AD 70. I do not know how much the history of this word can be known for sure, but of great importance to me is how Jesus used the word in His teachings. I think one of His main meanings was that people could be cast out of His kingdom to some other destined place if they refused to accept Him as Savior and Lord.

Many are offended at the idea of hell due to possible misunderstandings often presented by the church—for example, that hell is a literal fire. Hell may not be a place of literal fire. Terms used to describe hell are not always literal. Consider this: If hell is a place of everlasting black darkness (Jude 13), how can there be a literal fire that would destroy the darkness? Maybe fire is a figurative term for the mental anguish that will be endured there (Matthew 13:49–50). I once died in a nightmare and went to hell. A dream is not necessarily a source of how things really are, but I recall gnashing of teeth and no fire. The agonizing torture I experienced was the all-consuming thought that I would be there forever, that my fate was sealed. I do not pretend to have the ultimate answers to the subject of hell. Only God knows fully what this place is and what He intends to do, but I trust His goodness and fairness and that He will do what is perfectly just for everyone.

God does not sentence good people to hell because there are no good people, that is, none good enough in His eyes to merit life with Him in His perfect kingdom (Mark 10:17–18). To my college friend, I would say, "I am sure your father is a very good man with high morals and that you are right to admire him. God knows we need more good people in this world. But does that mean good people do not need to receive Christ Jesus as their Savior from sin and death? When you say your father is good, do you mean he is sinless and does not need a savior? Or do you mean he is good enough to go into God's kingdom on his own merit and that Jesus did not need to die for him?"

We are good in our eyes, but we do not see ourselves as God sees us (Psalm 14:2–3; Romans 3:9–12). We deceive ourselves when we don't admit the evil in our nature. I do not know what hell is or how it will be applied to individuals; it's probable that not all will experience hell in the same way. When I study Jesus' statements, I understand that He certainly meant something by His use of the word *gehenna* as well as by other descriptions He used that implied an eternally existing fiery realm that was not a good thing (Matthew 25:41, 13:41–43, 47–50; Mark 9:43–48). Jesus seemed to have in mind a definite place, and He warned people against it in the sense that it is possible to miss God's kingdom. It doesn't matter whether people are good or bad in the opinion of humans. Jesus invites us all to commit our lives to Him, seek forgiveness, have faith in Him, receive His gift of righteousness, experience a changed heart that leads in a Godward direction; and if we do, we will not perish but have everlasting life (John 3:16; 1 John 5:11–12).

## Chapter 11

## WHAT IS THE TRUE NATURE OF HUMAN BEINGS? WHO AM I?

In the modern age of movie technology I appreciate the ratings put on movies as they help us choose what we watch. Many PG-13, most R, and all X-rated movies claim to show violence or sexual conduct not appropriate for children. Personally, I don't think most are appropriate for adults, although there is nothing wrong with sex and violence in their proper, God-ordained contexts. In the few movies I have seen that have shown sexual images, I felt I was invading people's privacy; I don't think it's appropriate to go into someone's home or have others come into mine, to watch private sexual intimacy, but I think this is what we do when we watch it on film. I think it can feed lustful thoughts, incite self-centered gratification, motivate wrong fleshly desires, and promote shameful behavior. Many who feed a lot on such things are often led to more and deeper kinds of immoral subject matter, possibly becoming addicted, and possibly committing crimes against others including family.

The Bible warns of what can happen (Romans 1:28, 32). Sensitive people can find it hard to watch cruel, tortuous, inhumane acts against fellow human beings on the screen. If we see enough of immoral sex and violence, our hearts can become hardened and callous to both immoral sex and violence. When these kinds of things no longer bother people, what does that mean? Can it be dangerous for people to lose a sensitive conscience toward sexual immorality and violence? We seem to have a nature drawn to these sorts of things. Though I don't like to witness these behaviors, such happenings occur in life more than we know. Shame on us humans, and I include myself. Others would say that I am being prudish, judgmental, or worse.

Not only movies depict these behaviors; the Bible could be X-rated because it vividly describes the same kinds of sinful and evil behaviors (2 Samuel 11:2–15, 12:9; Judges 4:21, 19:22–30). For many people, what is seen on the screen and what is read in the Bible is offensive and repulsive. But immorality and wickedness should be repulsive to us because that is not how God intended us to live. In the Bible, God honestly reports to us how we really are, good creatures corrupted by evil. Winston Churchill, a famous English statesman who many considered a good man, read a newspaper article that asked, "What's wrong with the world?" He wrote to the editor, and very concisely answered, "What's wrong with the world? I am." It's easy for people to think they are better than they are. Jesus told a story to illustrate how people trust they are righteous and view others with contempt (Luke 18:9–14). But the Bible, even though it recognizes both good and bad people (Matthew 5:45), concludes that all of us are corrupt and have sinful and self-destructive natures (Romans 2:1, 3:23, 7:18–21). I agree with C. S. Lewis, who wrote in *Mere Christianity*, "No man knows how bad he is till he tries very hard to be good."[21] Some reading this may think this writing is very negative and depressing, but the Bible very clearly presents human nature in this way and tells us our only hope for change and a new life of freedom from sin and its consequences is to become honest and realize how bad and bad off we are.

A recovering alcoholic friend admitted to me he saw himself as a good person until he went to treatment and began to see how wretched he really was. I have been a pastor for over forty-three years, and I think many consider me a good person, but I am under no delusion; I am aware of my deep-seated sinfulness. I have at times felt I am the worst of sinners; I fit God's appraisal of human nature. Only when we come to self-honesty about our condition do we become willing to get help. It is best if we turn to God's solution, which presents good news for all who want help. That is why God gives us the Bible and Christ Jesus (John 20:30–31; Romans 7:24–25; Proverbs 28:13).

Many humanists and secular people say that we have evolved from lower life forms, that we have a material nature with no soul or spirit, and that everything we are made of is physical; everything we

---

[21] C. S. Lewis, Mere Christianity (New York: Macmillan, 1943, 1952), 124.

are and have is found in this present material universe, and nothing else exists. There is no God, and the problem of evil in humans is nothing more than the absence of a good environment and education, and as we work toward creating better environments, better living conditions, and better people, we can achieve a good, peaceful world.

In this view, people see themselves as basically good and able to accomplish what they want. We are the masters of our destinies. Religion with belief in a supernatural being is often cited as an enemy that prevents human progress. A proof, they say, that religion is an enemy of human progress are the wars and other conflicts religions cause, so religion cannot be allowed to mix with our scientific age and must be kept out of public places. Science, education, and good government become our hope for a better world. Each society's consensus and laws determine what is morally right. We can achieve great things if we work together toward our sought-after utopia. Someday, through science, we may even find a cure for aging and death. Our future hope for a better world relies on continued evolution, either natural or humanly manipulated, and the good things we do that future generations can build upon. We can only speculate what the future will be. There is no afterlife. Our death is simply passing out of existence.[22] How different this view is from the view God portrays of humans in the Bible.

What is the biblical view of human nature? "So God created human beings in his own image. In the image of God he created them; male and female he created them" (Genesis 1:27). According to the Bible, who we were made to be and who we are, differs greatly. We were made to be workers and to rule with God as good stewards over creation, to commune with God on an intimate, joyful, meaningful level, and to live without wrongdoing and death. We were made to share God's attributes such as love, wisdom, goodness, peacefulness, truth, self-control, and so forth. We were made to be in harmony with God, nature, others, and

---

[22] You can learn the humanist views from reading "Humanist Manifestos I, II, III" online. They are like pamphlets. If we were people who did not believe in any God, humanism would ideally be the best way of life. Christians could agree with many humanistic values.

ourselves and to be intelligent, imaginative, and creative—learning, discovering, and inventing. All was very good (Genesis 1:31). But if we honestly evaluate ourselves, how do we compare to those characteristics of being in God's likeness? We are not very good stewards of ruling the creation—we abuse it, greedily consume it, squander it, deface it, and ruin it. We don't seem to have intimate, joyful, and meaningful communion with God—we are often out of touch and unaware of His presence and purpose for our lives. Instead of being God-centered, we are basically self-centered. We certainly don't live free of wrongdoing, we carry guilt and shame for violating our moral conscience, and death comes as an enemy to us all (1 Corinthians 15:26). We don't enjoy the perfect array of godly attributes—we are often not very loving, wise, good, peaceful, truthful, or self-controlled. We frequently experience broken relationships with God, nature, family, others, and ourselves. We do not put our intelligence, imaginativeness, and creativity to the best use. We "lose" our minds in many situations and often fail to solve our problems. People say our present condition is what it means to be human, but the way God created us to be is what is truly human. Jesus, the perfect man, is what it means to be truly human. We need a restoration of God's image in us.

I once took my grandkids over to a local YMCA, where they were scheduled to participate in a kid's basketball league. On the wall of the gym, a sign read, "We build strong kids, strong families, and strong community." I thought, *What a fantastic goal!* Underneath those words was a list of rules: "Treat others with respect," "No profanity," "Watch your angry words," and "Avoid harmful physical contact." Everyone I met there seemed nice and friendly, so I asked myself, *Why the list?*

The answer was obvious; we are nice as long as things go our way or people don't provoke us, but situations can happen in life that suddenly bring out the worst in us. We have natures easily susceptible to behaviors that destroy what we are trying to build. I suppose they posted this sign and rules because they observed how nasty people could get in the heat of competitive sports. Generally, we humans think we are okay, are basically good, and have the ability to "get it all together." Are we blind or what? Every day, we see what the world is like. Does it look harmonious, right, and good? Most people I talk to these days say they can sense the world is changing and not for the better. I'd like to see it change for the better, but what guarantee do we have it will?

It should be obvious when thinking about it, that we have fallen a long way from what God created us to be. What happened? Why must humanity be in such a struggle to get better? The answer to these questions is in Genesis 3.

What does Genesis reveal about our corrupted nature? Genesis reveals we have become creatures who run and hide from God (Genesis 3:8) because we know we have done wrong and are guilty and fear facing a God who may bring judgment and punishment. We are afraid of God; we feel embarrassment and shame, so we avoid God (Genesis 3:7, 10). But if our nature is to run from God, how do we explain the fact that most people profess to believe in God? How do we explain the existence of religions all over our planet? If people are running and hiding from God, why do most believe in Him? I think that if people were questioned about the gods they believe in, we would find that their gods do not fit the description of the God who is revealed in the Bible.

If God created us in His image, it's likely we humans have an inborn sense there is a God, and because we live in a threatening world, we feel we need a God to help us deal with life's problems and fears. But because we don't want the real God who created us, we invent one we can deal with who we believe will respond to what we want.

An in-depth study of the world's religions reveals that their definitions of God do not fit the God revealed in the Bible. The biblical God is a God to be rejected (Romans 1:20–21). Even people who believe in the God of the Bible invent their own gods by changing Him to fit with a god they feel more comfortable with. For example, I have heard people say, "I don't believe in a God who would condemn anyone to hell. My god loves and would never do that." I would agree that hell is a hard concept to understand, but what right do I have to change God to fit what I want Him to be?

Another way people create their own views of God is by changing His views of who they are as humans. Denying their own evil nature, they may say they are good and on that basis believe God will accept them into heaven. But is that what the God of the Bible says? I conclude that most people believe in God but not the God revealed in the Bible. That is, a God people either defy or run from. Since people need a God to help them with their problems and to save them from fear or death, they invent one they can live with. Actually, their ideas of god are self-made idols (Exodus 20:2–6; Deuteronomy 6:14; Isaiah 45:5–6). If the

God of the Bible confronted us, we would be unable to stand before Him (Exodus 20:18–19; Psalm 143:1–2); we would run from Him rather than try to understand who He is.

The God of the Bible cares about us and wants to help us. He came into the garden and confronted the man and woman who were hiding in fear (Genesis 3:9, 21). He even covered their shame.

We cannot hide from the One who sees and knows all, so how do we respond when confronted with our wrongs? We deny our guilt. We find it difficult to accept responsibility for our wrongs. Instead, we justify our actions, we place blame elsewhere (Genesis 3:11–13). Our corrupt human nature does not wish to honestly look at who we are and admit our evil side. We make excuses and blame something or someone for the way we are or for what we did. We blame our upbringing, or others, or our circumstances, or the Devil; we blame even God if we feel He failed us.

Pride and fear prevent humility and truthfulness. It is as Jesus said; we choose to remain in darkness rather than coming into the light because we do not want our deeds or thoughts exposed (John 3:19–20). We make excuses and go into hiding. Our hiding from God sometimes means running from churches to bars, sports, or hobbies and thinking we are better than we really are. We hide behind lies, or by denying the truth, or by believing we are basically good. We even hide from reality by hiding in mental illnesses. I am not talking about the kind of mental illness caused by physical or chemical deformity but self-chosen illnesses as ways to escape reality. We use anything to get out of facing God and ourselves. The proof of our corrupt human nature and our rejection of the true God can be seen in the things we say, think, or do that are destructive to ourselves and others (Genesis 4:9–10; Romans 1:28–32).

Our sinfulness is deeper than we know. The apostle Paul knew it when he wrote, "I know that nothing good lives in me, that is, in my sinful nature. I want to do what is right, but I can't... what a miserable person I am" (Romans 7:18, 24). The apostle Peter knew it when he said, "Oh Lord, please leave me—I'm too much of a sinner to be around you" (Luke 5:8). The prophet Isaiah knew it when he said, "It's all over! I am doomed, for I am a sinful man" (Isaiah 6:5). King David knew it when he said, "Purify me from my sin. For I recognize my rebellion; it haunts me day and night" (Psalm 51:2–3).

When we become honest and allow ourselves to see the truth, we become broken and cry out to God for a Savior, as did the apostle Paul: "Who will free me from this life that is dominated by sin and death? Thank God! The answer is in Jesus Christ our Lord" (Romans 7:24–25). Even after years of believing in Christ, I am discovering by God's loving mercy things about myself that need admitting and changing. I am thankful for God's loving and gentle faithfulness in showing me who I am so I can get better (Hebrews 12:5–11).

Does this mean there is nothing good in our human nature? One might think so with Bible statements such as "No one does good, not a single one" (Romans 3:12; Matthew 19:17). However, Genesis does not say we know only evil, although for some it can reach that point (Genesis 6:5); we know good *and* evil (Genesis 3:22). Although our nature is corrupted, we are capable of good and great things (Genesis 11:6; Matthew 7:11). Art, music, inventions, architecture, beautiful buildings, gardens, good deeds, love of family and friends, and so forth, are all a part of who we are and what we are capable of doing (Genesis 4:21–22; Ecclesiastes 2:4-10; Romans 5:7).

There are a lot of good people in the world with varying degrees of niceness and goodness (Acts 10:22), but in spite of their goodness, all have their not-so-nice side. No one is good as God is good (Luke 18:18–19) or able to overcome the evil in his or her nature. No one is good enough to merit God's forgiveness and eternal life. Self-centeredness, wrong motives, and love for ourselves taint much of the good we do. People often do not help others because there is no advantage to themselves or it is too inconvenient (Luke 10:29–37). Although a lot of real caring goes on, many people do not genuinely care for others. Their caring goes only to those of their own kind (Luke 6:32–34) or because it is part of their vocations. But not all is hopeless. Since God is the ultimate definition of good, we can achieve true goodness in a proper relationship with Him. Believers in Christ do wrong (Galatians 6:1), but having been converted and possessing God's Spirit, they have His divine nature (2 Peter 1:3–4) and were re-created for good works (Ephesians 2:8–10), which characterizes true followers of Christ Jesus (Titus 2:7, 14, 3:14).

In summary, what does Genesis reveal about who we are? By failing to heed the warnings of their Creator, the first man and woman allowed evil and destruction into their world. The nature of humans changed from pure goodness to a mixture of good and evil (Genesis 3:5, 22). Our moral sense, relationships, thinking, and judgments—all aspects of our being created in God's image—have been negatively affected. The aspects of the image of God in us have been damaged beyond our own abilities to fix them. We are guilty of wrongdoing and fear God's judgment, so we hide, deny our guilt, and most of the time, we do not take responsibility for our wrongdoing and instead blame others. I remember in high school causing an accident in shop class and blaming someone else. We do good things, but our selfish and self-protective motives taint our goodness. One of the most difficult things I ever admitted to myself was that the only reason I did good things for others was so I would look good and people would like me, not because I genuinely loved and cared about them.

The apostle Paul had a difficult time finding people who did not seek only after their own interests but were also genuinely concerned for the welfare of others (Philippians 2:20–21). Our nature keeps us from seeing ourselves for who we really are; we are deceived (Jeremiah 17:9), and our destiny is self-destruction. Because of our corrupted nature, we need to be restored to God's image and true goodness. God offers us the hope of renewal; that's what the Bible is all about—it tells us the truth about who we are and gives us the solution.

God works to restore us to His image based on our response to His offer of salvation. We can resist God and forfeit becoming part of His new world. Those who receive His offer will be resurrected in new bodies perfectly fit for life in the coming restoration of all things (Acts 3:19–21). Jesus Christ possesses the true human nature, and we are to become like Him (Galatians 4:19; Romans 8:29; 1 John 3:2).

How can we break through our deceptive hearts to see ourselves as God sees us? To know who we are, we must come to see the truth about ourselves, both good and bad through honesty and courage. To have honesty and courage, we need a safe place to come out of hiding, a place where we know we will be loved. If we are fortunate to see our true nature and humbly admit it, what do we do? We call out to God for Him to save us.

I came across an article, "If Only Charles Darwin Could See His Descendent Now."[23] It contained an interview with Laura Keynes, his great-great-great-granddaughter. Laura has a doctorate in philosophy from Oxford University. People were surprised that she had returned to her childhood faith, Roman Catholicism. Having lived in the world of intellectuals and having been an agnostic, she said, "The influences in my life were highly rational, scientific, secular, and humanistic... I had absorbed the view that all phenomena are the product of the material brain." She explained the reason for her return to the Christian faith; it was during the time when "new atheists" were writing their books to attack God and prove the nonexistence of God and "God debates" were taking place.

> I expected to be moved from agnosticism to atheism by their arguments, but after reading on both sides of the debate, I couldn't dismiss a compelling intellectual case for faith. As for being good without God, I'd tried and didn't get very far. At some point, life will bring you to your knees, and no act of will is enough in that situation. Surrendering and asking for grace is the logical human response.

Her recognition of the true nature of human beings and the need for salvation reminds me of Jesus' words,

> You can enter God's Kingdom only through the narrow gate. The highway to hell is broad, and its gate is wide for the many who choose that way. But the gateway to life is very narrow and the road is difficult, and only a few ever find it. (Matthew 7:13–14)

---

[23] James Kelly, "If Only Charles Darwin Could See His Descendant Now," *National Catholic Register*, August 14, 2013. (Courtesy of National Catholic Register, www.ncregister.com)

## Chapter 12

## FACING AND ANSWERING THE PROBLEM OF DEATH

Do you know what a "materialist" is? No, not someone like my wife who collects material for sewing. A materialist is someone who believes everything in the world is physical. All matter, energy, and the building blocks for life have been here from the beginning, and everything has evolved to make up the world as we know it. Everything about the nature of humans can be explained in physical terms. Matter, chemicals, and electrical connections make up our brain, whose workings explain all aspects of our being. The materialist can point to experiments on the brain that demonstrate that the brain controls our morality, emotions, spirituality—everything.

Proof that the brain controls all is pointed out by observing that personalities can drastically change if the brain is injured. A person may change from easy-going and nice to a nasty and lewd person, from a spiritual God worshipper to an atheist, or from moral behavior to immoral, all due to changes in the brain. What we call free will is a function of the brain and our choices are not free, but determined. There is no divine Spirit working with our spirit that can influence and determine what our lives will be like; our brain alone is responsible, and there is no other dimension of reality. What Christians would call spirit or soul does not exist.

Death to a materialist is when brain waves, pulse, and all other bodily functions cease. When we die, we go out of existence, and we are nothing more than a memory in the minds of people who knew us.

But is there a dimension outside the realm of the physical known as *spirit*, otherwise translated as *breath* (Genesis 2:7; Psalm 104:30)? Can a spirit outside of us communicate with us, and is there a part of us that can exist outside our bodies? Some people who have temporarily died in surgery have reported seeing their bodies from a vantage point outside them. They claim to have left their bodies and were able to see and hear what was going on in the room around them. Of course, materialists can claim that these experiences were due to altered mental conditions and that we can produce the same effects in certain "hypnotic" states. Interestingly, neurosurgeon Eben Alexander claimed that his experience could not be due to functions of his brain because vital parts of his brain had been dead for seven days while he was in a coma. He is convinced that there is conscious life apart from the brain.[24] Naturally, people have questioned his character and claims, but he sticks by his story.

More important, evidence for the existence of a spirit dimension comes from what the Bible reports. For example, when He was being crucified, Jesus offered His spirit up to His Father (Luke 23:46). Jesus said a person dying on a cross next to Him would be with Him in paradise (Luke 23:43). This would seem to imply a conscious existence apart from the body. The Bible defines our physical death as more than the ceasing of bodily functions but as the separation of the spirit, or inner life principle, from the body (James 2:26). God put the breath of life into humans at creation. When Jesus raised a girl from the dead, the Bible says her spirit, or life, returned and she arose immediately (Luke 8:53–55). Does that mean her spirit or breath given by God left her body, existed somewhere in a self-conscious state, and returned at Jesus' word? Some would say the Bible was written from a primitive point of view, before science came along to explain everything, implying that the Bible is inaccurate because people did not know any better. But there are very good reasons to believe in God, who is Spirit (John 4:24), and who created us with the capacity to be connected to the physical and the spiritual world (John 3:8). Christians believe God created us to be multidimensional (Genesis 2:7; Isaiah 42:5). This means that body and spirit are united as one, and being a whole person requires that body and spirit not be separated from each other. As believers in Christ, our certain hope is that the resurrection of the body, united with spirit, is God's intended purpose. I know the Bible speaks of humans as body, soul, and spirit (1 Thessalonians 5:23), but I am not prepared to know or

---

[24] Eben Alexander, *Proof of Heaven, A Neurosurgeon's Journey into the Afterlife* (Riverside: Simon & Schuster, 2012).

discuss the mysteries of such a truth. For now, I am content to concern myself with our being as material and immaterial.

Death is a reality most people fear (Hebrews 2:15). Each one's fears may differ. Some people fear annihilation and the loss of their personhood because they do not want to lose their identity. Some who know of God's judgment may fear punishment or hell (Ecclesiastes 3:17; Hebrews 9:27). Others may fear the unknown, the pain they may have to endure in dying, or the anguish of leaving all they love behind. We may try to ignore death by keeping busy or putting it out of mind, but there is too much around us to remind us of its inevitability. We can't help but know death is always nearby, and when we do, we are likely to experience various degrees of anxiety. God calls death "the last enemy to be destroyed" (1 Corinthians 15:26).

What kind of comfort can satisfy us in the face of death? Philosopher Arthur Schopenhauer (1788–1860) believed that the basic drive in all humans was the will to live.[25] However, our will to live is frustrated because we all die. Therefore, he concluded, all we can do is comfort and console one another as best we can in the face of our hopelessness. It is common for people to do what Schopenhauer recommended; they learn to comfort one another in various ways. Some say, "Don't be afraid. Death is just a part of the cycle of life, a part of nature's way. We live on in people's memories, or through the artifacts we leave behind, or by disintegrating into the earth and becoming a part of nature."

Another comfort statement addresses the belief that we cease to exist when we die. Some say, "Just think what it was like before you were born, when you did not exist. You felt nothing. After you die, it's the same. It's not so bad to feel nothing, is it?"

When it comes to death, I don't find much comfort in such words; I find comfort in Christianity, which teaches that believers will be resurrected and live together with God and loved ones in a world free of evil (1 Thessalonians 4:16–17). I once heard someone remark, "Who would want to live forever? After a time, it would get very boring." I can

---

[25] Steve Wilkens, *Good Ideas from Questionable Christians and Outright Pagans, An Introduction to Key Thinkers and Philosophies* (Downers Grove, IVP, 2004; a short discussion about Arthur Schopenhauer's views on the will and death, 212–13). For a full look at Schopenhauer, read *The World as Will and Representation*.

appreciate such a comment because the thought of living forever seems incomprehensible. But such a remark fails to take into account our new nature and that God, properly defined, is infinite. The possibilities of what God could create for our activity and enjoyment are endless. There is another kind of very helpful comfort besides words and beliefs, that which comes from being surrounded in our dying days by those we love who loves us.

How can we know there is life after death? People believe in an afterlife for many reasons. Some say that nature declares an afterlife—seeds die in the ground but sprout to new life, trees die in winter but leaf out in the spring, and caterpillars go into cocoons but emerge as butterflies. Others say life after death is a moral necessity. We, humans, have a feeling that something is very wrong if there is never justice done to those who have been so evil as to hurt and destroy the innocent, so it makes sense to some that justice demands an afterlife to set things right (Matthew 12:36; 2 Corinthians 5:10; 2 Thessalonians 1:6).

Another reason people give for an afterlife is that human longings always seem to have a fulfillment; we hunger and there is food, we thirst and there is water, we feel lonely and there is love. Since we have a longing to live and not die (Ecclesiastes 3:11), there must be an afterlife to satisfy this longing.

Far surpassing all these reasons, the greatest evidence of an afterlife comes from the eyewitness accounts of those who told us they saw Jesus alive after He had died and was buried (John 20:26–29; Acts 2:32). Others saw Him ascend bodily into heaven (Acts 1:9–11). The existence of an afterlife is something God says we can know (1 John 5:12–13). Such an assurance should be a great comfort to us. Even in the midst of extreme sufferings, a man named Job had such assurance (Job 19:25–27).

How shall death be defined? According to the Bible, death involves three stages. First, spiritual death is the state of being disconnected from God, the source of life. As the Bible puts it, we are dead in sin (Ephesians 2:1–3). Spiritual death involves us in a dying process. The more we sin, the more we die, and this dying process leads to physical and ultimate death. We witness spiritual death when we see how our sins destroy us. For example, good relationships and trust die when we tell lies, steal, gossip, fail to keep confidence, commit adultery, or whatever. Death further progresses if we are plagued with remorse and guilt; we may suffer depression, withdrawal from people, or be unable to engage in the normal activities of daily life. If we develop a life-dominating problem such as gambling, pornography, alcohol, or drugs, we can lose our health, family, jobs, and self-respect, and we may come to the point of not wanting to live. We are killing ourselves. This process of dying little by little results from our decision to remain independent from God. We have rejected God as having the right to be our Lord by not accepting His way and doing things our own way. Spiritually dead people do not respond when others try to influence them to commit their lives to Jesus Christ; they can be too proud and rebellious to admit they are sinners who need forgiveness and renewal. The Bible says the consequence of rebellion against God is death (Genesis 2:16–17; Ezekiel 18:4, 20; Romans 6:23).

The second stage of death is physical death, an outcome of our being spiritually dead or disconnected from God. It happens when the spirit leaves the body and the body ceases to function (Psalm 104:29; Acts 7:59–60; James 2:26). We witness physical death every time we attend a funeral and burial.

The third stage of death is ultimate death, which occurs in our afterlife. Because of our refusal to connect with God, He grants us our choice, no longer tries to persuade us to repent, and we are separated from God forever. The Bible calls this the second death (Revelation 20:11–15). Sin always pays its wages and leads to separation from self, others, and God. The only answer to spiritual, physical, and ultimate death is to find a way to remove from our lives the sinfulness destroying us.

What is God's will concerning death? Some people think God has it in for them because of terrible wrongs they have done, or because of their immoral lifestyles, or because they have been ignoring God. But the truth is God is love and doesn't want anyone to die but for all to repent of their waywardness and choose the life He offers (Ezekiel 18:23, 32; 1 Timothy 2:3–4; 2 Peter 3:9). He loves us even while we live in sin, tries to get our attention to warn us, and has already sent us the answer to our need for the newness of life (Romans 5:8; 1 Timothy 2:5–7).

What is God's solution for death? Genesis 22 is about God telling Abraham to sacrifice his son on an altar; it was a test to see if Abraham truly trusted God and was willing to obey Him. We may think this was an awful thing for God to say to anyone, but to Abraham, this was a child God had promised him, and he believed that if God allowed Isaac to die,

He would bring him back to life (Hebrews 11:17–19). Abraham's faith in God's promise did not waver, and he received his son back. In fact, Abraham doubted that God would permit him to kill his own son as is evidenced by something Abraham said to his servants beforehand: "I and the lad will go over there and worship, and we will return to you" (Genesis 22:5). Abraham also assured his son on the way that God would provide a lamb for the sacrifice (Genesis 22:8). As Abraham was about to kill his son, God told Abraham to sacrifice a ram stuck in a thicket in his son's place.

The story is a picture of God's answer to death. Instead of us having to die, another was substituted for us so we could be set free to live. Many centuries later, that substitute for us came in the person of Jesus Christ (Isaiah 53:4–6; 1 Corinthians 15:3; John 10:11–18). We are delivered from death when we trust Jesus to rescue us and commit our lives to His care and leadership (John 3:16, 8:23–24, 11:25–26). When we take that step of trust, Jesus sends the Holy Spirit to reside in us and give us the power to be raised in two ways from the dead.

We are first resurrected spiritually through conversion. To be resurrected spiritually means that we are created new, and we begin a new kind of life. We are reconnected with God in a loving relationship. Our second resurrection is when Jesus returns; we will be raised bodily from the dead to live eternally in God's fulfilled kingdom. Both resurrections are spoken of in the Bible (John 5:24–29; Romans 8:9–11). Our sinful natures and bodies must die, but our spiritual selves and new bodies will live (2 Corinthians 4:16, 5:16–17; 1 Corinthians 6:14, 15:42–49).

How does death affect the way we Christians live? As we mature in faith, we do not fear death, we do not run from death or deny it; rather, we learn to face it and to participate in death. Participating in death does not sound like a happy or logical thing to do, and it is hard to come to that place of willingness, but for the committed Christ-follower, death becomes the path to a joy-filled life (Luke 9:24; John 12:24–25). Even unbelievers, when they give up their lives to serve others, experience Jesus' words, "It is more blessed to give than to receive" (Acts 20:35).

We find life by participating in death in five ways. First, we allow death to create in us a dependency on God, who has the only answer to death. There is no place else to go. Jesus asked His disciples if they wanted to leave Him. They answered, "Lord, to whom shall we go? You have the words of eternal life" (John 6:66–68). The apostle Paul told us we had the sentence of death in us so we would not trust in ourselves but in God, who raises the dead (2 Corinthians 1:8–10). Fearing death has the potential of bringing us to trust God as our deliverer.

Second, we participate in death by welcoming it as our doorway into a new world. We live with a sure hope and anticipate a wonderful life in the next age of the earth (Hebrews 11:13–16; Luke 23:41–43; 2 Peter 3:13).

Third, we participate in death when we deny ourselves to meet the needs of others. Because God supplies our needs and we have a future inheritance awaiting us, we do not have to selfishly hold on to our money or possessions (1 Timothy 6:17–19). Our life does not consist in the abundance of our possessions or in our having to grasp for security in this world (Luke 12:13–21). We willingly lose a part of our life by freely giving to bless people and meet needs.

Fourth, we participate in death by dying to sin. By walking in the Spirit, we continually override those negative traits God says produce death so we can live our new life in Christ (Colossians 3:3–15; Romans 8:12–14).

Finally, we participate in death by willingly and boldly identifying with Jesus in His sufferings. We become willing to stand up for Him even if it means persecution (Acts 20:22–24, 21:13). One of my favorite stories is about a missionary who traveled by boat to a faraway country to share the message of Jesus' love and forgiveness with a tribal people. A shipmate asked him where he was going. When he told him, the shipmate said, "Don't you know those people are dangerous? You could die out there." The missionary calmly replied, "I died before I came."

We seldom think about how precious life is. We grow up enjoying the things kids do but with very little thought and appreciation of what life means. The sacrifices of those who love us escape our notice. We marry and raise families, and if we are fortunate along the way, we develop close, loving relationships with our family members and a few friends. Life continues from season to season, taking us into old age. We may have taken life for granted, but now, through all the ups and downs and hurting and forgiving, we have grown fonder of those we love so much so that it deeply saddens us to think that one day our relationships with our life companion and beloved family and friends will come to an end. It doesn't seem right that death should rob us of all we have come to hold dear, treasure, and enjoy. We wish life would not end unless of course, our suffering is too great to bear.

Jesus gave us hope when He said, "I am going to prepare a place for you and I will come and get you, so that you will always be with me where I am" (John 14:1–6). Jesus will return for His followers, and together with those who love Him and look forward to His appearing, will rise to meet Him. There is no greater comfort anywhere (1 Thessalonians 4:16–18). Christ-followers believe in a God outside all material things who has created us and who has not abandoned us even though we abandoned Him. We believe in God because we have heard from Him, and He has convinced us by showing us through Christ's life, death, and resurrection that there is something more. We are not imprisoned in a limited universe, nor are we imprisoned in a life of our own making and subject to death. We have been set free and have had our eyes opened to see the existence of the supernatural. One who has personally seen Christ said, and I paraphrase his words, "If Christ is not real and if he has not risen from the dead, we are of all people most miserable, and our faith is worthless. But Christ has risen from the dead and His plan is, to abolish death" (1 Corinthians 15:12–26). We who belong to God due to our supernatural birth into His family possess the life He promised and will never die (John 11:26).

# Chapter 13

## HOW DOES GOD WANT US TO VIEW THE CHURCH?

The church was God's idea and His way of continuing Jesus' ministry on earth. Many have walked away from it because it has often been far from what God intended her to be and do. Jesus called it His church and He loves it (Matthew 16:18; Ephesians 5:25). We need a fresh vision of what God intends His church to be.

Let us begin with a basic biblical definition of the church. The church is all the people of the world who have taken Jesus Christ to be their Lord and Savior and who have miraculously been brought to new life by the Spirit of God (John 1:12–13; Ephesians 1:13). This worldwide group of believers is made up of smaller groups meeting in various locations (1 Corinthians 1:2; Philippians 1:1). The Bible says the church is the bride of Christ, and He will take her to be with Him when He returns (2 Corinthians 11:2; Revelation 19:7–9). The word *church* basically means "an assembly of people," and when Jesus returns, the church will be co-ruler of the world with Christ (Matthew 19:28; 1 Corinthians 6:2–3; Daniel 7:18; 2 Timothy 2:11–12; Revelation 2:26; 5:9–10). To be a co-ruler of the world with Christ means that the world needs changing to bring it in line with the goodness of God. The church is not to wait until that future day, but helping the world to experience goodness is part of our present calling as well (Matthew 5:44-48; Titus 3:1, 8, 14).

How did the church begin? It began when Jesus chose a small band of people to follow Him and carry out His agenda. After Jesus died and was resurrected, His disciples were to be witnesses of the things that happened (Acts 1:8) and proclaim the good news (1 John 1:1–3) that through faith in Jesus Christ, people could be forgiven their sins and experience a new life that would last forever.

These first disciples were to wait for the Holy Spirit from God to come into them before beginning their mission. God's Spirit was to assist them in doing the work of sharing the message and empower them to perform miracles to validate the truth of their message (Luke 24:45–49; Acts 1:1–5, 2:1–4; Hebrews 2:3–4). As Jesus' early disciples, called apostles, which means "sent ones," preached about Jesus, people believed and formed into groups who supported one another and grew in their faith (Acts 2:36–47; Colossians 1:6). Saul, later named Paul, was also an early apostle Jesus chose to spread the good news (Acts 26:13–18). He traveled the Mediterranean world preaching the message of Jesus, and local churches sprang up almost everywhere he went. These churches met in people's homes or other available buildings and eventually spread worldwide.

What form did the church take? In other words, how was it organized, and what did the people do? Various writings of the early church tell us that early believers in Jesus read the handwritten letters and gospels that circulated from church to church (Colossians 4:16), received and discussed the letters' and gospels' teachings, encouraged each other to practice lives that honored Jesus, celebrated the Lord's Supper, prayed, and sang. Leaders were appointed in each church to oversee them and make sure all went well (Titus 1:4–9). The church is an organism and an organization: it is a living body that receives its life from the breath of God, who indwells each true believer. It is an organization because its various parts are connected and put together so that it functions in an efficient manner to accomplish Jesus' intended purposes (1 Corinthians 12). The church may change its formations and methods over time; but its message and purposes are to remain the same (Galatians 1:6–9; 6:9–10). In the remainder of this chapter, I shall refer to the church as local churches made up of people who gather for fellowship and worship and then go out to serve Jesus. These churches may vary in their names, beliefs, places of meeting, and styles, but if they prove to have Jesus Christ and the Bible as their proper base, they are one in purpose, God's people called out of the world to serve and honor Him.

We can know how God wants us to view the church because He tells us in the Bible. It is important to know this because many people have mistaken views of the church that have caused them to deviate from her, or to want nothing to do with her, thus missing her rich, unparalleled benefits. Such muddled views of the church are common because people often see its negative or erring sides. Becoming a leader in the church has challenged me to seek in His word what God says about the church. I need to be continually correcting my own inadequate views, so I can be a proper, valuable part of what the Lord calls His church to be. I become more aware of the need to answer this question about how to view the church when I hear the church criticized or shunned by unbelievers and Christians alike. It was written concerning Jesus that if they knew who He was, they would not have crucified Him (1 Corinthians 2:7–8). We can say the same about the church. If we knew who she was, we would love her instead of ignoring her, love her instead of persecuting her, love her instead of leaving her, love her instead of failing to get to know her, love her in spite of her faults, and love her with our involvement.

I do not blame people for whatever feelings they may have against the church. Too often it has become just another religion instead of the living body of Christ. Here are a few reasons people avoid church. Some stay away from the church because they have been hurt. Although the church has tremendously blessed me, I too at times have been hurt by her, disappointed by her, embarrassed by her, and disgusted with her. I sympathize with people who have been hurt by the church. The church has unfairly judged, offended, rejected, slandered, and even killed people. Though most of these wrongs were not committed by the whole church but by one or a few individuals in the church, the church gets blamed because those individuals are considered representatives of what the church is all about. Others stay away from the church out of habit, or because of a disagreement, or because they are bored by its irrelevance to their needs. I too have experienced disagreements or boredom in the church because I felt it was not doing the right things or that it did nothing for me. Others reject the church because they say they do not believe in institutional religion. Do they mean that it is archaic and out of date, or that it demands involvement they are unwilling to make, or that it tries to control people, or that it doesn't demonstrate the life of Jesus, or what?

I have felt seemingly unreasonable demands, issues involving control versus freedom, or have had to wrestle with outdated, inept, or impractical structures, or have been disappointed by people. Others stay away from church because its people are hypocritical or they feel hypocritical if they attend. The only way for us to avoid such accusations is, to be honest, and admit who we are instead of trying to appear righteous. Jesus condemned hypocrisy (Matthew 23:13).

The fact is that the church is made up of imperfect people, including myself, and it always will be until Jesus perfects her when He comes. (Ephesians 5:25–27). Someone said, "To live above with the saints we love, that will be glory; to live below with the saints we know, that's another story." The Bible is perfectly honest in its portrayal of the church as being imperfect and needing help. Every letter in the Bible written to the church aimed at correcting something. For example, if you read the letters to the church in Corinth, you will quickly see that she had many faults and problems (1 Corinthians 1:10–11, 3:1–3, 5:1, 6:5–8, etc.). You will not find on earth a perfect church. There is no cause for anyone who has been a part of any church to be under the illusion that it is, or should be, perfect and exactly what he or she wants it to be.

Having been a part of the church all my life, I have seen her terrible side and her best side. As I have already said, I don't blame people for feeling turned off or betrayed by the church. I was once rejected by the organized church when I was told that they did not want me to be part of it. But I have seen the good side of the church, and it hurts me to see people turn away from something God ordained to be a help for all of us. On the good side, I have seen unloved people loved, messed up people get their lives together, marriages reunited, lonely people find caring families, compassionate people meet other people's needs, fearful people find peace, and guilty people find forgiveness. The church has done more good for the world than the world will ever know. It has created schools, orphanages, and eldercare facilities. It has fed the poor, given relief following catastrophes, taught health care, provided medical services, created agricultural projects, made loans to help the poor start self-sustaining businesses, and has fought for human rights. It proclaims the life-changing hope that Christ gives to a world of misery and evil, and on and on the list can go. The church is to be in the world, but not of the world. It is to do good in the world as it lives and shares the truth of the gospel. A believer's faith is to be proven by his or her works (James 2:14-17; 1 John 3:16-19)

Even in the most corrupt days of the church, there have always been pockets of believers in the church, doing what God intends it to be and do, but admittedly, because of a mixture of good and evil in the church, the church is both loved and hated. Jesus told us the church would be a mixture of good and evil. Jesus knew it would be imperfect because true believers were in different stages of maturity and many in the church were not true believers. Jesus implied the true and untrue would remain in the church until the end when the false would be removed and the true would remain (Matthew 13:24–30, 36–43). Though Jesus knew parts of the church would be corrupted, He still started it and trusts her to fulfill His purposes.

Jesus told Peter, "I will build my church, and all the powers of hell will not conquer it" (Matthew 16:18). In other words, evil will not overpower it, but the church, based on Christ Jesus and faith in Him, will win over evil. The church would take God's message of salvation and blessed hope to multitudes, and nothing would stop it. Jesus implied that when He came again, the true church would be called on to rule the world with Him (2 Timothy 2:12; Revelation 5:9–10).

I feel sad when people reject the church because they have experienced its negative side. They will miss the good and may miss ultimate victory in their personal lives and in the coming restoration of the world (Acts 3:19–21). Why should we give in to the church's evils and let it lead us away from God's greatest force for good? In light of what Jesus said, it certainly makes sense to be part of it in spite of its problems lest we miss its benefits and possibly its glorious future.

But that's selfish, isn't it, to be part of the church for our own benefit? The greatest benefit of being part of the church is finding fulfillment in helping one another become healed and whole. The apostle Paul died, giving his life for the people of the church so everyone might become complete in Christ (Colossians 1:24–29). At what point do we overcome selfish desires and care about others in Christ's family, our family?

What about people who sometimes have a seemingly legitimate reason for leaving the church? The Bible says some people leave because they never were true believers, but some may leave because a church has no programs for children or the Bible is not taught, or it is not alive and growing, or they need something more in tune with today's society. Some have personal issues with something or someone in a church. I have no problem with people seeking a church that best fits legitimate needs or ministry desires. The point is that they need to find a local body of believers that suits them and in which they become involved. Every believer is a part of the family of God, and if at all possible, they must take the place God has assigned them as a gifted member of His body. Many who live in societies where churches are aging and dying wonder if the church will survive? But God is raising new churches all around the world that are meeting the needs of today's people. Young people are flocking to them. The church is not dead, nor will it fail Christ Jesus. One caution: believers in churches must guard against seeking a church for the purpose of satisfying their personal desires rather than attending the church for the purpose of giving to God what He desires from us.

There are dangers in choosing to be part of a church, for there are some churches that are not in line with biblical Christian beliefs or practices. Here are some unhealthy church practices to watch for; Jesus warned us about being misled (Matthew 7:15–23, 24:4–5). Beware of any "church" that claims to be the only "true" church or that controls you by requiring submission and strict obedience to leaders who claim to know what God's will is for your life. Beware of any church that uses God's Word with guilt, shaming tactics, or threats to pressure you to submit to its teachings. Beware of any church that claims to have revelations from God that are in any way contrary to the Bible. Beware of any church offering secret initiation rites to those who prove worthy. Beware of any church having a different message of salvation than that spelled out in the Bible (Galatians 1:6–9).

Many churches do not fit God's biblical model of His church. But some people are susceptible to churches that want to be controlling. Some grew up in these traditions and do not know any better. Others are needy in some way, perhaps needing love or a secure environment where others make decisions for them. Some people see issues only in black or white, right or wrong, with nothing in between, and consider themselves right, and will not listen to other views. People like these may look for churches that agree with them. I applaud people for thinking they are taking a stand for what is right, but what if they do not have a complete picture of what is right? Those who reject the traditional Christian church still want a religion that will justify their lifestyles or concerns, so they lean toward whatever seems to fit them or are taken in by what outwardly looks good.

I have already mentioned that God wants His church to have the dual purpose of proclaiming the truth and doing good works. I now want to discuss two Bible passages that also give clear descriptions of how God wants us to view the church. First, God wants us to see the importance of unity in a community (John 17:20–26). Jesus asks God the Father that all who believe in Him may be one just as He and the Father are one that we may be perfected in unity. Jesus prays that God's love would be in us. There should be no greater vision we have for the church than that we practice God's love for one another and live in the essential aspects of unity (John 13:34–35).

The church is foremost to be relational, but we in our individualistic society have a difficult time grasping the concept of a close-knit community. Some argue that the first and foremost priority of the church is not to develop relationships but to preach the gospel. There can be no doubt that God called us to proclaim His message of salvation and make disciples of all peoples (Matthew 28:18–20), but if His people were authentic in their love for one another, their message would be more contagious. If they lived and not just spoke their faith, many more people would undoubtedly receive it.

Friedrich Nietzsche, the famed "God is dead" philosopher and not the greatest friend of the church, made an outstanding point: "If you want me to believe in your redeemer, you have to look a little more redeemed."[26] Paul, one of the church's founders, said his joy would be most complete if people of the church would be of the same mind, maintaining the same love, united in spirit, and intent on one purpose (Philippians 2:2). Paul also said we are to be "united in the Spirit, binding ourselves together with peace" (Ephesians 4:3). As a pastor, my heart is most broken when I see people in churches having unresolved conflicts and not loving each other (1 Corinthians 1:10). It is inevitable, to be sure, but one of the more beautiful, godly things to see is people confessing their offenses to each other, forgiving others, seeking to change their offensive ways, and moving on in love and unity. When the love of Jesus is evident, people are drawn in.

The second biblical passage that provides a fascinating description of how God wants us to view the church is to see it as a place of caring (1 Corinthians 12:12–26). The church is likened to the human body with eyes, ears, hands, feet, brains, hearts, and so forth. The church is made of

---

[26] This Nietzsche quote appears in Greg Ogden, *Discipleship Essentials* (Downers Grove: IVP Connect, 2007), 153. The quote is attributed to Nietzsche numerous times on the Internet in slightly varying forms.

many parts, different people with differing functions, but each one important, each one needed so the body can function as designed. Even the weakest part is needed, and we all need to rely on each other for the proper functioning of the whole. God puts each member in the body as He desires. It is emphasized that there be no division in the body and that each member have the same care for one another (1 Corinthians 12:25-26). When I injure my body, my whole body gets involved. If I am cut, my body feels the pain; my brain tells the body what's needed. My arm and hand respond by holding the wounded area to comfort the pain and by applying ointment, a Band-Aid, whatever.

Just as the body cares for itself, the church, when functioning effectively, will care for its members. Jesus is the head of the church, and the church body is to work with one another as He directs. Each member does their part, and caring happens. God used the human body as an analogy for His church as a clear illustration of how He wanted it to operate. When we think about how our bodies operate, we can apply that to the church. For example, we can understand that to leave the body of the church is like an arm leaving the human body. When disconnected from the body, the arm is alone, useless, and unable to play its role. Another point to ponder is that the human body is organized and visible; so is the church. Thinking about these two passages may help correct our mistaken views of the church. Beyond caring for members in the body of the church, we are to care about those outside the church (Matthew 22:37–39; Galatians 6:10).

I once asked a very close friend of mine, my wife, a person with keen insight into people and life, "What do you think is the greatest thing about the church?" Without hesitation, she answered, "It is the place where we come to learn how to die." Certainly, one aspect of this is learning how to face our physical death with the hope of eternal life. The church gives such hope and comfort (1 Thessalonians 4:13–18), but what my wife meant by dying is learning how to give up our lives for others. I admire her life of daily seeing and meeting the needs of others. Jesus put it this way: "If you try to hang on to your life, you will lose it. But if you give up your life for my sake, you will save it" (Luke 9:24). When Jesus' disciples argued about who was the greatest, He pointed out that the greatest is the one who serves, and He used Himself as the supreme example (Luke 22:24–27).

When it comes to dying and serving, there are many instructions for people to consider and practice in God's view of the church. It is a place where its members greet one another to show that things are all right between them (1 Peter 5:14), a place where we encourage and build up one another (1 Thessalonians 5:11), where we bear one another's burdens (Galatians 6:2), teach one another (Romans 15:14), help the weak, and be patient with everyone (1 Thessalonians 5:14). Our choice is whether we will do what God put us into the body to do (1 Peter 4:10). All believers must discover their roles, and submit to Christ and to one another in fulfilling those God-given roles in the church (Ephesians 5:21; Hebrews 13:17).

Unfortunately, when it comes to teaching about submission and serving, some church leaders abuse their authority. This truth about submitting to God's will and to church leaders has nothing to do with controlling people (Hebrews 13:17). It is proper to resist anyone who tries to use the Bible or their authority as a tool to control others' lives and get others to do what they want or believe what they say is good for the group. Some groups expect unconditional obedience with whatever they say and call others unspiritual if they don't obey. There is a proper place for authority in the church but not as manipulation. As a pastor-teacher, I am told not to lord it over others (1 Peter 5:3).

Authoritarianism leads to bondage, whereas Jesus' concept of dying to oneself and serving leads to freedom and fruitfulness (John 12:24–25). Dying to self-centeredness can only produce freedom when serving is out of voluntary choice. True serving begins with love for God and others, which means willing acts of serving, as Jesus directs. True serving will produce personal joy and the blessings of God for yourself and others.

Jesus said we could not be authentic disciples if we did not take up His cross (Luke 14:27). John Talbot sings a song, "Few Be the Lovers of the Cross."[27] How true that is. Paul sent Timothy to help a church, and he told them to receive him because he had no one else to send who would genuinely be concerned for their welfare because they all sought after their own interests, not those of Christ Jesus (Philippians 2:19–21). What a few have discovered is true; we do not really live until we learn how to die. Dying to self is very difficult without the Holy Spirit's life

---

[27] This song is on the CD "The Talbot Brothers Collection."

and influence. A helpful way to learn how to die in practical ways is by being with people who care about others. Their influence on me inspires me to do the same (Romans 15:1–3). We rub off on each other. That is why belonging to smaller groups within the church is essential for growth (Proverbs 27:17).

However, such groups must be able to speak into the deep centers of each member's heart to provide the greatest help for healing and growth. This takes a willingness to be vulnerable and honest as well as an understanding of the Bible so they can more effectively speak God's Word into each other's lives.

Why would anyone want to be part of the church when it has so many unresolved problems? The simplest answer is because Christ Jesus loves the church, even to the point of dying for her. Reformers such as Martin Luther fought corruption in the church not by leaving it but by seeking to bring her more in line with Scripture. We might better love the church in spite of her imperfections if only we knew how God wanted us to view her. If we as God's people endeavor to see the church rightly, as He describes her in his book, such a view will go a long way to helping us want to be a contributing part.

The word *"church"* and the concept of church is not a bad thing. The church is the only institution that has what the world needs; she has been entrusted with the gospel of Jesus and His truth (1 Thessalonians 2:4; 1 Timothy 3:15). The church may not always do things right; but with the right view, we can go in the direction of doing better. As believers, we are the church, and the church will only be as good as we in God's Spirit make it. Each Spirit-filled believer has a role to play in the church to help it function as Christ designs. If people in the church lack this spiritual dynamic, the church becomes more of an organization that seems dead for its lack of what is life-giving. But if spiritually alive people fill the church, it will change as needed to reach its culture and it will attract others, especially those seeking what she has—a God who can impart life and love to them.

## Chapter 14

## WHAT PRAYER TELLS US ABOUT OURSELVES

Bible teacher Haddon Robinson tells a story about a game he used to play with his young children. He would put pennies in his hand, and the kids would try to pry his fingers open to get the pennies. These few coins were a great treasure to the kids, and once they got the coins, they danced and delighted in their newfound treasure. What do you think was more important to the kids, the coins, or their relationship with their father? Both are okay, Haddon would say, but not the material gains to the neglect of the relational. The Bible tells us that if we love the world and the things of the world, the love of God the Father is not in us (1 John 2:15). However, a right relationship with God will result in a right relationship with the material aspects of the world. What is of primary importance to me, the blessings I can get from God or my relationship with God?

As we pay attention to what we want from our Father, we learn more about ourselves. When we pray, are we wrestling and pleading with God to give us what we want, or are we more interested in knowing God and discerning His interest in our lives (Jeremiah 9:24)? Jesus said that eternal life is to know God the Father and the Son, Jesus Christ (John 17:3).

What is prayer? Consider the prayer our Lord taught His disciples (Matthew 6:9–10). Yes, prayer is asking God for the things we need or desire, but the first part of the prayer implies the importance of knowing God as "our Father," sensing His infinite greatness, setting Him apart as special from all else, and wanting to know Him intimately. Prayer, first of all, is about drawing near to God for fellowship and desiring His will to be done in our earthly lives (James 4:8). When we examine our praying, we can notice whether we are interested only in getting things from God or whether we are also interested in knowing and loving Him, that is, whether we are mostly self-focused or mostly God-focused. Of course, self-focus is great if it involves wanting to grow in godliness or asking to glorify Him through whatever is happening in our lives.

When Jesus prayed to His Father, it was sometimes a struggle to overcome what He wanted and to become one with the person and purposes of His Father. He worked through a problem or temptation in His life, to not let it take Him out of fellowship with His Father. Jesus faced such a struggle in the desert of temptation when He had to overcome Satan's efforts to get Him to stray from God's purposes (Luke 4:1–12).

Another example of this is Jesus' mental and spiritual battle in prayer as He faced the cross (Luke 22:39–44). He was facing excruciating torture, the pain of having God abandon Him, and the pain of knowing His impending death was causing His beloved followers deep sorrow. He asked God to take this suffering from Him, but at the end of His time in prayer, He accepted God's will, had peace within, and experienced great joy. The time with God in prayer renewed His vision that this unjust evil He would soon face would accomplish salvation for a great number of people. He came to the point of realizing that God was working all things for good and that God would give Him strength to go through this trial. The great joy He received from His time alone with God and from seeing life from God's perspective carried Him through His crisis (Hebrews 12:2).

Jesus prayed, "I want your will to be done, not mine" (Luke 22:42). Many see this as a cop-out. They may ask, "Shouldn't we be persevering and pressing God until He grants us our request?" (Luke 18:1–8). Sometimes, in the right context, that is appropriate, but it is not necessarily the normal course of praying. When Jesus prayed, "Your will be done, not mine," He was not wavering or doubting God but rather coming to the place of acknowledging that God's way was best. If what I am asking is wrong or not for the best, God is good to override and say no to the request. If we persist and God grants an unwise request because we want it so badly, we may not experience the best results (1 Samuel 8:4–21).

I learn things about myself when I pray during personal trials and suffering. Am I interested only in God getting me out of a painful situation, or am I interested in seeing it from God's perspective? Am I interested only in getting comfort for myself, or am I seeking intimacy with God as my refuge and strength? My struggle is one of learning to give up what I want and to accept what He wants (Job 40:1–5; 42:1–6). At first, I ask God to remove my pain and sufferings, but as it turns out, what happens in my conversations with God is that I come to accept my condition and find peace in knowing He loves me and will not let anything happen to me that is not for my good or for the good of others. I find myself allowing God to strengthen my faith and relationship with Him (Lamentations 3:19–25). Praying becomes more than asking; it becomes a time of drawing near and enjoying God. Knowing He is with me and has my best interests at heart becomes my comfort and my staying power. Being with God is the safest place I could be. When I honestly express my hurt and pain during my conversational prayers with God and seek Him as my refuge, I discover that building my relationship with God is more beneficial and helpful than getting the things I want or think I need. I fall short if my prayer never gets beyond asking for things and into the reassuring companionship of God as a loving Father.

It's not that God isn't interested in meeting our needs or desires; in fact, He very much wants to do that. But if that's the main thrust of our relationship, we have missed a huge purpose of prayer. Prayer is often about being near God so the peace of His presence and the knowledge of His goodness will replace our fears and worries. This kind of praying results not so much in God's material blessings, but more importantly, God becomes our greatest treasure (Psalm 73:25–28).

It's easy to become disappointed with God when He doesn't answer our sincere requests. It is disappointing when we hurt for others and pray fervently for God to help them, but what we pray for does not happen. It may seem God does nothing as a result of prayer, and we wonder if He cares or is even there. We may think, *Why pray? It does no good.* But how we take God's responses to our prayers can show us things about ourselves. If we conclude God is not there or is not caring, we need to correct our thinking to be in line with God's revelation of Himself. For us to say that it does no good to pray is contrary to many instances in the Bible when God granted people's requests (1 Samuel 1:27; 2 Chronicles 30:20; Mark 10:51–52; Luke 18:1, 7). God may answer no, but that does not mean we should refrain from asking for what we need or want. It is always proper to ask God to meet our needs because we typically do not know what He will do and because the Scriptures, as well as stories of modern people, show us He does grant requests. If He does not, it is because He has good reason. Unless we truly believe that God is most wise and good, knows each of us perfectly, and understands what is best for us, we will think we know better than He does what He should be doing to help us.

What do we learn about ourselves when what we pray for does not happen? When children come to their parents to ask for something, the parents decide what is good for the children and answer *yes* or *no*. Either answer is what the parent thinks is best for the child. Why can't we give God the same leeway? Whether we get what we pray for or not, God is good and does what is best for us. As children do, we can stomp away disappointed or angry instead of thanking God for His goodness and wisdom. What do we learn about ourselves? We learn what we think of God, that He is good and wise or mean, uncaring, absent, or lacking in wisdom to know what is best. We naturally think we know what is best (Proverbs 16:2). We need to learn that our trusting relationship with God is not yet complete. Do we have confidence that God loves us beyond all measure so our relationship with God is not shaken by what He does or doesn't do?

Is God wrong or insensitive when He does not grant our requests? At times, after I have helped another person, I wondered if I had done the right thing. Would it have been better for them if I had not helped? I do what I do with limited knowledge of what a person really needs, but God knows.

We can think we know better than God because we see how right it seems to us to be helping someone in need. To avoid thinking we know better than God, we need to be convinced that God knows us better than we know ourselves, that all He does is right, and that He always has our best interests at heart even though it may not seem so. We need not give up believing God will answer our prayers, but at the same time, we should not lose the knowledge that God is all-wise and good and knows what is best for us.

I like to read about people in the Bible who did not experience answers to their prayers. I learn from them different ways to think in those times when I might be tempted to doubt God or feel self-pity by thinking God doesn't care. Here are a few of my favorite responses when God does not answer prayer. When Job lost his children, possessions, wealth, and health, he argued with God to give him an answer, but none came. In spite of unanswered prayer, Job said, "Should we accept only good things from the hand of God and never anything bad?" (Job 2:10). "God might kill me, but I have no other hope" (Job 13:15). "I know that my Redeemer lives and he will stand upon the earth at last. And after my body has decayed, yet in my body I will see God! I will see him for myself. Yes I will see him with my own eyes. I am overwhelmed at the thought" (Job 19:25–27). This response tells us that Job was obviously a man with hope. He would keep hoping in God no matter what; not like the person who said, "Curse God and die" (Job 2:9).

God told the prophet Habakkuk that enemies would destroy his country. Imagine if God told you that your nation faced sure destruction and your life as you knew it would be over. Habakkuk trembled at the news and could hardly bear the thought of what was coming. We might be tempted to cry out to God, "No, you can't allow this—help us!" but no answer would come. Habakkuk prayed that even though his country would be destroyed and nothing would be left, he would exult in the Lord and rejoice in the God of his salvation. He said, "The Sovereign Lord is my strength" (Habakkuk 3:16–19). Nothing could destroy his faith in God; he could rejoice in the face of adversity. When God does not answer our prayers, what is our response, and what does that tell us about ourselves? There are many other examples in the Bible of people whose prayers were unanswered or not answered as they wished, and it is instructive to compare our responses to theirs.

At times, I think I am the worst prayer in the world. Perhaps this came about because I got bored as a child at the prayer meetings I attended with my mother. I would listen to people pray through all the prayer requests, and it seemed that each one took a turn and prayed the same things for everyone on the list. Although praying this way is perfectly all right and has positive results, I think that because I felt bored, to this day, I have an attitude that prayer is not something I am eager to do. Perhaps what this sadly says about me is that I don't care for those who need and deserve my prayers. Furthermore, whenever I have many on a list to pray for, I find it takes such focus and concentration to stay on task. Also, because there are so many things to pray for, I find myself hurrying to get through. Hurriedly mentioning names to get through a list does not connect me to God nor to those for whom I pray. I feel I am offering inadequate, uncaring prayers when I pray this way. We all have different personalities, and I suspect we all pray according to who we are. I need to learn to slow down, take more time, and care more. I find I am more deeply and sincerely engaged when I become contemplative and draw near to God, conversing with Him as a revered, caring Father. That's when I am more passionate and earnest in bringing up people's needs, requests, and concerns to Him. When I pray for others in a contemplative mode, I think about them more and feel more connected to them. I suppose each of us finds what manner of praying fits us best. I am sure there is no one right way to pray; I think God is most concerned with our hearts.

The amount of time we pray also tells us something about ourselves. Here are three possibilities. Number one, taking time to pray tells me something about my level of caring because the amount of time I take to pray for others tells me whether I sincerely care about them. Number two, the time I take for prayer tells me something about my relationship with God; those who don't pray must realize they have little or no relationship with God. Either they are too busy or don't believe in God. And third, lack of time spent with God may tell me something about whether I feel worthy to come into His presence. Some may not pray because they know God does not approve of the lives they are living, in which case they may feel they don't deserve for God to hear them. Scripture says that if I regard sin in my heart or if I live an unrighteous lifestyle, God will not hear me (Psalm 66:18; Proverbs 15:8, 29). Fortunately, this can be changed by becoming humble, admitting our faults, seeking God's forgiveness, and turning from our wrong ways. Under those circumstances, God will not turn anyone away (Luke 18:13–14). Anyone can begin to know God and develop an effective prayer life.

There are other reasons we do not pray besides our lack of caring about others, being too busy, or feeling unworthy. Prayer may be tiring, we may have a hard time staying focused, or we may believe prayer doesn't produce results and thus doesn't seem worth the effort. We may think we are capable of handling life by ourselves and don't need God. So think about how much time we spend with God in prayer. What does that say about us? Do we grasp the Bible's admonition to "Never stop praying" (1 Thessalonians 5:17)? What would being obedient to such a command mean for us?

In regard to what we pray for, Jesus taught that some things are weightier than others (Matthew 23:23). Do we pray for things like God to make us more holy, or help us love others, or give us the heart to forgive or overcome our critical negative ways so that we are more positive and encouraging to others, or help us be a light for our coworkers so they might want to know Jesus? Do we use prayer to wage war against our sinful nature (Galatians 5:13–17)? Do we pray for God to raise up more workers interested in people's salvation (Ephesians 6:18–20; Matthew 9:37–38)? Our prayers can show us if we are too shallow, selfish, or limited in scope.

The Bible says if we ask anything according to His will, or if we ask in faith, He hears us and will grant our requests (Matthew 17:20, 21:22; James 5:14–16; 1 John 5:14–15). Verses like these can play devastating tricks on our minds and hearts. As children of God, do we believe He will give us what we ask in faith? What do we think or believe if He does not—that our faith is not strong enough, that we had wrong motives (James 4:3), that some sin is blocking our prayer, that God does not care, that God is not good or may not exist? Do we get angry at God or blame Him? There is no person who has ever had God answer every prayer the way he or she may have wanted. On the other hand, if He satisfactorily answers many of our prayers, is our response to be humble and thankful, or do we feel a tinge of *I am special to God* or prideful thoughts that we are above others?

Do these verses tend to cause us to see God as our servant instead of us serving Him? Do we desire power of the supernatural world to be at our disposal (Acts 8:19)? How many of us could rightly handle the feeling of having such power in our prayers? Do we find ourselves playing mind games with God, thinking that we can persuade Him to answer our prayer? Are we presuming to know what we need more than does our Creator, Redeemer, and loving heavenly Father? Or do we believe God knows exactly what we need and trust Him to answer as He sees fit? Certainly, our responses to these verses reveal many things that we believe about God and our relationship with Him.

In my attempts to understand these kinds of verses, I try to notice the scriptural contexts, and it seems conditions go with each one. Maybe some were meant for only the disciples and apostles of Jesus' day to bring about demonstrations of the truth of their message. Maybe others are limited to knowing and praying according to God's revealed will, not so much to give us what we want or need, but to give us what will enable us to accomplish the ministry or work God has given us to do. Globally, it seems the prayers that work are mostly in special circumstances, such as a spiritually darkened culture in which God wishes to perform a miracle to help people come to faith in the gospel message.

What do prayers offered in faith tell us about what we believe? In thinking about God answering our prayers made in faith, do these verses confuse us, make us bold to claim what He promised, make us feel we are trying to tell God what to do, or are we simply to pray in obedience to His Word that tells us to ask in faith? Perhaps a simple, childlike faith with no ulterior motives or doubts would be the way to pray, asking our heavenly Father for what we want or need, trusting that He will answer as He sees fit, and accepting the results.

Do I believe it matters if I pray? Is life a matter of fate, whatever will be will be? Definitely not! The Bible teaches us that God changes His mind or actions based on our life decisions or persistent praying (Jeremiah 18:7–10, 26:2–3; Luke 18:1–8). We have all experienced answers to prayers; prayers do change things. God seems to have built into His universe the working of His will by means of prayer. We are co-laborers with God for His glory, and we can be change agents for good through prayer. Peter boasted to the Lord he would stand up for Him (Luke 22:31–34), and Jesus told him he would deny Him three times. Jesus said He prayed Peter's faith would not fail. Jesus could have thought Peter would come through this all right, but He believed in the necessity of prayer. If Jesus thought prayer made a difference and had confidence God would do something to help, I can do no less.

In summary, how we pray reveals something of our character and what our relationship with God is. It shows whether we are doubtful of God's love, goodness, and care for us or if we want only a good end to our situations. It shows whether we are only using God to get what we want or if we are interested in relating to God as an intimate friend. It shows whether we are respectful of God or have flippant attitudes toward Him as though He were only a distant power for us to try as a last resort. It shows whether we believe in God, are doubtful, agnostic, or atheistic. It shows whether we are on good terms with God or feel judged and condemned. It shows whether we believe prayer works and are earnest about it or if we easily give up in despair. Insights from the way we pray can help us by serving as a corrector to improve our knowledge of prayer, our character, and our relationship with God.

If we want to learn more about how to pray, the Psalms provide a great book on prayer. Probably every feeling we experience in daily living is expressed to God somewhere in Psalms. These prayers model for us how to praise, how to give thanks, how to honestly relate to God, and how to make all sorts of requests. Recorded prayers of saints through the ages can also become great models of prayer. One prayer the first disciples made to Jesus is still relevant today: "Lord, teach us to pray" (Luke 11:1).

## Chapter 15

## THE VALUE OF SUFFERING

Every human will experience some degree of suffering. Suffering is caused by evils that can be put into three classifications. The first includes natural evils, the result of the corruption of nature (Genesis 3:17–18, 5:29; Romans 8:20-21) such as tornados, hurricanes, floods, famines, earthquakes, fires, and diseases.

The second is moral evils that result from the corruption of human nature (Romans 3:23; Matthew 15:19; Galatians 5:19–21; 2 Timothy 3:1–5; Hebrews 11:36–37). They include such things as lying, stealing, hating, murder, sexual abuse, verbal abuse, racism, wars, failure to love, disrespect for authority, persecutions, fears, guilt, depression, breakdowns in communication and relationships, and so forth. We, humans, cause much of our own suffering (Genesis 6:11–13).

A third classification includes supernatural evils that are a result of the acts of supernatural beings (John 8:44; Job 1–2; Luke 8:1–2; Mark 1:12-13). They include demonic possession, witchcraft, satanic temptations, acts of satanic power, and evil "rained upon us" by the judgments or acts of God though always with a righteous purpose (Judges 9:23–24; 1 Samuel 16:14; 1 Kings 22:23; 2 Kings 6:33). Death is a consequence of evil (Romans 6:23).

Evil is a horrendous problem; every culture, religion, philosophy, and individual must deal with it; we try to find an answer to it or ignore it. The existence of evil is a big reason some choose not to believe in God, and from their viewpoint, such a choice is understandable. How can there be an all-powerful, good, and loving God when these evils exist and cause such unthinkable sufferings? We will do all we humanly can to alleviate the suffering of our loved ones and others, but a supposed almighty, loving God remains silent, absent, and does nothing. We could never let ourselves be like that and stand by and do nothing. Either such a God does not exist, has left us on our own, or does not care. Such a viewpoint is understandable. People having a hard time understanding why anyone would not believe in God have perhaps not seriously experienced or dealt with the magnitude of evil and suffering. Suffering is not easy to accept. Many confessing Christians have been angry with God in the midst of evil and have found themselves questioning and being tempted to disbelieve. Suffering has caused some to fall away from faith in God. We can easily ask, "Why isn't God helping us?"

All kinds of answers, called *theodicies*, have been proposed to justify God in the face of evil; some are better than others, and although God allows suffering to continue, He promises the ultimate answer, a time of judgment when all wrongs will be righted, all evil will be eliminated, and a new world will be brought into existence. God does not say why evil was allowed to exist in the first place, but it's here, and God assures us that those born of God, many having suffered unjustly, will live again in resurrected bodies and enjoy His righteous world forever. God is all-powerful, good, and loving and will prevent and destroy evil but not yet (Acts 17:31; 2 Corinthians 5:10; 2 Peter 3:7–14; Acts 3:19–21).

I agree with the theodicy that says that in an imperfect world like ours, it is possible that God has a good and sufficient reason for allowing evil to continue. Viktor Frankl, a noted Austrian psychiatrist, witnessed and experienced extreme inhumane treatment in four concentration camps. His pregnant wife, his parents, and his brother were all murdered. He said he was able to endure the horrendous sufferings by believing that meaning could be found, even in suffering.[28] Could it be that one reason for God allowing evil to exist is that for warranted reason we need the opportunity to experience the value of suffering?

Jesus makes it clear that even in the face of suffering God cares about us. Jesus was an exact representation of His Father (John 14:8–9; Hebrews 1:2–3). What Jesus said and did shows us, God, as He really is. Since Jesus had compassion for people who were suffering, He showed us by His many acts of kindness, healings, and feeding the poor that God cares about us (Matthew 9:35–36; 15:32–38; Mark 1:40–42). Even in

---

[28] Viktor E. Frankl, *Man's Search for Meaning* (Ypsilanti, Beacon Press, 1959).

the Old Testament, where God is sometimes unjustly criticized as being vindictive, angry, and condemning, it says He is compassionate (Exodus 34:5–6; Deuteronomy 4:31; Lamentations 3:21–24; Jonah 4:2). Peter agreed that God cares by telling us to "Give all your worries and cares to God, for he cares about you" (1 Peter 5:7–10). Admittedly, it is hard to accept that God cares if He seems not to be helping us in our sufferings, does not answer our prayers, and if we experience overwhelming pain.

People respond in four ways to the problems of evil and suffering. The four responses are skepticism, seeking, overcoming, and grieving. The same person may have one or more of these responses. First, there are skeptical responses found in people who look at the problem of evil or personal pain and use it as a reason to question the existence of God. People with these types of responses may end up with minds bent toward agnosticism, which says, "We can't know whether God exists," or minds bent toward atheism, which says, "There is no God."

Second, there are seeking responses found in people who are open to hearing answers to the problem of evil. They want to pursue the issues involved and try to come to an understanding of evil and suffering in a way that makes sense or helps them. Third, there are overcoming responses found in persons who accept evil and suffering as a part of life, and they work at coping with suffering when it comes. Christian overcomers continue to believe in and rely on a good, caring, and helpful God. Finally, there are grieving responses found in those who are experiencing the deep pain and hurt of losing something or someone very dear and important to them. They need comfort more than answers to the problem of evil or to their questioning of why this happened. They need the freedom to express their pain and anger even toward God. Initially, it is not best to say to a grief sufferer, "God has a reason for this," for they cannot accept that kind of an answer at this time, if ever. They need people not to give them explanations and platitudes to help them feel better about what happened, but people to come alongside them and love them by listening, accepting, and comforting them (Job 2:11–13). There is no need to panic about friends losing their solid faith in God. They may question God or express anger at God, but more than likely, they will return to their faith. Those with previous doubts about God or who have weak faith are at risk of falling away, but they still need loving comfort, not answers.

God does not choose to eliminate evil and suffering from this world and our lives (Job 5:7; Romans 8:17-18), so we must choose how we will respond to our sufferings, hopefully in the most beneficial way possible. Of course, there is always the question of whether we deserve our suffering. We may or may not have a right to be angry at it. But be that as it may, the concern of all of us who find ourselves in the midst of suffering is to find a way to cope with it. Why God relieves the suffering of some of His people while others suffer unto death is not known, but faith's reward is the same for both (Hebrews 11:32–40). Our great hope is through faith in Christ (1 John 5:4). If you have ever had a miserable night and were very glad to see the morning, you can imagine the hope people of faith enjoy, knowing that morning is coming. In spite of the evil, injustice, or pain, could it be that there are benefits to suffering that are good for us, thus making the experience more bearable?

What value is there in our suffering? One of my favorite illustrations comes from the caterpillar emerging from its cocoon. Someone once decided to help that process along by opening the cocoon of the butterfly to ease its struggle of trying to get out. The result was that the butterfly could not fly and died. Apparently, it needed to struggle for its wings to become strong so it could fly. The Bible teaches us about many good, necessary things that can result from suffering, and you may have experienced some of them. I will share five thoughts on the value of suffering.

First, because of suffering, some are led to a belief in God, or in the case of those already believing, they may be led closer to God, or back to God. I suffered panic attacks and mental anguish at the thought of my death. This led me to want an answer to the question, *Is there any way for me to escape death?* This kind of suffering made me open to the gospel message, to the very words of Jesus, "He who believes in me shall never die." Trusting Him and His words brought new life and peace to my troubled mind and heart. Sufferings can make us open to the need for repentance and faith lest we perish (Luke 13:1–5; 2 Corinthians 1:8-9).

Sufferings can humble us and cause us to draw near to God for help and strength (Psalm 4:1, 22:11, 119:28; Matthew 26:36–44). Many have shared how they turned to God's Word during times of suffering and found the answer they needed to enable them to go on. Those without hope can find that God alone is sufficient for their needs and wants. The psalmist recognized that God was his greatest good (Psalm

73:23–28). Perhaps that is the place we all need to get to but cannot or will not without suffering.

A second value of suffering is that it serves as a test of our hearts. Suffering reveals what is in our hearts and often our need to grow stronger. Do we have faith, love, and hope, or do we doubt, lose heart, and give up (Job 2:9–10)? Our reactions to suffering reveal who we are. They may reveal unbelief or a lack of character necessary for increased maturity or health. Through sufferings, we often are "forced" to make decisions and changes that cause us to overcome bad habits or to grow in character or faith so future sufferings are more ably endured (Psalm 119:67, 71; 2 Corinthians 12:7–10). According to the Bible, sufferings lend to the genuineness of our faith by helping to bring about perseverance and the assured hope that God's love will never fail us (Romans 5:3–5). Instead of resenting or trying to escape sufferings, we are encouraged to endure them because they help make us perfect and lacking in nothing God promises us (James 1:2–4).

Third, suffering can also help loosen our grip on the world, enabling important things of life to surface. Suffering can help us see that money, fame, material things, or self are not the important things to live for. Jesus talked to a man who had much wealth; when Jesus asked him to decide between wealth and following Jesus, he chose wealth. We can easily hold on to this world's goods more than God's goods (Mark 10:21–22). How many times have people in trouble discovered the more important things in life such as loving families, the value of friendships, appreciating the simple everyday things that happen, or enjoying the beauty of God's creation? In Jesus' story of the farmer who strove to increase his assets, Jesus reminded us that some things in life are more important than others. Life is not found in wealth or possessions (Luke 12:15–21). Without sufferings threatening to take away, or taking away, the lesser things we live for, would we ever give our efforts to living for the most worthy things?

A fourth value is that suffering helps us discover the necessity of relationships and brings us closer together. More than we may realize, we need each other to help us cope and encourage us to stay the course. Being lonely is one of the greatest sufferings imaginable. Sharing our struggles and pain with each other in our sufferings helps us realize we are not alone. I once needed a friend to listen to me regarding a life-threatening situation that had me scared and depressed. My wife was gone for a couple of days, so I called another friend. He was there for me, allowed me to infringe upon his time, listened, and accepted my feelings without trying to fix me and without any attitude of condescension. By doing those things, he encouraged me immensely, and my bond of friendship with him deepened. If I can't be there like that for others, how true am I to what life is all about?

When we suffer, we are given the opportunity to love each other through our involvement in helping alleviate those sufferings. Because God works through people, experiencing the care of others helps us know that God cares and that we are not alone in this universe. Suffering also gives us an opportunity to learn to be more sensitive to others and more understanding of what others may be going through (2 Corinthians 1:3–4). Through suffering, we become more accepting and loving.

Fifth, suffering can show us God at work, accomplishing good that evidently cou ld not have come about any other way. God often seems hidden and absent when we are suffering (Psalm 22:1–2; Mark 15:34). When we are able to see that He is working in ours or in others' sufferings, it encourages us to know that He cares, has not abandoned us, and is in control even in our nightmare situations. Perhaps the greatest example of this is seeing God at work in the sufferings of Jesus. Through His sufferings, we see many people are able to be saved and possess eternal life, which couldn't have happened apart from His sufferings (Isaiah 53:10–12).

In the Old Testament, Joseph suffered at the hands of his brothers by being sold into slavery, being grievously separated from his family, and being falsely accused and imprisoned in a foreign land for two years (Genesis 37, 39, 42:21). But as much as Joseph suffered, we see God working to produce unimaginable good. He saved many from starvation through his unfortunate suffering and achieved reconciliation between himself and his brothers (Genesis 50:20–21).

In Jesus' day, a man was born blind from birth. He suffered this condition in order that God could show His miraculous work and reveal Jesus as God's Son, the light of the world (John 9:1–3, 5, 35–38). Seeing God at work through people's sufferings gives us hope. When He seems absent, we should take encouragement by remembering what we have seen Him do and believing He is doing something good through our suffering (Romans 8:28). He is still there, just as the sun is still there even though hidden by clouds at times.

Suffering seems necessary in a world in which evil has gotten a foothold in our lives. If it were not for suffering, we might not gain the benefits listed above. None of us likes to suffer, but efforts to escape involuntary sufferings would leave us incomplete. It seems that imperfect people, living in a world in which they are ingrained with evil and self-centeredness need suffering to overcome the evils that plague them. Whatever can be shaken needs to be removed so what is unshakable can stand in its place (Hebrews 12:27–28).

What is acceptable and not acceptable to say about evil and suffering? It is not acceptable to say God created evil and suffering to bring about these kinds of good. In my mind, to create evil just so these kinds of values can be experienced would be inexcusable for a loving, righteous, and good God. We do not know a lot about why God allowed evil to come into the world, but since it exists, we must learn to overcome it. Evil and sufferings are never good. No! Evil causes the most painful sufferings. Rather, we can say that through God's caring and loving power, good can come from the worst of evils (Romans 8:28; Genesis 50:20). We might say humanity's choice allowed evil into the world (Genesis 3:1–7) and that we are responsible, but God took responsibility for evil when He came in the person of His Son to suffer evil Himself and to die a torturous death in order to destroy evil and its cause (1 John 3:8; Revelation 20:10, 21:4–5).

Believers can say there is hope for the obliteration of evil and suffering sometimes in this life but completely and forever in the next. It's okay to pray for relief from suffering, but we need wisdom to know when to seek help to alleviate it in ourselves and others and when to accept it as one of God's allowed ways to enrich our lives.

## Chapter 16

# HOW CHRISTIANS NEED TO THINK ABOUT SIN IN THEIR LIVES

Stop focusing on it. Stop thinking it's a big deal and letting all your energy go into defeating it. Stop letting it define who you are. Start focusing on living your new life in Christ. Television used to broadcast "extreme makeover" programs. People who were common in appearance became beautiful and extraordinary. People who dressed in clothes that did not flatter them donned high fashion that dramatically improved their images. Old homes where people lived in poor conditions were made over into homes providing comfort and modern conveniences. Such makeovers helped people have better lives, feel better about themselves, and be happier. Certainly, such changes do help people feel better. And we enjoy being entertained and encouraged by seeing other people's lives improved. Though such makeovers may meet valid needs, do they touch people's deepest needs?

Our deepest need is not to have our outer circumstances changed but to have our total being remade. This means things like knowing we are loved for who we are regardless of our status or performance, allowing our performance to be checked by those who love us, possessing a genuine love for others rather than being overly self-centered, and gaining freedom from guilt, shame, anger, and depression, including feelings of worthlessness because of present or past failures or wrongs.

Christians as much or more than non-Christians can suffer from the ill effects of their failures or sinfulness. Many do not like themselves or their situations. People need truth, wisdom, and understanding to help change their lives. One of my favorite songs expresses what it's like when Jesus enters our lives as a change agent: "All I've ever done before won't matter anymore... I'll never be the same again."[29] God alone is

---

[29] From the song, "I've Just Seen Jesus."

the ultimate makeover artist, and His desire, like ours, is that our total being is made new (Ezekiel 36:26–27; John 10:10; 2 Corinthians 5:17; Revelation 21:5).

Sin and its effects hinder makeovers and create problems for unbelievers and Christians alike. Paul could not help some believers become mature and enjoy healthier lives because they were still wrapped up in themselves and in their sinful behaviors and attitudes (1 Corinthians 3:1–3). Christians can have two problems with sin: first, they cannot stop being a certain way, even though they know they are hurting themselves and others. And second, they experience sin's effects, which may include pride, damaged self-image, guilt, shame, anger, hatred, resentments, inability to love, feelings of worthlessness, failure, lack of self-control, denial of their evils, and so on. How many times has there been the fall of respected Christians due to sin in their lives? Rather than be surprised, critical, and condemning, we need to have the attitude of helping each other and most of all being concerned about our own lives. It is encouraging to know that Jesus was concerned about our being free from sin and told us we can be (John 8:31–36). The apostle Paul knew the agony and defeats of sin in his life (1 Timothy 1:15). He understood God's truths and taught us in Scripture how to deal with our sinfulness.

Genuine followers of Christ Jesus must understand that two opposing forces are within them, not good versus evil but sinful versus spiritual. All humans are created in the moral image of God so we all have a sense of right and wrong and a sense of goodness. Originally, we knew only good, but because humanity fell away from God, evil became a part of who we are so that we are now a mixture of good and evil. The Bible calls this corrupted nature within us our "fleshly; or sinful nature" (1 Corinthians 3:3). Jesus says evil comes from within, from the heart (Mark 7:20–23). This sinful, or fleshly nature within is described in the Bible by numerous lists of attitudes and behaviors that include things like lovers of self, lovers of money, boasting, arrogance, malicious gossiping, lack of self-control, murder, disobedience to parents, ungratefulness, immorality, drunkenness, jealousy, forsaking the church, and so forth (2 Timothy 3:2–5; Romans 1:24–32, 13:13; 1 Corinthians 6:9–10; 2 Corinthians 12:20–21; Galatians 5:19–21; Hebrews 10:24–26).

We are not all guilty of *all* these destructive attitudes and behaviors but we are guilty of many. The apostle Paul honestly acknowledges that there is a principle of evil within him preventing him from being the good person he wants to be (Romans 7:21). Our natural selves have our God-given sense of moral goodness with which to fight evil, but unfortunately, our goodness is not enough to eliminate evil's power and corrupting work within us. This is because we do not have a spiritual mindset and cannot understand the things of God that make for victory over evil (1 Corinthians 2:14). Therefore, the battle in any natural person is only between the inner forces of good and evil, and even though we want to be good and try to be good, our goodness is unable to win the battle. Our corrupted human nature is too strong, and sin controls us and hinders goodness in too many ways.

As Christ-followers, by faith and the gift of God's grace, we are given a new resource, the Spirit of God who creates a spiritual dimension in us by bringing us a new and miraculous way of life (Ephesians 2:1–22). Being spiritual does not mean we are sinless but that we now have a new identity, a new way of thinking, and a new power within us that we can rely on for a changed life. When those operating in this new spiritual dimension realize their sinful human nature is in control, they consciously move into relying, not on their inherent goodness or will power, but on their spiritual nature and God's resources to take over.

Here is one example of how this works. If I am being impatient, getting angry, and talking nasty to someone, God's Spirit reminds me, *You're operating in your old, sinful self; you must switch over to your spiritual self.* How am I reminded? A key resource, the Bible, was produced by the Spirit of God and when we know it and develop our mind to think it, the Spirit uses it to speak to us. It becomes God's word to me when I need it in particular situations. As I let the spiritual in me—that is, the Spirit of Christ and the mind of Christ which comes from His word—be in control, my thinking and behavior change to patience, kindness, and gentleness. This recognition of identifying our old way of thinking and replacing it with God's revealed way of thinking is one way to keep putting off those sinful desires and to be living by the new nature (Romans 6:12–13, 8:12–14, 12:2; Colossians 3:5–17).

I have long puzzled over a statement made by the apostle Paul. After confessing he is a sinner and he sins, he said, "So I am not the one doing wrong; it is sin living in me that does it" (Romans 7:17). Did Paul have a mental disorder? Was he deluded? By claiming that the evil part of him was not really him, was he saying he had a split personality? When I sin, I say I did it, but Paul says he did not do it but that the sin in him did it. He was not deluded, but what did he mean? Your true self is your new nature—the spiritual self. The new "I" is the one who has been newly created, who loves God, wants to do things His way, and who wins in the end. The new "I" is the one who will inherit all God's promises, be bodily resurrected, and live forever in God's new and righteous kingdom. The sinful part of you will one day be gone and no longer bother you. That is why Paul could say when his sinful nature acted out, "It is no longer I doing these things." It appears that Paul is trying to tell us to separate who we really are from our sinful nature so that it is not taking over our lives. I am no longer who I used to be.

The true "I" is Paul's mind and body controlled by his spiritual nature. It was not his spiritual nature doing sinful things but rather his "sin which dwells in me" nature. I once heard of a businessman who was dishonest and cheated people. He became a Christian by faith and the receiving of Christ's Spirit and thus acquired a new spiritual nature. His changed heart (Ezekiel 36:26-27) now wants to please God and do things God's way, so he deals with people fairly. Those who knew him in the past accuse him of being a cheat, but he claims he is no longer the same person, but has been changed. Others who know him as he now says he is honest and fair. Who is he really? He is no longer the person he was but the new person God created him to be (1 Corinthians 6:11; 2 Corinthians 5:17). As Christians, we are not to see ourselves as sinful beings incapable of living God's way but as spiritual people, saints of God able to live to please God, learning how to give up our sinful ways through the Spirit and not let them control us. Our will to be good is not what fights our battles, but our Spirit-motivated will that relies on the powerful spiritual life within us. In a mysterious and surprising way, we may experience that we cannot control our new spiritual nature; we can only yield to it and marvel at the results.

Let's examine how Paul tells us to think about our sinful nature. God's truth, written by Paul, tells us that we have been baptized into Christ Jesus (Romans 6:3–4). Our baptism consists of Spirit and water.

All who believe in Christ Jesus are baptized with God's Holy Spirit. This Spirit baptism was promised to us as an act of Jesus (Luke 3:16; John 1:33). Paul makes it clear that all who have faith in Christ Jesus have been baptized by one Spirit (1 Corinthians 12:13). This is the miracle of being born again, born of God, born of the Spirit, as recorded in John's gospel (John 1:12–13, 3:3–8). Without it, no one can see or enter the kingdom of God.

Believers in Christ who have been baptized by the Spirit are instructed to be baptized with water to mark the fact they are cleansed disciples of Christ Jesus; part of the new people of God (Matthew 28:19; Acts 2:38–41; Galatians 3:27). The important point Paul makes about our faith-in-Christ baptism is that to be baptized into Christ Jesus is to be united with Him in His death and resurrection (Romans 6:4–6). This certainly means our physical bodies like His will die and like His will rise, never to die again (Romans 6:8–9). But that is not the primary meaning because, although the Bible says we die with Christ, we are still living, and although it says we rise with Christ, we are not yet bodily raised from the dead. A meaning beyond the physical is that like Christ, we have died to sin, and like Christ, we have risen to please God and accomplish His purposes.

What does being dead to sin mean? How does it help us deal with our sin problem? Christ died to sin, and we who are united with Him have also died to sin and therefore are dead to sin (Romans 6:2, 10–11). Perhaps it will help us to understand if we think about what it means when we say that another living person is dead to us. We mean that even though that person may still be a part of our lives, we no longer choose to have anything to do with him or her and we will not allow them to affect our lives in any way. When we say we are dead to sin, it means we will no longer have anything to do with it and will not let it affect our lives. Ideally, this is our wish, but we do not experience being dead to sin in this way, for sin still rears its ugly head, and we find ourselves sinning. Therefore, we are not dead to sin in the sense that we will not have anything to do with it anymore. We still sin and suffer its ill effects. So we still ask, in what sense are we dead to sin?

Certainly, we can say we are dead to sin in that it no longer has the power over our lives it used to have. What power did it have? It had the power to create guilt, make us feel guilty, and condemn us to death because all who commit sin are judged by God and are under God's penalty of death (Romans 6:23). But if we consider ourselves dead to sin, we can say we are dead to its power to condemn us. This is because Christ Jesus was condemned in our place, and all who are forgiven through faith in Him are no longer under the punishment of death. We are accepted by God as His beloved children, and our sins can no longer cause God to be against us (Romans 8:1–2). We have been made right with God.

Considering ourselves dead to sin is all a matter of how we think about it (Romans 12:2). If Christ is dead to sin and was raised to new life; so are we. "It is finished," said Jesus (John 19:30), so I have no business letting sin control my life and feelings. If I am guilty of sin, whether intentionally or not, and I feel guilty and a failure, I confess it to God with a repentant spirit and acknowledge His forgiveness by thanking Him that Jesus paid for my sin (1 John 1:9). I mentally rehearse that God still loves me and does not hold this against me, nor seek to punish me for it (Psalm 103:10-12). I tell God I want to do better and I do not want to repeat my sin. And if I do repeat it, even, again and again, I follow this same mindset. In this way, I am practicing what Paul said: "Consider yourselves to be dead to the power of sin and alive to God through Christ Jesus" (Romans 6:11). Sin no longer has the power to destroy my life by separating me from God. Sin no longer has the power to create feelings of guilt, shame, or self-condemnation, for by my confession and God's forgiveness I am free from such accusations against myself, and God accepts me in spite of my sin. As Paul said, "When we died with Christ we were set free from the power of sin" (Romans 6:7). We may not always be free from committing sin, but we are free from its eternal consequences of death and feelings of guilt and failure. To consider yourself dead to sin is to remind yourself after every sin you may commit that it cannot make God love you less, forsake you, or condemn you. Whenever we sin, we must keep on believing this and accepting that God is not taking our sin into account.

Sometimes, because sin is still in our lives, a satanic voice likes to accuse us of not being good Christians or maybe not even a Christian at all. We may feel God could not love a person like me who keeps sinning. We need to tell Satan that Christ paid for the sin, we are forgiven, so "get lost; you have no power to use my sin against me" (Revelation 12:9–11).

What Jesus did on the cross destroyed sin's and Satan's power over me. Do not let your sin make you feel guilty, ashamed, or depressed. Do not worry about it and get so bogged down trying to fight it that you find yourself forgetting who you really are. You need to claim your victory in Christ and move on to your new life of living for God. This way of thinking also heals our feelings of worthlessness because God accepts us as we are and loves us. Once we know this, nothing can make us feel unworthy, even the fact that we are imperfect and fail. If we mess up, so what? We put it behind us and resolve to do better. Reckon it true that we are dead to sin's penalty and effects. Reckon it true that you are not your sin nature. This is why Paul can say we have freedom from sin not in the sense we can never sin but in the sense that sin can no longer destroy us in death or in our emotional well-being.

We can easily be prone to think about our sin from our human point of view and miss seeing it from God's perspective. Let's return to Paul's point mentioned earlier. When the apostle Paul was converted to Christ God showed him things he did not see before. For example, he never understood how to see sin from God's perspective. He thought he was the greatest of sinners, and humanly speaking he was, until he was converted and became a new person in Christ Jesus. Then he learned to see his life from God's point of view. Here is what he wrote, "If I do what I don't want to do, I am not really the one doing wrong – it is sin living in me that does it." (Rom. 7:20) What does he see that I may not? It is this: I am no longer a sinner because that was my past life and it was very destructive to me. Now, I have become a new creation in Christ Jesus and the life I now live is rich and satisfying because I live by trusting in the Son of God who loved me and gave His life for me. (John 10:10; Galatians 2:20) His old sinful life died with Jesus on the cross and the real Paul wants to love God and live his life loving God and doing God's will and pleasing Him. Paul is actually trying to tell us what God has revealed to him – that we must separate ourselves from our sinful nature – we are new creations in Christ and we need to see that our sinful nature is no longer who we are. We put aside our old self and focus on the new self – we stop letting our wrongs define us and start letting our new life define us.

Some may say that if we can dismiss our sinful self so easily, and if God so easily forgives us, it doesn't matter if we sin because we can just keep claiming that it is not us and we are forgiven. Paul told us this was a misunderstanding of what it meant to be Christian. "Should we keep on sinning so that God can show us more and more of his wonderful grace? Of course not!" (Romans 6:1–2). Why go back to our past destructive behaviors? The Bible encourages us to be guided by the Spirit and not by the sinful nature (Galatians 5:16–17). Recognizing when we sin and disappoint God, receiving forgiveness each time, and recommitting to live God's way is what happens when we let the Spirit guide us. The sinful self must be put to death first by reckoning it so and then by learning to let the spiritual self be dominating our thinking and living (Romans 6:1–8:39).

We must guard against being discouraged and trying to overcome our sins in our own strength. I have discovered that if I keep committing the same sin over and over, and keep asking God's forgiveness, at some point I feel bad and begin to wonder how God can keep forgiving me. I find it hard to believe that He does keep forgiving me and am tempted to think that He cannot. But when I say no to this temptation and continue to believe He does, this greatly deepens my sense of how much God loves me. This deepened sense of His love has brought me to tears and motivates me to love Him more, and I find that I want to be done with sin. I eventually get to a point of disgust with myself. I come to hate the sin so much that I develop a deeper desire to be more diligent in not letting it control me. I feel so bad about how I treat God's love that I am more determined to look for ways to stop the sin. I have to remember at that point who I am and to defeat sin with my faith in the truth, and then rely on God's Spirit to show me how to stop sinning in those areas that are problematic for me.

In summary, followers of Jesus live by faith – faith that never stops believing in God's forgiveness, faith that separates my true self from my sinful nature, and faith that trusts the Holy Spirit to help me focus on my new self and live to please God. By becoming Christians, we now have a spiritual dimension because the Spirit of God dwells in us (Acts 2:38–39; Romans 8:9; Ephesians 1:13; 1 Corinthians 2:12). This is God's answer to our inability to be rid of the sin in our lives; we become a new creation in Christ Jesus (2 Corinthians 5:17). The natural or sinful person becomes the old person who used to be, and we are now new people who have acquired new natures—a spiritual nature (1 Corinthians 6:11). The spiritual person cannot be corrupted, so our goal as believers in Christ is to lay aside the old or former sinful self that still resides in us and put on our new self, our spiritual self, created by the Spirit of God for righteousness and holiness (Ephesians 4:17–24). We overcome sin not by dwelling on our sinfulness and relying on our human goodness and willpower to overcome it, but by faith in the mighty Spirit of Christ and His truth about our sin.

When we act as spiritual persons and are led by the Spirit, we cannot be sinful persons, for our spiritual nature can do only what is good and right. The spiritual nature cannot sin; sinning is what the sinful nature does (1 John 3:9). As Peter said, "You share his divine nature and escape the world's corruption caused by human desires" (2 Peter 1:4). Even so, the sinful nature can rise up and battle for dominance with the Spirit so sometimes we do not do what we want or should (Galatians 5:16–25). When that happens we remember that our sinful nature was nailed to the cross with Jesus and it no longer has power over us. We focus on letting the Spirit lead us.

Our makeover starts with yielding our lives to Jesus, being born from above, and acquiring a new heart that no longer wants to be part of sin. We learn from Scripture how we are to think about ourselves and how we win the battle over sin. A movement toward victory is achieved in our minds, emotions, and actions by how we think (Romans 12:2). We deal with putting off bothersome sins by turning to the truth, to our spiritual self, and to Christ in us. We learn to recognize wrong thoughts as soon as they begin to enter our minds, and we dismiss them immediately (Romans 13:14). Very importantly, we stop dwelling on the negative and keep focusing on the positive ways God intends for us to live (Ecclesiastes 5:19-20). We enjoy the everyday life God gives us and concentrate on the needs of others. We live God-directed lives with faith, hope, and love, and we live contentedly and happily by taking opportunities given us each day to do the good God has created us to do (1 Timothy 6:17–19; Titus 2:11–14; 3:4–8). By seeing the truth about sin from God's perspective, we learn to stop letting our sins get us down and take over our life, we focus instead on putting our energy into living as the new "I."

## Chapter 17

## TRUSTING A HIDDEN GOD

Paul G. Hiebert, a former missionary to India, wrote an article that appeared in the book *Landmark Essays in Mission and World Christianity*.[30] He wrote of an epidemic disease in a village and the Christians were asked to contribute to buying a water buffalo to sacrifice to one of their goddesses so the goddess would take away the sickness. Because the Christians refused to contribute, the villagers didn't let them draw water from the village well and the merchants would not sell them food. When a Christian girl got sick, the villagers said it was a punishment from the goddess because the Christians would not help them with the purchase of the water buffalo. Hiebert was asked to pray for the sick girl and everyone in the village watched to see if the Christian God would heal the girl. When the girl died, Hiebert felt totally crushed. He had prayed for healing and had not received an answer. He needed God to show Himself so others would come to believe in the true God, but God remained hidden. However, the Christians radiated hope and joy that their beloved little girl would be resurrected and live forever in God's future kingdom. Soon, reports came that other villagers were becoming Christ-followers because they had seen how the Christians responded to this tragedy. Hiebert concluded that God had remained hidden and had not healed the girl because the people of the village believed in spirits and magical powers, and if God had healed the girl, they would have made God just another one of their magical powers they could call upon as needed. (A similar situation is in Acts 8:9–24.)

---

[30] Paul G. Hiebert, "The Flaw of the Excluded Middle," in Robert L. Gallagher and Paul Hertig, eds., *Landmark Essays in Mission and World Christianity* (Maryknoll, New York: Orbis, 2009).

One problem that occurs due to God's hiddenness is that people can use it as an excuse for their unbelief. The reason they do not believe, they say, is because God does not make Himself known in such a way that they can clearly see Him. If only God would reveal Himself by some direct, unmistakable voice, appearance, or miracle, they would believe in Him. But He doesn't show Himself, so how can they be expected to believe?

I would respond by saying that some will believe due to a sign, but for many, unbelief in God is not because there is a lack of evidence, rather; unbelief is due to a person's unwillingness to see and believe what God has made known. In the Old Testament, God clearly revealed Himself many times, but people still did not believe. In Exodus, God delivered His people from Egyptian bondage by many great miracles and led them through the wilderness by His unmistakable presence in fire and cloud; He spoke to them in an audible voice from a mountain and gave them His Commandments through Moses. But they still ended up making a golden calf to worship in place of God, even when He told them not to have any gods but Him (Exodus 32:1–14). They remained skeptical and still would not entrust their lives to His care and build a loving relationship with Him.

In the New Testament, people asked for a sign from Jesus that would enable them to believe (John 6:30). Jesus gave them many signs, including the resurrection of bodies from the dead (John 11:44–48, 53; Matthew 28:1–15), but many still would not believe and entrust their lives to Him. Jesus told a story to teach that people would not believe even if someone were to rise from the dead (Luke 16:25–31). God is under no obligation to show people more if they will not believe what He has already given them (Matthew 21:23–27). The truth is that many do not want God to rule over them. They want to continue running their lives without God's interference. If God did reveal Himself, would there be those who suppress the truth and refuse to submit to God? According to Romans 1:18–21, yes.

Another problem concerning God's hiddenness comes when believers think God has abandoned them in their time of need. Should we believe in God and trust Him only if He shows up to protect us from evil and pain? What if He heals my child or me from cancer? What if my family is in a serious car accident and everyone escapes unhurt? Surely, we thank God and believe in Him. But what if the next time my loved one dies of cancer or in an accident? Will I stop believing and trusting God because God did not show up to protect them or do what I wanted Him to do? Does my trust in God depend on whether He is always there for me when I want things to turn out a certain way? A God who meets all my wishes and answers all my prayers the way I want is not a God worth trusting; that God is my servant. A God worth trusting is a God who knows the end from the beginning, a God who truly knows what is needed for my good. I'd like to determine what is good for me and what isn't, but do I know the difference? Does God know more than I do about what is good for me no matter what evils or trials I may be going through?

True faith and trust in God is the ability to see beyond present appearances and conditions. It is like being in the midst of a blackened sky with dark clouds and thunder and wind and storm and knowing that this is not how it will always be. We know that the sun is still in the sky and will shine again. Likewise, God is still there, and His good purposes for our lives will prevail. Although God does intervene miraculously in lives, the truth is that when God remains hidden, He has a purpose and an unshakeable belief in the reality of His promises that need to remain our primary focus. A person in the Bible named Job experienced the goodness of God and also some of the worst pain and suffering a human being could endure. What was His attitude toward God? He said, "The Lord gave me what I had, and the Lord has taken it away… Should we accept only good things from the hand of God and never anything bad?" (Job 1:21, 2:10).

The hiddenness of God is common. When bad things happen and God fails to show up to help, atheists, agnostics, and some skeptical believers doubt that there is a God of love. Their argument is that tragedy and death happen to well-meaning people and to children all over the world every day. God does not seem to care and lets it go on. Where is God? I agree it is easy to think that way. But the Bible definitely portrays God as a supernatural being with great power who frequently enters our world and does miraculous things. However, because these acts of God are written about so frequently in the Bible, we can easily think that is God's normal expected activity. We must remember that the Bible primarily emphasizes the saving acts of God during certain periods of history, but there were long stretches between these wonderful acts when God was silent and hidden from view (2

Peter 3:4). Though we are encouraged when we hear of miraculous things that God does in our current day-to-day world and we have confidence God answers prayer, God will not appear again with the same frequency of mighty miraculous acts we read about in the Bible until the end of this age (Matthew 24–25; 1 Thessalonians 4:13–18; 2 Thessalonians 1:7–10; the book of Revelation).

In the meantime, we must learn to trust an often hidden and seemingly inactive God. Actually, He is hidden mostly from the unbelieving world (Matthew 11:25-26; 2 Corinthians 4:3–4). Those of us who love Him believe He is at work every day. There are times, however, that God seems absent when needed most, and this can be troubling, even to the strongest believers (Job 13:24; Psalm 13:1, 22:1–2, 44:23–24; 88; Isaiah 8:17; Habakkuk 1:2, 13; Matthew 27:46). It is good to remember that God's choosing to be unresponsive to us does not mean we are bad persons or that God is punishing us for certain wrongs we have done. It also helps to remember that God is not absent. We may be dragging ourselves through a dry and desolate desert but He is doing something to grow us or help us and the drought will end. So keep on loving Him and trusting His love for you (1 John 3:1).

For many of us humans, trust is not an easy thing to do. Maybe we grew up in an environment where we trusted the adults, but they violated our trust to such a degree that we have determined not to entrust our lives to anyone ever again. When people have betrayed us or let us down repeatedly, our ability to trust is greatly dampened, making it difficult to trust anyone, even God. The feeling we can't trust anyone is reinforced when God doesn't seem to hear our prayers and we struggle and suffer through bad things without God giving us what we want or need. We feel alone in our problems. It's easy to wonder, *Where's God? Why isn't He answering my prayers? Why does He let these things happen? Hasn't God promised He would always be with us?* Many of us have experienced that God does not always make things turn out as we hoped they would. Unfortunately, we may have come to believe that a good God, if He cares about us, should have made things turn out differently. When we go through difficulties and witness others' horrendous sufferings, it reinforces this belief in an uncaring God. By such repeated disappointment and feelings of betrayal, many have concluded they cannot trust others, including God. Some even come to the conclusion that there is no God.

Because we have learned that we cannot trust others, we turn to the only people we can trust—ourselves. The fact that we humans possess the curse of self-centeredness further enhances our resolve to depend on ourselves for our safety and well-being. When we do rely on others, it is only to help us out of trouble, and when we are out of danger, we return to self-reliance. Our basic belief is that since God and others have not protected us from hurt, we must protect ourselves. Thus, we go to great lengths to protect ourselves from every kind of physical and emotional pain. We have come to believe that when we trust others, it doesn't work. Since we rely mostly on ourselves, we are very cautious about whom we trust, and we guard ourselves against letting anyone fail us or hurt us again. This seems like a good rule given the kind of evil world we live in, and we do have to be cautious. However, we live in a world of necessary dependence on others, and this extends to God, whom the Bible encourages us to trust (Proverbs 3:5). The fact that He chooses to remain hidden or unresponsive to us does not mean He is inactive in our situation, uncaring, or nonexistent. The truth is that God loves us (John 3:16) and wants us to live (Ezekiel 18:32; John 11:25–26). But what explanation is there for His apparent absence or hiddenness in the midst of people's cries for help? What is there for us to see that is beyond our present painful circumstances?

God is at work in multitudes of daily events, but one reason we don't see God is because we seldom see the meaning of those events. God will be hidden until the true meaning of our events becomes clear. Once we see the true meaning behind the events, God will no longer seem hidden. The apostle Paul had a distressing problem and wondered why God would not hear his prayers and heal him, but God revealed the meaning behind it (2 Corinthians 12:7–10). When he did, he was able to accept it. God can be seen in the events of life, but not always and not by everyone. As the Bible says, only those with ears to hear and eyes to see will discover the hidden God at work behind the scenes (Matthew 11:15, 13:10–16). Consider Christ dying on a cross. Some observers may have concluded that Christ must be a criminal and was now receiving what He deserved. Others who knew more might have said that Jesus was a good man being unjustly put to death by wicked people who wanted Him out of the way. Still, others would have seen this as the end of their hopes and dreams for a Messiah who would come and set their world right. They saw His death as a disappointment and felt betrayed, thinking that Jesus really was the Messiah when in fact He had tricked them and was actually an imposter. Others might have talked about the cross event as "Hey, did you hear the latest news?" without any realization an act of God was taking place. And many would ignore it altogether as having nothing to do with them, being totally unaware that God's love for them was being demonstrated in this horrible event. God seemed hidden, but He was working all the while. God and His acts of salvation for all mankind would have remained hidden had it not been for the resurrection of Jesus and for His followers being enlightened about the truth concerning the meaning of His death (Luke 24:25–27, 44–47).

People were not able to see God in that event until the meaning of the event was revealed to them coupled with their desire to accept and believe it. How many events in daily life would reveal God at work if only we had eyes to see and ears to hear? Those who wonder why God at times seems to have abandoned them by letting bad things happen need to trust God is good and is at work, though unseen. We may not like our circumstances, but once we love the God we know is good and right in all He does, we can accept our situation, endure the sufferings, and mature from them. We can even pray as did Job (13:15): "God might kill me, but I have no other hope," or like Habakkuk (3:17–19): "Though bad things are happening, I will rejoice in the Lord." We usually cannot see the future, but often, when we look back, we see how God has worked. Can we believe God is for our good, even though we may not see Him or trust Him? Can we wait to see what He will do?

Sometimes God remains hidden to examine or test our hearts (Psalm 11:5; Proverbs 17:3; Job 1:8–12). The good and bad things that happen in this life are tests of our hearts to reveal whether we will trust God and be committed to Him or whether we will disbelieve in God and doubt or leave Him. If good things happen to us and life is going great, will we forget God because we think we don't need Him (Deuteronomy 6:10–12)? If bad things happen, will we leave God, concluding that we cannot trust Him, that He is not there for us, that He doesn't love us? God tests the hearts of people to see whose side they are on—His, their own, or Satan's (Joshua 24:15). We could look at every challenging event as a test of our hearts, whether we trust God's love and goodness or not.

One of the reasons God tests hearts is that He wants to create a people for His new age and a new world (Ezekiel 11:19–20; 2 Corinthians 6:15–16; Revelation 21:3). God uses life's events to grow us in faith, hope, and love. He wants to develop a godly people who will be suited for life and participation in His kingdom, both present, and future (1 Peter 1:3–10, 13–17). If God saved us from every bad thing that came our way, the kind of person we each need to become would not likely happen. Stay faithful to Him and keep serving Him. He will show up again at the right time.

It is all right to seek relief from pain, but we don't want to focus so totally on getting out of our sufferings that we lose the opportunity to deepen our faith and love toward God. Even non-believers learn that we grow stronger through life's adversities. I like to look at it this way. God cannot create a new world and have ungodly and unloving people living in it, as is the case in this world (Revelation 21:27, 22:12–14), or it would become as spoiled as ours. This world is a preparation for entering the next (2 Peter 1:5–11).

I have wondered why God can't create a new world in which wrongdoing is not allowed and all people can enter into it. It makes sense to me that somehow, human free will and God's determined destiny are both involved in the formation of God's created universe. God may determine what will be, but free will means that some may choose to be on God's side while others may choose decidedly against God, refusing to be under His rule. Christians do not believe in fate, as if we have nothing to say about what happens since it will happen anyway. We are created by God to be agents of change taking responsibility for our choices and for our responses to what happens around us. God wants a kingdom of people who freely choose to love Him. Life's events reveal peoples' responses one way or the other; to grow more in love with God, or to grow more in rebellion toward Him, and He will base His final judgment on the responses we have made to certain events of our lives (Matthew 16:24–27; 25:34–46; John 5:24, 28–29).

We will have no argument with God about His final judgment, for the tests of life will clearly show what side we are on. I can hear some people saying, "I can't believe in a God who allows people to suffer." You can think that about God if you want, but what if such sufferings in an evil world like ours are the only way and therefore the kindest way for people to be awakened to the point of choosing God and avoiding being lost to His eternal kingdom (Luke 13:1–5)? Consider also that some tragic deaths may not have the same frightful connotations to God as they do to us (Psalm 116:15; 2 Samuel 12:13–23; John 11:25–26). As God is preparing a people for the next age, His tests serve as wake-up calls for some, while for others they build godly character and hope, and for others, they result in judgment and banishment from God's kingdom. I heard someone say, "Love not tested is not really love at all."

Any time when God seems hidden and to have left you alone, there are many prayers in the Psalms you can say to honestly state your true feelings of abandonment, anger, pain, or disappointment. It is okay to cry out to God. Here are a few prayers from Psalms that address God's hiddenness in times of trouble (Psalm 22:1-5; 42:9–11; 44:23–26; 69:1-3; 40, 88). Let them out, but do not give up hope. It will be rewarded.

## Chapter 18

## LOVE YOUR ENEMIES—FORGIVING OTHERS AND YOURSELF

In the movie *Second Chance*, starring Michael W. Smith and Jeff Carr, an incident occurs in which a pastor is betrayed and his inner-city church was going to be destroyed. Those who were going to destroy it decided to do it without the pastor's knowledge, and when he found out, he grew very angry at their insensitivity to his ministry and the injustice of it all. Managing with difficulty to restrain his anger, he responded to his "enemy": "The Bible says I got to love you, and right now all I want to do is beat the hell out of you." Jesus gave us a very difficult assignment when He commanded us to love our enemies, do good to those who hate us, bless those who curse us and pray for those who hurt us (Luke 6:27–28). It can seem impossible to love someone who has hurt us and is continually offending us. We are angry, and justice rightly demands their wrongs be righted. How can we let go of angry or bitter feelings and become free to be loving and forgiving? This is no easy or automatic task; it seems to go against our natural human tendencies.

When you care about Jesus' teachings, there is no doubt that He wants us to learn forgiveness. Here are some of the things he says. "Forgive us our sins as we forgive those who sin against us... If you refuse to forgive others, your Father will not forgive your sins" (Mathew 6:12, 14–15). When Peter asked Jesus how many times he should forgive a brother who sinned against him, Jesus replied, "seventy times seven" (Matthew 18:21–22). Jesus told His followers to proclaim repentance for the forgiveness of sins to all the peoples of the world (Luke 24:47). Forgiveness, according to Jesus, is very important and is a huge calling to master. But it is so unnatural to the wounded, hurting, and angry heart.

Throughout my years of ministry, I have had people ask me questions about forgiveness. Most of them had to do with why or how we could forgive people who continue to talk or act wrongly toward us without ever-changing. "All it seems to do," they say, "is let people who say they are sorry off the hook so they feel better and think everything is okay, but it's not, and they keep on being the way they are. This makes it difficult to keep forgiving them. Should we forgive them?" Yes, but that does not mean letting them continue in destructive behavior. This question typically refers to persons who certainly feel like enemies and are most likely close to us, someone at home or work.

There is a Bible passage that refers to fellow believers in Christ who wrong us. We have the right to confront them and if the person honestly and sincerely apologizes and repents, we are to forgive him or her (Luke 17:3-4). Forgiveness hinges on their repentance. A confronted believer needs to be committed to the process of changing. It is easier to keep forgiving others when we see they are trying to change their character defects. I think this same rule is valid for anyone, whether we know them in a home or work situation or whether they be strangers who hurt us. But the question still remains, if a person does not repent, should I forgive? Why should I when he or she does not try to change?

Consider what happens to us when we do not forgive. We remain hurt, angry, and frustrated if something is not being done to correct the wrong and make things right. We become upset every time we think about what someone did or continues to do to us. Perhaps we are unable to think about or be around those people without ill feelings rising up again. Un-forgiveness may affect not only our minds and emotions but also our physical well-being. We may find ourselves unable to sleep or eat; our stomachs may churn, and so on. We may become so bitter that we are hard to live with (Hebrews 12:15). We blame others for what they did or are doing to us and we cannot seem to get past it. Forgiving them doesn't seem like an option; if we forgive them, we think they are getting away with their wrongs. Letting them go free doesn't sit right; we'd rather see them suffer certain consequences.

Of course, if people would humbly and sincerely apologize and repent, we might be able to more easily forgive them and move on, but they don't, so we feel justified to hang on to our resentments and pay them back by ignoring them or making their lives miserable. A big problem with that is they often don't care, so our attempts to let them know we aren't happy will likely have no effect on them, and that makes us more angry, frustrated, or depressed. As we hang on to these offenses, we end up hurting ourselves more than them. We will increasingly find it hard to live with our growing feelings of bitterness, rejection, and our desire to retaliate or get even. To remain in such a position is terrible because we are continually troubled and we feel ourselves becoming someone we do not want to be.

Forgiveness is not about letting evil win. Even when we do love and forgive, there are instances when justice must be done and relationships made right. Just because we may forgive people doesn't mean they can keep doing wrong. There are definitely times, for the sake of safety or well-being, that the people committing the offenses or crimes must be stopped, whether by society at large or in a private situation such as marriage. To let them continue is to forfeit happy and healthy relationships by allowing ourselves and others to continue to be hurt by unchanged behaviors. Some can overlook offenses more easily than others; it's their nature. But that may not be good if it allows wrongs to continue.

How do we get free of our hurtful feelings when the wrongs done to us are not righted? We want justice. We want change. How can we bring ourselves to love and forgive? What makes it possible for us to do it?

If we follow Jesus, we have His example to help us know the right thing to do. At times we may want to see others suffer for things they did or do to us, nevertheless, for our own well-being, love and forgiveness has to happen at some point. Our faith in Christ helps us deal with being unjustly treated and having to live through sleepless, tormenting times. It is important to realize that Jesus died on the cross for our offenders' sins just as He did for ours; He cares for them in spite of what they have done. God wants everyone to repent of their wrongs and experience His forgiveness (2 Peter 3:9). Seeing them as Jesus does helps us see them in a new light—they also need God's salvation and healing.

Sometimes, when I remember Jesus' words, "Love your enemies and pray for those who persecute you" (Matthew 5:44), I obey and actually pray for them and ask God to do good for them and help them. This softens my heart toward them and helps me gain more willingness to love and forgive. I realize that because Jesus died for them too, He wants to extend His mercy and grace to them through the message of His love. The gospel involves Christ saying, "I love you, I died for you, I want to forgive you and free you from the evil chains that bind you.

Therefore, repent and receive the things that I provide and want for you." As true Christ-followers we have done that and have been forgiven for the wrongs we have done to God and others and even to ourselves. We know what it is like to be loved by God and to be set free.

God wants my enemies, those who cause my pain and grief, to experience that too. The problem is that they do not receive it and they reject the offer, continuing in their evil ways. They do not change; they think they are all right and seem to be indifferent to my pain, and they do not care. I feel I cannot forgive that. But please see what Jesus did on the cross; remember how people unjustly, wrongly, and falsely treated Him and put Him to death. He was treated every bit as unfairly and as painfully and as wrongly as we are and to the severest degree (Hebrews 12:3). Yet what did He say to God about those who treated Him like that and who refused to admit their wrongs and who kept on in their evil, and who seemed to be winning because nothing was done to them? He said, "Father, forgive them, for they don't know what they are doing" (Luke 23:33–34). I take it that He felt compassion for them because He was making a way for them to be loved and changed but they could not see it. If they do not accept His message of forgiveness and reconciliation offered to them, they would die in their sins (John 8:24), face God's judgment, and be banished from His love and life forever.

If we truly saw it this way, would it not change our hearts toward those who unjustly treat us, give us more compassion for them, and make us want to see them come to Christ? We can love them as Christ loves them when we are willing to enter into Christ's sufferings by going through what He went through. As we suffer others' ill-treatment of us and choose to forgive, we will suffer pain like His. To identify with Jesus' suffering will be like suffering our enemies' sins put on us, causing some degree of death to ourselves. And like Jesus, seeing they need mercy or will be lost forever, separated from God and all that is good, we can pray for their forgiveness. We can have pity because of their ignorance. We can wish them God's mercy and salvation. It is best if we can work toward forgiving them in our heart, so we can free ourselves of anger and perhaps even love them by peacefully confronting them about what needs to happen. We all need to do what it takes to get past hurtful attitudes or behaviors. Too often, instead of thinking about their need to know Jesus, we live with a *"poor me it"* attitude.

Is there any other way I can get past my anger and my need to see them punished for the wrongs done to me? It helps me when I realize they will not get away with what they have done but will face God and be dealt with by Him for their wrongs. I can let go of my need to punish them, turn that task over to God and free myself to become a more loving and forgiving person. It is somewhat helpful and satisfying to remember that even though the wicked may win for a while, their day will come (Psalm 73:2–19; Proverbs 2:21–22, 24:19–20). But be careful; it's tempting to gloat or feel glad when bad things happen to our offenders and we see them getting what they deserve. The Bible says that to rejoice and be glad when our enemy falls or stumbles will cause God to be displeased with us and turn His anger away from them (Proverbs 24:17–18). We need to remember God still cares for them (Ezekiel 18:23, 32).

One of the best statements I have read concerning this hope of God's coming judgment to set all things right is by N. T. Wright, a leading New Testament scholar and former bishop of Durham in the Church of England.

> God's coming judgment is a good thing, something to be celebrated, longed for, and yearned over. In a world of systematic injustice, bullying, violence, arrogance and oppression, the thought that there might come a day when the wicked are firmly put in their place and the poor and weak are given their due is the best news there can be.[31]

For us to experience a change of heart and mind, we might have to tell ourselves, *God will repay them; I will let Him do it. It's not my job* (Romans 12:19). Giving up our desire to repay, we can say, "Father, I forgive them for what they did and do to me. If you want to humble them, I leave that up to you. Give me strength and wisdom to know what to do in my current situation."

How will I know if I have loved or forgiven them? My feeling of animosity toward them will be replaced by coming to think toward them as Jesus does, that they are in deep trouble and will be lost forever if they do not turn their lives over to Christ's love. I will want to do good for them instead of retaliating or always avoiding them. Thinking

---

[31] N.T. Wright, Surprised By Hope (New York: Harper One, 2008), 137.

about problems that have caused them to be the way they are is another way to help us feel more sympathetic toward them. Loving my enemies does not mean I have to tolerate and accept them with their evil ways. But loving them does mean releasing them from my ill will. Loving my enemies means that I have to learn to pray for them and to do good to them as a way of gaining victory over evil and myself (Romans 12:21). I will know I have loved them if God's grace gives me the courage and strength to do what Jesus says to do in Luke 6:27–28. I have experienced victory over evil treatment when I have been able to think as Jesus does toward those whom I have been greatly embittered against. It is truly freeing, and if you can believe this: joy can come into your heart.

But we will have a hard time doing this if we do not see the situation from the perspective of Jesus and if we have not experienced His love in our own lives (Colossians 3:12–13). We cannot give to another that which we have not received. "We love each other because he loved us first" (1 John 4:19). For additional help, one of the most practical books I have found useful in dealing with forgiveness is Doris Donnelly's, *Putting Forgiveness into Practice*.[32]

Let us turn now to the subject of forgiving ourselves. I often hear people say, "I know God forgives me, but I struggle with forgiving myself." Maybe we live with guilt or shame in a relationship thinking we caused it. Or maybe we are haunted or regretful over something terrible we have done. Difficulty forgiving ourselves may stem from two sources. Either we have not acknowledged that something we did was wrong and so have not asked for forgiveness, or we have asked but haven't believed God has forgiven us. By not believing we are forgiven, we are perhaps trying to punish ourselves because we feel we deserve it and are hoping such self-condemnation will enable us to live with what we have done. Unfortunately, it does not. Self-forgiveness is not so much an issue of needing to forgive ourselves, as it is to believe that we are forgiven and still loved; we are playing God if we judge ourselves unworthy of forgiveness when He is willing and has already forgiven.

Another thing that makes forgiving ourselves difficult is that we are constantly faced with our past—that is, we cannot seem to overcome

---

[32] Doris Donnelly, *Putting Forgiveness into Practice* (Allen: Argus, 1982). This is a workbook that helps us work through many issues involving forgiveness.

recurring thoughts of regret or self-blame for what we have done. It may be true that we were guilty as charged and what has happened can never be changed. So how do we live with it and not have to feel the recurring pain of regret and guilt? The pain may sometimes be there, but since God has forgiven us, it need not come as a condemner but as a reminder of the greatness of God's forgiveness through the cross of Jesus, of our continued need to be thankful and to depend on God, and of our need to live differently. We can learn to dismiss thoughts of self-incrimination as soon as we sense them entering our minds. Say no immediately, thank God for His forgiveness, and move on to other thoughts and activities. Once we are forgiven, Jesus does not want us to carry our wrongs (Psalm 103:10, 12). If we stated our part in the wrongdoing and have been forgiven by God, we must guard against allowing ourselves to relive the wrong and focus on our guilt (Romans 8:1–2; 1 Corinthians 6:11).

Another reason it may be difficult to accept our forgiveness is that God's standards of right and wrong never go away. We may be reading the Bible or hearing God's Word being proclaimed, and we hear again that we have sinned. God's moral laws do condemn; they are producers of death, but we must remember that their purpose is to set forth the right way to live so people see their wrongs and come to a place of humility before God, seeking His forgiveness and power to change.

When we hear those standards, we can easily feel condemned again and want to run from the truth so that we do not have to feel judged and unaccepted. However, we need to work through this by knowing that even though God has a good purpose for His Law, we are no longer under the Law but under the grace of Jesus. It is then we need to remind ourselves, *Yes, I have sinned, but I have been forgiven and am being changed into a new creation of God bound for newness in His glorious kingdom. He loves me and I am now one with God in Christ Jesus.* God no longer holds our sin against us (Psalm 103:1–14). We need to keep hearing Jesus' words to us as stated in John 8:11. If we believe and know God's moral statutes to be true, we can hear them and agree with them but know that all is past, forgiven, and that we are now on a new journey.

Part of the problem of still feeling condemned is those around us who do not forgive us and continue to see us as sinners or having wronged them. If they choose to treat us like that, we must see that as their problem, not ours. But to dismiss them or run away from them allows the problem to continue unchecked and allows us to continue in unhealthy relationships. Even though we may consider them to be in the wrong, we can improve our relationship with them when we arrange a meeting with them, admit to them our wrongs, be honest with them about our feelings, tell them the story of how God has forgiven us, and ask for their forgiveness. This helps to remove their sinful judgmental thoughts and behaviors toward us and puts it onto them to be as God wants them to be, to forgive us as God has forgiven them (Ephesians 4:31–32; Colossians 3:12–14). When we can work through these kinds of issues with them, it helps them and us. We are all sinners, and we are taught by our Lord Jesus the importance and need to forgive one another (Matthew 18:15–35). Receiving others' forgiveness helps us to forgive ourselves, to know we are forgiven, and to feel forgiven.

Forgiving ourselves has a deeper dimension than just dealing with our sinful thoughts or actions. There is what some call existential guilt. I was coaching a team at a kids' game event. My daughter was in the final race, which required running laps around a circle and finishing in the center. If she won, the team would win the games. I was to count her laps. As she was running, she came around and looked at me as if to ask, "Am I done or should I go one more lap?" I realized that I had not kept track of her laps and I told her to run one more. She did what I said and came in last place instead of first. She had looked to me for help and trusted me, and I had told her wrong and failed her trust. Not only that, I had caused the entire team to lose their first-place trophy.

I felt shattered on the ride home, knowing I had failed everyone, especially my daughter's trust. Then it came to me, I realized at that moment that I am not a perfect person and that I cannot always meet the expectations of others or myself. I was feeling down not over a sin that needed forgiveness but over being an imperfect person, something I could never change or eliminate. I came to realize that Jesus not only died for my sins but also for the very fact that I am an imperfect human being. I thanked Him that He loved me just as I was. That day, I felt I had taken care of something I had been unaware of, my need to accept myself as an imperfect person. People can make mistakes or cause accidents for which they blame themselves. People can feel guilty for things that are not wrong in God's eyes. These are not in the same category of sins. Christ died, not only for my sins, but for all that is wrong with me, and He accepts me as I am. I should not have to keep hiding who I am, but because Jesus loves and accepts me, I can live honestly and openly before others. It was a good and freeing feeling to know that Christ loves and accepts me, but now, to feel totally healed in my situation with my daughter and the team, I needed my daughter's and her team's forgiveness. I admitted I was responsible for their loss and how sorry I was for having let them down. To my relief, they told me it was okay, and I believed them. Being forgiven and accepted by Christ and them for who I am and for what I did, was for me a great healing. These things enabled me to forgive myself. Self-forgiveness is always helped when I am forgiven and feel accepted, not only by God but also by others involved.

Walter Trobisch, in "Of Flight and Forgiveness," tells about a person who approached him to convince him God was not Almighty because He was not able to make what has happened "unhappen." As a new Christian, Trobisch was confused as to how to answer, but after some years passed, here is what he finally came to.

> God showed me that that is exactly His particular work; the heart of all His dealings from the first to the last chapter of the Bible. God can make what has happened "unhappened" through His forgiveness. It has wiped out my past, and made possible a whole new beginning.[33]

---

[33] "Of Flight and Forgiveness," in *The Complete Works of Walter Trobisch* (Westmont: IVP, 1987), 720.

## Chapter 19

## WHAT IS LOVE—THE KIND THAT MAKES GOOD MARRIAGES?

Once upon a time, I got married, and I have been married to a special and remarkable woman for over fifty two years. Although there have been times when our marriage has been strained and tested, our commitment, like most persons who marry, is to keep our wedding vows through the good and the bad until death parts us. I am pretty sure we loved each other when we got married, but we have learned that love is much more than the feelings that brought us together. If we had relied on those feelings to carry us through, we might not be married today.

Marriage can be very hard, and I can understand why many feel they must end their marriages. But I believe in love. Love is a frequent biblical word God is very high on (Matthew 22:36–40; 1 Corinthians 13:13). True love has the power to hold a marriage together through troublesome and desperate times. I know of nothing more hurtful and painful and anger producing than the feeling of rejection and not being loved. Many people live in marriages and families in which lives are shattered by an inability to give or receive love. Many leave their marriages and families not so much because of legitimate life-threatening abuses or immoral situations but because of refusing to learn the true meaning of love and excusing themselves with all manner of self-focused reasons.

I pronounce no judgments on anyone's marriage decisions; we all have to deal with varying difficult circumstances. My purpose in this chapter is simply to help all of us who are married or contemplating marriage to rethink the meaning and practice of love in light of God's point of view. Hopefully, some currently rocky marriages might be saved.

What is love? What better authority is there on the subject than our Creator? God is the key to learning love. The Bible says that the one who does not love does not know God, for God is love (1 John 4:8). All human beings have the capacity for love because we were created in God's image. To help us understand a little more about the meaning of love, I will focus on three Greek words all translated as love. The first word is *eros*. It has a bodily, sexual, passion-filled connotation we recognize in the word "erotic." This form of love is sensual, passionate, a desire to have another person for oneself. There seems to be a natural, mysterious, and God-given human drive that draws us to that special one and makes us want to connect with them. When God created the first man and woman, they had a strong attraction to each other, a kind of "Wow! This is the person I have been looking for!" (Genesis 2:23). Perhaps this initial erotic form of love lends to the romantic side of the relationship, but unfortunately, after getting married, these initial passions many call falling in love often disappear. The marriage becomes difficult as imperfections become more visible, partners become offensive to each other, and the realities of daily life cause those initial feelings to cool and fade.

Interestingly, the Bible does not use the word *eros*, possibly because of man's fall and separation from God, resulting in love's corruption. But I think the Bible does define *eros*. The Bible presents the corrupted form of love as self-centered, lustful, and uncontrolled desires that lead to immoral sexual encounters such as adultery, rape, and sex outside of a marriage commitment. What God may have meant as a good urge with the purpose of drawing mates to each other and giving a romantic flair to their relationship got twisted and became an out-of-control passion that often causes persons to lose their rational senses and to give in to their lustful desires and pleasures (Genesis 34:1–4; Romans 13:13–14). Physical aspects of love by themselves are very likely not to make for lasting and satisfying marriages. I believe most couples do experience some mystical attraction that brings them together, but it needs to develop into a second level of love.

A second Greek word for love is *phileo*, found for example in "Philadelphia," which means "brotherly love." Such love develops into friendship and longing for togetherness, the feeling of wanting to spend the rest of life with one special person. It is a feeling of bliss, happiness, and fulfillment. This form of love is a friendship kind of love, a fond affection for another. I have heard people say, "If I marry someone, I want us to be friends before we marry" because a friend is associated with qualities such as loyalty, and a true friend will stick with you no matter what (Proverbs 17:17; 18:24). This level of love realizes the qualities of the other: he or she is smart, listens to me, understands me better than anyone, accepts me with my faults, likes to do things with me, will be a good parent, comes from a good home, has a spirituality that matches mine, and so forth. People want a relationship based not on sexual attraction or selfish possession alone but also on trustworthiness, kindness, and generosity. A phileo kind of love acts more out of thoughtful tenderness than mindless passion. Friends discuss issues and make decisions on what is good for them as a couple (Proverbs 27:9).

*Eros* and *phileo* working in conjunction can keep marriages together so long as each person is mature enough to work through problems. But married partners cannot meet all of each other's needs, and friendships can end (Job 19:14; Proverbs 17:9, 19:7; Psalm 41:9). The problem with this kind of love is that people change, we are let down, differences cause conflict, or resentments build and begin to erode our friendly and loving feelings. Those original love feelings seem to last only if the reasons we liked our mate continue. If our mates no longer meet our expectations or wants, our feelings can change and we feel we no longer love them as we once did. If things progress from bad to worse, as often happens even in good marriages, we can end up thinking, *I don't love you any more* or *This is too hard, so I want out.* One partner may feel trapped and unhappy and divorce becomes the answer. In some cases, the leaving one has found another person. He or she may think that true love is all about these exciting *eros* and *phileo* feelings and looks to recapture the excitement of love with someone else.

"*Agape*" the word most used in the Bible for God's love, is a third Greek meaning of love that includes aspects of the other two. *Agape* is partly defined in 1 Corinthians 13, a passage many couples use in their weddings. This definition of love includes the following statements. "Love will last forever." If that is true love, then why do so many marriages fail? Has *agape* been unreached? "Love keeps no record of being wronged." Then why do so many marriages divorce with the reason that my partner is to blame? Is it because they have not yet experienced *agape*? "Love is patient and kind." If that is true of love, why are so many married partners unkind to each other? Where is *agape*? "Love does not demand its own way." If what they have is true love, why are so many married people selfish and demand things be their way? Few seem to experience and practice *agape*. Why? Of course, from a biblical perspective, the answer is found in the truth that all human beings are infected with an evil side to their nature. Our "dark" side needs fixing, but that is not the main purpose of this chapter.

One thing true of God's love is that it is commanded. Few persons have the kind of relationship with God that leads to *agape* (Matthew 7:21). *Agape* does not act necessarily by how we feel toward our mate but by how we respond to God's love. We love because God first loved us (1 John 4:19; John 15:12; Ephesians 5:25). We experience God's love when we come to the point of admitting our failures and turn to Jesus for mercy, forgiveness, and help. The experience of being loved and forgiven by God awakens in us the desire to love as He loved us. Without this experience of God's love found in the cross of Jesus, we cannot get to what true love is all about.

*Agape* does not love only as long as the other person pleases me and is deserving of my love; it is a love that gives to meet the needs of my spouse. Experiencing God's love is a powerful motivator that moves us to action. It is this true love that can rescue marriages from divorce and help bring back original loving feelings, making marriage the kind of marriage we dream of minus of course a continuous passion and happiness, which normally comes and goes. At times in my marriage, I had to say to God, "I am not able to love my wife as I need to, and I don't know how to love, so please help me." God wanted me to love my wife as Christ Jesus loved the church and gave himself for her. That is what I wanted to be able to do.

One of the keys to a lasting and fulfilling marriage is to determine who the boss is in your marriage. Who says how things should be? What if neither married partner considers himself or herself to be the boss? What if both partners become willing to be subject to a third person? What if each person acknowledges Jesus to be the rightful Lord of their lives and allows Him to tell them how they should conduct their marriage? What if they trust His Word to be what they need for their relationship to become increasingly loving and harmonious? What if we all decided to play by His rules? We likely will fail to do it perfectly all the time, but what if we knew His way was right and we kept working at learning how to live married life His way?

The most important questions for each married partner to ask are, Is Jesus Lord? If so, is He mine? Jesus made this point very clear when He said, "So why do you keep calling me 'Lord, Lord!' when you don't do what I say?" (Luke 6:46). Of course, one of the reasons we do not is that we cannot (1 Corinthians 12:3). Our corrupted nature will not allow it. Therefore, if we are genuinely sincere about following Christ, we need to discover how He changes our corrupted nature so we desire His will above ours (2 Peter 1:4). We need to have the nature He displayed in His relationship with His Father, a humility and love that showed when He faced a very difficult task requiring total commitment, "I want your will to be done, not mine" (Luke 22:42).

How can we develop the kind of love that makes our marriages lasting and meaningful? John 15:1–13 gives us an answer from Jesus' teachings. Love is part of the fruit Jesus has in mind when He told His disciples He was the vine, God was the vinedresser, and they were the branches (John 15:12–13; Galatians 5:22). According to John 15, the fruit of love is produced in our lives when we are pruned and when we abide in Christ. Pruning is the act of cutting back the things in our lives that prevent love from happening, including selfishness, impatience, and unkindness. God works to cut out our poor attitudes and character defects by using other people, our own consciences, pain that comes from the consequences of our actions, or troubles that arise. God may use many ways to correct us, and one key way is through one's spouse.

Our mate is a likely source God uses to prune us so we can be better lovers. Consider the words of clinical psychologist Sven Wahlroos, in his book *Family Communication*.

> People with family problems often come to a psychologist to find out what is wrong. The fact is, however, that if they would only listen closely to the diagnoses which other family members offer concerning what is wrong and accept their suggested remedies, they would often not have to seek professional help at all... the people you live with have observed your behavior for a long time, know you intimately, can hear things in your voice and in your choice of words that you can't hear, and can see feelings reflected in your facial

expressions that you yourself may not be aware of... whatever a family member says about you must be taken very seriously and must be seen as valuable information.[34]

The Bible agrees: "An open rebuke is better than hidden love! Wounds from a sincere friend are better than many kisses from an enemy" (Proverbs 27:5–6). If we are willing to accept words from our spouse not intended to hurt us but to help us, we are more likely to grow in love as God wants.

In addition to pruning, God produces true love in our lives through our abiding in Christ (John 15:4–5). God commands us to love because He knows love is not going to come about naturally; there is too much of self in the way. The pruning takes care of our self being-in-the-way issues, and the abiding takes care of Christ doing for us what we cannot do for ourselves, that is, produce true love. To their credit, many married people care and try to fix their broken or disappointing marriages, but often their efforts do not seem to work. Developing a closer relationship with the Lord Jesus is what can enable us to experience His love in such a way that it becomes part of our nature and we can give it to one another.

In marriage, we may feel we are tired and don't feel we can give any more. We may feel the relationship is too far-gone. Nevertheless, our goal can be to experience Christ's love for ourselves, learn to love as He loves, and depend on Him for godly results. It is good to learn to please our heavenly Father by practicing His love in our present relationships. We need to abide in Jesus by believing His love for us, by meditating in His Word, and by obeying His teachings (John 15:7, 10).

God can use our unfortunate situations to develop His love in us. Maybe loving in obedience to God and practicing His love toward our spouses will not restore long-gone marriages, but at least it will make us better people for having learned how to live His way. And if our marriage ends, at least we can say to God, "Thank you for using this situation to teach me to learn to love as you have loved me. I know I cannot make my mate love me. I have prayed that you might help my

---

[34] Sven Wahlroos, Family *Communication, revised* edition (Chicago: Contemporary Books, 1995), 87.

mate, and I am sorry for any pain I caused that cannot let my mate back into a relationship with me. I have recognized and confess my part in the problems. I may have failed for so long that I destroyed my mate's ability to trust me. But Lord, thank you that you forgive my failures. Help me to accept whatever happens. I know you will help me survive the pain and go on, not be bitter, and keep learning how to become a more loving person."

The communication we practice in marriage makes a big difference in whether love becomes intimate. Partners must learn to avoid words intended to hurt the other—gossiping words, name-calling words, accusing words, blaming words, defensive words, and threatening words (Ephesians 4:29). Most often, these words come out of pride or anger because our partner criticizes us or has not met our desires, wants, needs, or expectations. Rather than these evil words, partners need to use truthful and helpful words even though they may be hurting words (Proverbs 27:6). We do not like to hear words of criticism; we do not like to have our faults pointed out to us. Pride and power struggles in marriage are obstacles that prevent us from listening. But does not love have the right to say words that hurt when they are said to help the other become a better person? To fail to hear hurtful words from one who loves us is a mistake, for God may have put that person in our life to help us see what we need to change to strengthen our relationship and increase love (1 Thessalonians 3:12). Be cautious— "We will speak the truth in love" (Ephesians 4:15) does not mean we have the right to hurt another with harsh words unwisely spoken, or spoken without insight into our partner's personality and needs.

Jesus offered a primary reason for divorce. When questioned as to why God permitted divorce in the Old Testament laws of Moses (Deuteronomy 24:1–2), Jesus, referring to God's created order, responded, "Moses permitted divorce only as a concession to your hard hearts, but it is not what God had originally intended" (Genesis 1:27, 2:24, 5:2; Matthew 19:3–8). Jesus knew hard hearts were the cause of most marriages dissolving. What did He mean by a hard heart? The Bible says, "Whoever stubbornly refuses to accept criticism will suddenly be destroyed beyond recovery" (Proverbs 29:1, 28:14). "It is stupid to hate correction" (Proverbs 12:1). The hardness of heart is stubborn pride that thinks self to be in the right; it is a dangerous place to be. I once heard on the radio a humorous but wise quip: "If you find

Mr. Right, make sure his first name is not 'Always.'" Of course, one person can contribute to the other person's hardening heart. The hardened person has suffered wrongs for so long that his or her heart has turned off toward the constant offender. If there is to be any hope of restoration at all, there must be genuine repentance, confession of wrongs, forgiveness, and continual effort made to change one's ways. This takes willingness by both parties, but it's what Jesus teaches us to do when we want His will in our lives.

We have called love a passion. Interestingly, the word *passion* is also used for Christ's sufferings on the cross. Married love involves suffering. People who love each other are willing to suffer by dying to their own desires to meet the needs of their beloved. Unfortunately, we are more often concerned with what we want over against what our mate wants, or needs; selfishness wins the day over love. To die to our self-centered desires can be agony, but to suffer such a death is to love.

The Bible teaches us that we are to love one another as Christ loved us. Wives are to respect their husbands, and husbands are to love their wives as Christ loved the church, giving himself up for her (Ephesians 5:25, 33). True love is rare. That is why we must be humbled, want it, and unceasingly ask God for it. I used to be afraid to help my wife with household chores because I did not want her to control me. I was fearful that every time she wanted me to do something, I would have to do it. I shared this feeling with her, and she said she didn't want to control me. I believed what she said, and when I help her, it is because I choose to do so, recognizing her need for help.

Supposedly, the reason couples get married is that they love each other, but there are many reasons. The phrase "love is blind" has validity because often we do not allow ourselves to be totally honest about some of those other reasons; we push some into our subconscious and ignore others, depending on how amiss we think they are. What were some of the reasons you got married? It is good to ask ourselves that question because if we get married for poor reasons, we might have to come up with better ones to make our marriage work. Before I married my wife, I definitely had a feeling that I wanted to be with her, but I was not sure I knew what love was. I recently asked my wife if we loved each other when we got married. She answered, "We loved each other with as much love as we had." Yes, we did. And as with everyone, our love had to grow for us to continue to enjoy our relationship.

To you who want to leave your marriage: Did you love your spouse when you married? Did you feel he or she was the one for you? Was your beginning wonderful? Is it not worth the fight to have it return and through effort and learning, to love as God loves, have your marriage be better than ever? Some who have not been married for long want to give up too soon, but many who have stayed in there have testified their marriages became great and they were glad they stuck it out and gave it a chance.

A man once shared with me that he was experiencing intense mental and emotional pain because his wife was committing adultery and he did not know what to do. He was torn with vengeful thoughts and angry emotions. His Christian beliefs of wanting to have the right attitude and do the right thing were wavering. His dilemma was, "Shall I divorce her or not?" Part of the cause of his frustration and confusion was his firm belief God did not intend divorce (Matthew 19:3–8). He loved his wife, but she was trampling on his love. I am reminded that God experienced a similar problem. God loved and took a bride, Israel, who was unfaithful to Him (Ezekiel 16:32). God was deeply grieved but honest with her about His feelings and about her wrong, hurtful behavior. Rather than enabling her, He allowed her to face the consequences, even administering some of them Himself. He warned her she would eventually face disaster and the loss of the good things she had in their relationship. But after giving her warnings, patience, and many opportunities to repent, due to her persistent unfaithfulness, God gave her a writ of divorce (Jeremiah 3:6–8). Yet He continued to love her; He kept the door open to receiving her back and planned to make that option a future certainty (Isaiah 54:4–8); He did not give her up as lost forever (Romans 11:25–27).

Such is God's love. Perhaps the truth in this for us is in God's longsuffering. Perhaps in a similar situation, we ought not to be too quick to seek divorce but renew our efforts to hang in there and see what will happen. Perhaps we can be encouraged with the thought that sometimes people we love need to experience, like the Prodigal Son (Luke 15:13–19) and Israel, that their ways of living do not result in the happy life they thought. They see that their choices are destructive for self and others, at which point they may decide to return, hopefully, changed and better than what they were.

If such a scenario happens to us, our renewed relationship can become richer than ever, making it worth the effort and pain to give the situation time to see what happens. Admittedly, this wait does not always work out as we might wish, but to keep on loving will make us better no matter which way it turns out.

Only those with insight, great fortitude, and a deep commitment to Jesus Christ as their director and sustaining resource can walk this path. We cannot control people who exhibit contrary minds; we can only offer them, love, own our faults, and keep trying to do what is right according to the truth and wisdom of God. Things may not turn out as we wish, the hardened person may leave (1 Corinthians 7:10–15), but we can survive by clinging to our hope that no matter what, God will not forsake us. He loves us still, and He can make all things new by bringing beauty out of ashes (Isaiah 61:3).

## Chapter 20

## FINDING A BIBLICAL VIEW OF SICKNESS AND HEALING

I suppose most people have experienced praying to God for some kind of healing and nothing happened. What are your options especially if you believe in a God who is supposed to love, care, provide, and protect but does not come through as you hoped, thus leaving you with distressing pain and sorrow? Do you begin to question and doubt and lose faith by thinking, *What good is it to believe in God?* If your crisis has not ended, do you choose to keep believing God will heal you, but if nothing happens how long can you keep faith with no response? Do you give up on God and rely on yourself, other people's abilities, science's promises, or other religions? If you do not find the help you long for, do you find yourself feeling depressed and hopeless?

Perhaps you need to rethink your assumptions and beliefs about God and search for a different understanding of reality and what God desires from and for you. For example, is God supposed to give you what you want even if you say you do not expect Him to give you everything? Does God reserve the right to give you the best possible good according to His wisdom and knowledge? Maybe God wants us to be healed, but even more, He wants us to see and understand life from His perspective, something we cannot or are unwilling to do as long as we think the world revolves around us. Maybe a world we would design for ourselves is not the best world God intends for us; maybe He has planned something better for us. Maybe He loves and cares about us far beyond what we know. I realize that to say God cares can seem trite and absurd in the face of great pain and suffering we may experience, but has God promised to always in this life give us what we perceive is best for us or what we want?

I once told a group of grade-schoolers two seemingly minor experiences I had with God. When I was young, I made a paper airplane that would not fly. Out of frustration, I finally prayed and asked God to help my airplane fly, and it glided beautifully across the room. I remember feeling surprised and pleased by what God had done. The other experience was when I was trying out for a baseball team and I kept striking out. I prayed hard that God would let me hit the ball. I struck out almost every time and was cut from the team. I asked the kids, "Why do you think God answered my first prayer but not the second?" Their answers were more mature than many adults' answers. "Maybe God answered your first prayer to help you believe in Him," they said, "and He did not answer your second prayer because He had a better plan for your life than playing baseball."

Our subject is sickness and healing. Why is there disease? When sin and evil came, God's good world was spoiled (Romans 8:18–23), so we now experience many causes of sickness, including viruses, bacteria, transmitted diseases, infections, defective genes, and so forth. Aside from natural causes, we can also bring sickness to ourselves by lack of cleanliness, improper diet, or other failures to take proper care of our physical and emotional selves. Psychosomatic diseases are bodily ailments caused by stressed emotional or mental states. Jesus also called sin itself a sickness that needed curing (Luke 5:30–32), and there are sometimes supernatural causes of illness (Mark 9:17–29; Deuteronomy 28:58–61).

What attitudes do Christ-followers commonly have about illnesses and how to get well? Various biblical beliefs regarding sickness and healing may include the following: Some believe strongly that if they have faith or if others have faith on their behalf and if they are seeking to obey God, God will heal them. This is based on certain Scriptures, including "You can ask for anything in my name, and I will do it" (John 14:13, 16:24), "A prayer offered in faith will heal the sick, and the Lord will make you well" (James 5:14–15), and "I hope all is well with you and that you are as healthy in body as you are strong in spirit" (3 John 2).

The belief that God wants all Christ-followers to be healed is supported by Jesus' healing ministry on earth and the apostles' continuation of healings after Jesus ascended to heaven (Mark 6:56; Acts 8:6–8). It is also pointed out that Jesus died not just for our sins but also to make us whole and healed (Isaiah 53:4–5), thus His provision is for us to enjoy complete healing (Matthew 8:16–17). In this belief about healing, doctors are sometimes not an option.

Others ask God to heal them believing He can, but they do not always know what God's will is. Does He want us to get well, or does He have a purpose for the sickness? God did not heal Paul after he prayed three times for healing because God had a reason for that (2 Corinthians 12:7–10). Therefore, those with this belief will ask for healing but leave it up to what God wants to do and accept their condition whichever way it goes. Their acceptance of "Thy will be done" is what Jesus prayed when He asked God to take away his sufferings; He concluded, "Yet I want your will to be done, not mine" (Luke 22:42). In this belief, doctors and technology are viewed as part of God's gifts to help in healing, but God is always involved as our healer.

Some may take the approach that God brought illness on them to get their attention about something in their lives that needed correction and that when they confess and change, God will take away their illness. Job's friends thought this (Job 4:7–9; 5:8-9, 17-18). Those who believe this can point to God's dealings with Israel; if they do right, God will not bring diseases upon them (Exodus 15:26). This also appears to be true in the church when God causes sickness for believers who fail to properly examine themselves at the Lord's Supper (1 Corinthians 11:28–32).

Some understand their illnesses to be tests from God, to see if their faith will hold and if they will continue to trust God's goodness (Job 2:3–7). Others believe that if God does not heal, sickness may be the way God chooses to take persons home to Him. Many of us have heard the expression, "It must have been their time to go." Some believe that Jesus' and the apostles' healings are no longer to be expected to happen as often because they were signs confirming who Jesus was or confirming that their message was from God (Hebrews 2:3–4). Now that we have Jesus' identity and His gospel message confirmed in Scripture, we no longer need these signs, although they may occasionally happen, especially on mission fields in Third World countries.

One attitude God definitely wants us to have toward sickness and healing is to look to Him as our healer. For most people, at least in more developed nations, the first thought when an illness is detected is to take medication or get to a doctor. In the Bible, God disapproved of a man named Asa for going to physicians instead of coming to Him for healing (2 Chronicles 16:7–13). Please understand that God is not against going to doctors; Jesus affirmed the value of doctors in Luke 5:31. In Asa's case, God was concerned about being left out. Asa did not seek God's help for the troubles in his life. He would much rather trust in sources of help he could see. God did not like this because God cares about him and knows that He was the true source of life and health, and He didn't want Asa to harm himself by missing what He could offer. People will never experience what is truly good, rewarding, and satisfying without God as their friend and helper. When God permitted sickness in Asa's life, perhaps to help him turn to God, Asa continued to show contempt for God by seeking human physicians and dismissing God as a healing source.

Through fearful and agonizing times regarding my health, God's grace helped me get to the point that whenever I am concerned about sickness or some health concern, I say to myself, *The Lord is my healer.* In Exodus 15:26, God revealed Himself to those who were His people as "I am the Lord who heals you." Whether or not God will heal me in my present situation, He is still my ultimate healer as is acknowledged in the Isaiah 53 passage.

My personal practice about doctors is that if and when I do consult a doctor, I am also giving God the option to heal me. I am not one who believes we ought never to consult doctors thinking that God will heal us. To me, it would be morally negligible to die or let a loved one die when a doctor could have prevented it. I believe God approves discovered means to bring healing, for He created this world with hidden resources, allowing humans to discover medicines. And He gave us the capacity to learn how to develop skills at whatever our job (Exodus 36:1-2), including surgeries. But even though God has built into this world the scientific discovery of medicines and surgical procedures as valid sources for healing, I must not neglect Him as my true healer. Man cannot perform healing as completely as God can. My wife and I and some of my friends have prayed and have experienced God's healing on a number of occasions.

Some have come to God for help and feel He did nothing to alleviate their suffering or allowed a loved one to die, and they became angry with God. I have discussed this in another chapter, "Trusting a Hidden God." I feel terrible for anyone who has had this experience, and I sometimes wonder why God would allow Himself to be seen as uncaring, lacking the power to help, or even appearing to be nonexistent. For their own well-being, I pray that those with such opinions of God might be able to come to a better conclusion by taking an honest look at what God has revealed about Himself, us, and our world rather than relying on appearances or limited understanding.

Scripture says we are healed by Christ's whipping (Isaiah 53:5). This is emphasized in the New Testament (Matthew 8:16–17) and with Peter's words, "By his wounds you are healed" (1 Peter 2:24). These Scriptures refer to Jesus' death on the cross and what it accomplished—the complete forgiveness of sins and healing of our diseases. However, that total healing does not necessarily take place in this present lifetime. It can be argued from this passage that if we have total forgiveness, why shouldn't we believe we have total healing of our bodily sicknesses? One reason might be that even though we are forgiven, sin still exists in us and we still do wrong things. Our sinful nature is not totally removed until we are resurrected with new spiritual bodies. Likewise, with disease still present in our world, we should not expect the total healing of our bodies until the coming day of resurrection.

Actually, to accept sufferings is a pathway to a spiritual kind of healing, for God purifies our souls through our sufferings. Yes, by His whipping we are healed, and we can expect some physical healing benefits now because Christ's kingdom is in some measure here now, but the future completion of God's kingdom is where full healing will be realized when Jesus physically returns to accomplish the restoration of all things (Acts 3:21).

Because we are God's beloved children, we have a right to ask confidently for healing. If we have a gift of faith, revealed knowledge from God, or knowledge that He hears us because we have asked according to His will, we can know He will heal us when we ask (1 John 5:14–15). Otherwise, we must take into account that it may be His will not to heal, and we must accept His reasons if He does not. A leper said, "If you are willing, you can heal me and make me clean" (Matthew 8:2–3). He did not use the word *if* in a doubting manner, for he knew God could heal him; He simply did not know *if* God was willing. In his case, God was.

God may have other plans for our lives and unfortunately, we are not always able to discern what those plans might be. But overall, I believe the Bible tells us that we should ask God for healing, for example, in James 5:14–16. I can testify that following this practice according to James has worked in mine and others' lives. We also need to consider our motives and lifestyles. Our prayers can go unanswered if we ask with wrong motives or if our lifestyle is not pleasing to God (James 4:3). Why do we want to be healed? To accomplish His will? The will of God is that we know and love Him above all else and want to glorify Him with how we live our lives each day (Matthew 22:37–38; 1 Corinthians 6:19–20). We can expect He will answer any prayers asking Him to give us what we need to do His work and promote His kingdom on earth. Is that not the point of John 14:12–14?

God desires deeper kinds of healings than just physical. Most often, we focus on physical healings rather than on other needed healings. Jesus at times focused on the healing of sins (Mark 2:3–5) and came to die for that purpose (Luke 24:46–47). If He came to heal only our bodies, such healing would serve no grander purpose. God's grander purpose is having our bodies become vehicles through which He can bring healing to others, which is most effective if we let God heal our inner selves, guilt, fears, attitudes, faulty thinking, self-centeredness, detrimental behaviors, and broken relationships. God wants people to become whole and fit to dwell in a world not of our making but of His. What good is a healed body that cannot bear His fruit for a renewed world (John 15:8)? God heals some simply out of His compassion and for the joy of helping them, and He desires to give us rich, satisfying lives (John 10:10), and He wants us also to serve Him for the good of others (Titus 3:14).

We all need healing of our anxieties and fears that accompany bodily illnesses. At those times, we need the peace, comfort, and hope that come from believing and trusting a good and encouraging word from God (Proverbs 16:20). He tells us that anxiety weighs down our hearts but a good word makes them glad (Proverbs 12:25; Psalm 56:3–4, 94:19). God is a God of comfort in the midst of afflictions (2 Corinthians 1:3–5). He tells us we have the sentence of death in us so we would not trust in ourselves but in God. When our burden is beyond our strength and we despair, God's promises of deliverance bring a welcome peace (2 Corinthians 1:8–10). We must accept the fact that although our outward selves are dying, our inner selves are being renewed every day (2 Corinthians 4:16).

Knowing Jesus is in us and guarantees our life to be preserved forever enables us not to lose heart. His promises strengthen and renew our spirits in the midst of afflictions (2 Corinthians 4:7–18). Our focus needs to be on pleasing God, knowing that His Spirit is with us (2 Corinthians 5:1–9). A great source of peace and comfort that God gives us is His Holy Spirit, our comforter and source of peacefulness (John 14:16 –18, 26 –27). During upsetting or panic-stricken sicknesses, I have prayed many times that He would remove my anxieties and give me peace (Philippians 4:6–7), and at times I have been overwhelmed by immediate and complete peace as a gift from God's Spirit. My anxiety and fears were suddenly gone, and I experienced complete rest (John 14:27). That is a healing I sometimes feel desperate for in the midst of anxiety. Such peace sustains me and helps me accept my condition as being okay if that is what God wants for me. God grows my faith not always through removing my bodily ailments but through accepting them. Can God physically heal me? Yes. I always claim Him as my healer, and sometimes, my bodily illnesses have gone away; at other times, He has healed me mentally and emotionally. But more importantly, I know my ultimate healing is in His kingdom in the day He will come to destroy all evil and raise His people to life.

Why love and trust a God we feel ignores our pleas for healing? That is a good question. I know someone who served God through his music ministry. One time, something bad happened to him, and he said, "What good does it do to serve God? He still lets bad things happen to me." I interpreted his comment to mean that his reason for serving God was so God would protect him from evil. His reason for serving God was actually self-serving; his motivation was errant. We love God in spite of His allowing evil to continue in this world. We love Him because He is good and worth loving; He is our only hope for the ultimate cure of our whole person and for making a new world free of all sickness and pain (Revelation 21:3–4). Victory over sin, sickness, and death is already ours because His plans are certain.

Obviously, God knows things about this world that most people do not know. He knows that this world is full of evil and unfairness and humans can't fix it. He knows this world will come to an end and a new heaven and earth will be ushered in to take its place (2 Peter 3:10–13). If that's so, why would He want us to receive everything we want in this life if all it does is settle us into a world system that is perishing? Wouldn't that be insane if He desires for us to settle into a better world (Hebrews 11:13–16, 39–40)? Healing earthly sicknesses is something we desire, especially if we want to serve God but ill health prevents it. But there is a deeper healing than what we often know or want, and that's what God desires for us.

Whatever you find to be your biblical view of sickness and healing, you are free to practice it with the measure of faith you have from God. But also be willing to accept His answers whether that means healing or not, and know that God is good no matter what. Keep seeking to grow in your trust and love toward God, our only ultimate healer (Exodus 15:26).

There is much sickness and suffering in this world. I have asked myself, *Would I be willing to take that person's raging headache on myself so he or she could be pain-free and at rest? Would I be willing to take another's cancer into my body and suffer its ill effects so he could be healed? Would I be willing to take that person's sins so she could be free of guilt and at peace with God, others, and herself? Would I be willing to suffer hunger and die and give that starving person my food so he or she could live?* I know of one who was willing and who did it for all who suffer. I pray, *Lord, if there is any way I can help ease another's suffering, help me do it in the name of the one who did it.*

If anyone reading this is suffering and in need of healing, I pray for you now, *Father in heaven, ease their pain and suffering and let them experience your rest. Flood their bodies with your healing power and restore them to good health. Let them know your love and mercy by revealing to them the one who took their pain and suffering. Bring them into oneness and intimate relationship with that one—Jesus. Amen.*

## *Chapter 21*

# HAVE YOU DISCOVERED THE POWER OF WHY?

When I talk about the power of "why," I mean the power of thinking. In his best-seller, *The Road Less Traveled and Beyond*, psychiatrist M. Scott Peck wrote,

> One of the major dilemmas we face both as individuals and as a society is simplistic thinking— or the failure to think at all. It isn't just a problem; it is the problem.
>
> It [thinking] is perhaps more urgent than anything else because it is the means by which we consider, decide, and act upon everything in our increasingly complex world.[35]
>
> With the freedom that we have to think for ourselves, ultimately we must hold ourselves accountable for how and what we think and whether we are using our capacity for thinking to get the most out of life.[36]
>
> Many people show little interest in contemplation... they rarely stop to think about why they're going where they're going, where they really want to go, or how best to plot out and facilitate the journey... we must acknowledge that thinking well is a time-consuming process. We can't expect instant results. We have to slow down a bit and take the time to contemplate, meditate, even pray. It is the only route to a more meaningful

---

[35] M. Scott Peck, MD, *The Road Less Traveled and Beyond* (New York: Simon & Schuster, 1997), 23.
[36] Ibid., 53.

and efficient existence.[37]

The Bible promotes thinking. "Don't think you are better than you really are. Be honest in your evaluation of yourselves" (Romans 12:3). "Fix your thoughts on what is true, and honorable, and right, and pure, and lovely, and admirable" (Philippians 4:8). "Let God transform you into a new person by changing the way you think" (Romans 12:2). When I feel depressed, not necessarily clinically but as a normal part of life, if I change my thinking to positive and true thoughts, my depressed feelings leave and I feel on top again. The psalmist learned to change what he was thinking when he was down: "Why am I discouraged? Why is my heart so sad? I will put my hope in God! I will praise him again—my Savior and my God!" (Psalm 42:5). The practice of thinking in ways the Bible promotes can change our lives.

If we are to engage the power of thinking, we often need a catalyst, something to get the thinking process started. Questions often start us thinking. God created us with inquisitive natures. Consider children's curiosity. They are busy getting into everything, so parents lock things up and put dangerous or precious objects out of reach. Children as young as two are famous for asking "Why?" Many scientific discoveries begin with questions that lead to better technology, health, and solutions to many societal problems. Philosophers can seem to be way out there, but they are good to have around because they ask things others do not think to ask, things that make us think more deeply about life.

God and Jesus often approached people with questions to get them to think. God asked Adam, "Where are you?" He asked Eve, "What have you done?" (Genesis 3:9, 13). Jesus asked people, "Who do you say that I am?" or "What do you think about the Messiah?" (Matthew 16:15; 22:42). If Jesus told a story, He sometimes asked, "What do you think about this?" (Matthew 21:28). God through His prophets may ask "why" to get people to think about their lifestyles (Haggai 1:9).

Questions can motivate us to see more than we see and enable us to think about our world and ourselves so we gain helpful knowledge, insights, and understanding. We can have a lot of knowledge but not always understanding of our knowledge or how to use it. Understanding

---

[37] Peck, *The Road Less Traveled and Beyond*, 54.

can be missing if we do not include God's input because only God's input furthers our understanding of the most important questions about life. (Proverbs 1:29–33, 2:2–6; 28:5).

I could have called this chapter, "The Power of Questions," but I chose to focus on the "why" question. "Why" is powerful in many areas. Knowing why things work as they do is what enables us to know how to fix things that become broken. We can deal with our health problems when we know why they came about. To ask why can yield some profound insights into life and ourselves that can lead to significant self-discovery and beneficial growth toward the kind of world and persons God created us to be. The power of why comes to us when we ask about many of the things we think or do. Why did I say that? Why did I just act like that? Why am I so angry? Why do I believe as I do? Questions like these can lead to life-changing insights, but answers do not always come easily. It can be frustrating to ask why but not be able to come up with an answer. We often need to rely on others, particularly God, for the knowledge we seek. He reveals things we can learn from no other source (Psalm 139:1–3, 23–24; Hebrews 4:12–13; 1 Corinthians 2:14).

People generally want to understand what life is all about. They want to make sense out of what happens to them. They want explanations for things that concern them, especially when they experience bad and painful things. At those times, we are quick to ask, "Why"? We shall discuss that kind of "why" at the end of the chapter.

We need to be aware that why questions often threaten people. When directed to their personal lives, they can make people defensive or want to avoid the issue. Some refuse to see doctors for fear of what they will find out; they would rather not know, even die, than face the emotional pain of dealing with bad news. Some married couples don't discuss their marriages because that would likely bring up matters they fear facing.

Peck asks,

> Why would someone choose not to think deeply? Why would someone choose to think only simplistically, superficially, and reflexively? The answer is… we have a preference for avoiding pain. Thinking deeply is often more painful than

thinking shallowly.[38]

I think he has a valid point about some kinds of deeper thinking being painful. The Bible makes the same observation: "To increase knowledge only increases sorrow" (Ecclesiastes 1:18). We often do not like to face our memories of failures, wrongs, unfulfilled dreams, or whatever. Perhaps that is why some "why" questions are made light of or ignored (John 3:19–20). But without such insight, people may not be able to move past their crippled thoughts and behaviors; they might progress into deeper depression, anxiety, guilt, fear, or avoidance. The fact is self-assessment can produce helpful self-understanding that can improve our mental, emotional, and physical well-being. Answers to why questions about ourselves can reveal where we are, help us understand our actions and beliefs, and lead to new directions in living.

Believers in Christ are encouraged to examine themselves to see if they are in the faith (2 Corinthians 13:5). They are encouraged to examine and probe their ways, and if they are errant, to return to the ways of the Lord (Lamentations 3:40). "Why" is a powerful tool for self-discovery. Are we afraid to be alone with our thoughts? Is that why we like constant noise and busyness?

Actually, fears of self-discovery are unfounded if Jesus is allowed to enter the situation. Having to deal with the why of things is good if it pushes us to realize our need for a Savior who can rescue us from self-destructive patterns. He answers many of our problems and is the answer to our fears. He often reassured His followers, "Don't be afraid" (Matthew 10:28, 31; Luke 5:10, 8:50, 12:32). He is the answer to our guilt: "The Son of Man has the authority on earth to forgive sins" (Mark 2:10). He is the answer to our doubts: "Just believe that I am in the Father and the Father is in me. Or at least believe because of the work you have seen me do" (John 14:11). He is the answer to our emotional pain: "Come to me, all of you who are weary and carry heavy burdens, and I will give you rest" (Matthew 11:28–30).

Because we live in a world of evil within and without, Jesus does not promise a pain-free life. He does, however, promise a way through and into a new existence of His making. He gives us the hope we need to

---

[38] Peck, *The Road Less Traveled and Beyond*, 69.

persevere in our trials because there is coming a day of restoration of all things to which we can look forward with joy (Acts 3:19). With His light, we can face darkness: "I am the light of the world. If you follow me, you won't have to walk in darkness, because you will have the light that leads to life" (John 8:12).

Let us examine a few of Jesus' why questions and see what we can discover. It would be interesting to think about how we might answer them. He asked, "Why are you afraid?" (Mark 4:40). Fear is common to us all. Jesus' disciples were caught in a life-threatening storm at sea and were letting their fears take over instead of facing the situation courageously. In so doing, they acted cowardly or timidly. Jesus asked them why. After all, He was with them. If they answered this question for themselves, they would have seen they still lacked faith in Jesus because they had not yet fully understood who He was.

Like those disciples, we too often lack faith, but we can let our life-threatening situations become teachers of where we stand in our relationship with Jesus. What knowledge and understanding do we have of Him, and how can we grow to the point where we can face our trials with the confidence that no matter what happens, with Jesus at our side, all will be okay? It may take us a while to trust and have confidence in Him so that fear leaves us, but to get there is our objective, and true faith in Him is the way to experience peace.

Jesus asked, "Why did you doubt me?" (Matthew 14:31). At Peter's request, he was commanded by Jesus to walk to Him on the stormy sea. Peter did what Jesus said, but he took his eyes off Jesus, started to sink, and became afraid for his life. Jesus rescued him and asked him why he had doubted. We too may doubt amid things Jesus commands us to do. Our life efforts may not be working out, but we need to keep trusting Him. If Jesus gives us something to do and promises a certain outcome, we have no good reason to doubt it.

Jesus also asked why to doubt, in Luke 24:38 when His followers did not believe He had risen bodily from the dead even though He had told them He would rise (Luke 24:44–46). Paul asked unbelieving people a similar question: "Why does it seem incredible to any of you that God can raise the dead?" (Acts 26:8). What would your answer be? If God has promised bodily resurrection, why would you doubt it? Of course, modern thinking would say, "We doubt it because things like that do not happen." The truth is that in history, something need only happen once for it to be real. Because we don't ever see it happen in our day doesn't mean it never happened or that it cannot happen again. People who doubt it may do so because in their world there is no God. Given the existence and love of God, why is it impossible?

Another of Jesus' questions was, "Since I am telling you the truth, why don't you believe me?" (John 8:46). In this conversation with unbelieving people, Jesus gave them the answer. They did not believe because they were not godly people and had no interest in hearing what He said. I have experienced this many times in talking with people about spiritual things; it seems to go right over their heads as if their minds are elsewhere. (2 Corinthians 4:4; 1 Corinthians 2:14).

Here is a difficult question. "Why do you keep calling me Lord when you don't do what I say?" (Luke 6:46). Ouch! This question requires some careful thinking on our part. Some people call Jesus Lord as an expression of their belief in the existence of a benevolent God. Their belief involves praying to Him at certain times when they need His help with a problem, but their belief that Jesus is Lord is not in their thinking. Their relationship with God has nothing to do with knowing Jesus personally in such a way that they consider Him their Master whose words they try to obey and practice. It is a difficult question as well for believers who claim to know God personally. Jesus said He wanted us to learn to practice His teachings, and if we did, our lives would be able to withstand inevitable life-threatening events (Matthew 28:20; 7:24–25). When we do not want to do something He says or we come short in our attempts, how do we handle our failures? Rather than feel guilty and fall away or drop out and disappear because we don't want to face people who were counting on us, it's best to confess our lapses and simply get back on track. It might be helpful to honestly attempt to answer this question for ourselves to see where we stand in our relationship with Christ as Lord. Maybe we have never settled the question of His Lordship and we commit to His will only when it is convenient.

What a strange question by the crowd in answer to Jesus' statement, "You are trying to kill me." They thought He was crazy. "Who's trying to kill you?" they asked (John 7:19–20). People do not outright confess to wanting to kill Jesus, yet in their beliefs and ways of living, they would be rid of Jesus rather than submit to His commands. Many people seek to eliminate Jesus as the God to whom they must answer for how they live. If you do not follow Jesus, what are your reasons?

How about this question: "Why worry about a speck in your friend's eye when you have a log in your own?" (Matthew 7:3). This question is about being critical and judging other people. We do need to make judgments about people to make proper decisions about our relationships with them—what to participate in and what to avoid. But the judgments here are about putting people down and demeaning their worth as individuals created in the image of God. There may be many reasons why we see others' faults without seeing our own, and it would be worth thinking about it.

Consider Jesus' words, "Why do you call me good? Only God is truly good" (Mark 10:18). Here are some questions for you to think about and try to figure out. Do you consider yourself a good person? If so, why? In what sense do you do good things if no one is good but God? In what sense are you not good?

We now come to discuss that other kind of why we mentioned earlier, the kind we have when things go very badly. When Jesus was suffering execution on a Roman cross, He cried out to God, "Why have you abandoned me?" (Mark 15:34). That is a common human cry of most people who suffer traumatic loss. Somehow, we humans have a belief that life is supposed to work out for our good. We get attached to people we love, and when we lose them in accidents, murders, natural catastrophes, or whatever, we feel deep emotional pain that causes us to complain to God with an outcry of "Why?" Our search for a satisfactory answer is elusive; we hear nothing in response, only silence. Whys in these situations are mostly screams of frustration, pain, or anger. It is best not to try to answer the whys, but simply allow ourselves to feel our pain. When we see others suffering pain, the best thing we can do is be there and offer sympathy.

In many cases, we expected answers to our prayers for protection or healing, but there were none. My friends and I prayed for a baby with leukemia to be spared, but the baby died. Many years ago, five missionaries were killed by people they tried to love. Their families knew their efforts were dangerous and they prayed for God to protect them, but it was not to be. When we experience such loss, how do we keep faith in God? How can we continue believing in goodness? Elisabeth Elliot, the wife of one of those five missionaries wrote a reflection titled, "On asking God Why."[39] She struggled with why her husband had been killed and eventually concluded there was no answer for why God allows evils to prevail, but she concluded through her tragedy that there was only one safe place to be—where Jesus was when He suffered His own cruel death with a cry of why. The place to be was to keep loving God and to be faithfully doing His will.

If we become angry at God because of a tragedy, we can come to a crossroads. Anger at God is normal because we feel God has failed us, and some may wonder if they could ever trust God again. Most who have faith in God will in time return to their faith. They challenge the whys of grief by not letting them make a wrong decision about God. John the apostle wrote to believers, "This world is fading away along with everything that people crave. But anyone who does what pleases God will live forever… Every child of God defeats this evil world, and we achieve this victory through our faith" (1 John 2:17, 5:4).

Jesus lived in an evil world and it seemed that any good done in it would never prevail. But by His example of committing His life to God and doing God's good will day in and day out, He was in the safest place he could be, for God always rewards those who do His will in this life or the next. To this day, Jesus is still reaping the joyful benefits of His sufferings, and so shall we if we remain faithful to the end (Revelation 2:10–11, 26–28; Matthew 24:13). To give up on a lifestyle of faithful love and obedience to God in doing good results only in evil being the victor instead of faith and goodness. Doing God's will is the safest place to be, even in a world of uncertainty and evil, a world that makes no sense to us. Maintaining that attitude and way of life in the midst of evils comes from having hope in God's promises and knowing He will never disappoint us in the end. To live with hope in goodness winning out enables us to persevere the whys of painful tragedies.

The power of why is that it leads us to think; M. Scott Peck, in *The Road Less Traveled and Beyond*, points out, "Thinking is perhaps more urgent than anything else because it is the means by which we consider, decide, and act upon everything in our increasingly complex world."[40]

---

[39] Elisabeth Elliot, *On Asking God Why and Other Reflections on Trusting God in a Twisted World* (Grand Rapids: Revell, 1989).
[40] Peck, *The Road Less Traveled and Beyond*, 23.

So, why not try asking why more often? Then think and follow where it leads. It often leads to some very surprising destinations.

## Chapter 22

## STRESS AND THE CALMING PRESENCE OF OUR FAITH

Think about a bridge, something very important for completing a journey. A bridge allows us to get from one place to another. As objects cross the bridge, they put stress on it. The bridge must be designed and structured to handle the pressure put on it or it will collapse. Life is like a bridge. We are all trying to get from one place to another. As we do this, pressures on us weigh us down. Stress in family situations, health issues, finances, jobs, and our social life are part of living. Normal stressful pressure helps us perform our proper duties and responsibilities, but disheartening events can put us beyond our normal stress range until we feel we have more than we can handle. If the pressure or stress is too great, we might react poorly or break down.

As believers in Christ Jesus, we claim to have a faith that can get us through, but we can fall apart like anyone else if we are unable to connect with God in calming ways during upsetting events. Although many Christians have learned to rely on God in ways that enable them to cope, the faith of others does not seem to kick-in automatically when needed. We can hear the words that tell us to trust God, but that does not mean we are able to do so. There is a need for us to construct our lives so we can handle those pressures to avoid our lives collapsing under the stress.

We who follow Jesus have admirable God-given resources to use in constructing and strengthening our lives: faith, hope, love, and wisdom. Faith knows that God has valid reasons for what is happening to us and that He is with us and helping us (Matthew 8:25–26). Hope knows that things will not always be as they are now, there is the confidence that a better day is coming (2 Corinthians 1:10; Psalm 42:11). Love knows God cares about us and is doing what is best for us even when life does not seem right (Psalm 6:4; 1 John 4:16). Wisdom knows good things to be doing in the midst of our stressful sufferings (Proverbs 8:12, 14, 17, 33; James 1:5). When under great stress, our goal is to be able to fellowship with God and come to a calming peace, even joy, by using our resources of faith, hope, love, and wisdom. So how can we better experience these resources in those times when we are overstressed?

Chicago's prominent Catholic Joseph Cardinal Bernardin was once on the cover of *Time*. Before his death on November 14, 1996, an autobiography featured on the Internet read,

> In a September 1996 ceremony at the White House, President Bill Clinton awarded Joseph Cardinal Bernardin the Presidential Medal of Freedom, the highest civilian honor bestowed on individuals who have made significant contributions to their communities and the nation.[41]

The cardinal shared his experiences of stress in *The Spirit of Cardinal Bernardin*.[42] His responsibilities and pressures had increased throughout his work. He talked about experiencing loneliness in spite of being surrounded by people, having anxieties caused by the fear of not being able to live up to other people's expectations, and how it hurt when he was misunderstood or criticized. He felt frustration when his best efforts seemed to accomplish little or nothing, at times he felt abandoned by God, and he experienced a depressing loss of morale when taken for granted as an insignificant person.

At the end of his life on earth, he suffered battles with cancer. He said it took him twenty-five years of ministry before he realized he needed to put Jesus Christ first in his life not just in theory but also in practice. When he did that, a profound spiritual change took place. He describes it as "letting go of Joe Bernardin and grabbing onto the Lord." His stressful situations didn't go away, but putting Christ in charge made a difference that enabled him to successfully cope with life's stresses. Faith knows how to "let go and let God." This phrase is a

---

[41] Pub. by crbrunelli, *A Tyronean Prince… (www.scribd.com/doc/158575103)*.
[42] A.E.P. Wall, *The Spirit of Cardinal Bernardin* (Notre Dame: Ave Maria Press, 1997).

cliché, but learning how to do it in unsettling situations works to settle us. It took Joe Bernardin twenty-five years to learn it, but it need not take that long for everyone.

Jesus' disciples needed to learn how to have trusting faith, but it took many experiences for them to learn it. Learning to trust is often, though not always, a process by which faith becomes stronger due to many testing situations. When a sleeping Jesus and His disciples were in a boat, a storm suddenly caused Jesus' learners to fear for their lives. They woke Jesus and implied He did not care about their well-being. Sometimes, we feel that way when bad things happen to us. But Jesus did care for them and spoke to the wind-tossed sea, which became instantly calm. The disciples were amazed. "Who is this person?" they asked. Jesus asked, "Why are you afraid? Do you still have no faith?" (Mark 4:35–41). As I think about this, I ask myself, *Could God's voice, speaking "Silence, be still" to me in the midst of my stressful crisis, calm my troubled heart and mind just as it did the sea?* The answer is yes if I trust in His caring presence, love, and power to help me, not necessarily in His power to take away my hurtful circumstances but in His power to fulfill His promise that all will be all right no matter what happens (Romans 8:22–25, 31–39).

What if we are doubtful, scared, or too depressed to believe? What can be done if we find ourselves in a frame of mind or heart where we cannot bring ourselves to trust God? I think of the man who came to Jesus and said, "If you can, heal my son." Jesus responded that all things were possible for those who believe. The man cried out, "I do believe, but help me overcome my unbelief" (Mark 9:22–24). The point here is that unbelief can be helped. Although the kind of healing this man experienced does not happen to everyone, in this case, Jesus helped him to have faith by healing his son. At times, I have felt such great stress and spirit-crushing fear that all I could do was cry out to God to give me His peace. I was not asking Him to take away the problem for I knew He might want the problem to remain to mature my faith. I just needed Him to give me His peace so I could endure the frightening aspects of the situation. His grace did this for me a time or two because I could not get there by myself. He instantly calmed my inner spirit, just as He did the sea (Philippians 4:6-7). It was amazing, and I was so grateful. I had done what the man did when he wanted Jesus to heal his son—I asked (Matthew 7:7–11).

What might help our unbelief? Here are a few things I have found helpful when I have doubts or struggle to trust God. I review the evidence for my faith and remember the times God has helped me. If He helped me before, what would make me think He would not continue to be faithful? When I review who He is and what He has done, through trust in such knowledge, I become settled and at peace with my situation, confident that He is able (1 Chronicles 16:11–12; Lamentations 3:22–24). The more I have found Him to be faithful in the past, the more I trust Him in the present. Even when I do not experience the answers I want or need from Him, I am at peace with the fact that in His time God will do what is good for me no matter what.

Another way to help our unbelief is to read the Bible. The Bible tells us that faith comes by hearing the word of Christ (Romans 10:17; John 20:31). As was once said of Jesus, "The Sovereign Lord has given me his words of wisdom, so that I know how to comfort the weary" (Isaiah 50:4; Matthew 11:28–30). Knowing what the Bible says and teaches is valuable knowledge. The Bible often brings to me calming words that relax my soul and troubled spirit and they help me remain calm. His comfort and promises help me rest in God's presence and revive in my heart the certain hope that He is with me and helping me. Even though I may not know how help will come, I look for it with expectation, confidence, and joyful anticipation. We can all find special words in the Bible that comfort us, give us courage or settle our minds and hearts. Reading God's Word in times of stress helps. We need to hear from God, but for His words to empower us, we need to believe them and surrender to them (Proverbs 16:20). I struggle at times to find what word He wants me to trust in my particular stressful situation. I sometimes desperately want to hear Him say something that gives me assurance everything will be all right (Romans 15:4).

A great way to help our faith is by honestly revealing our feelings of hurt, pain, or anger about what is happening (Job 7:11; Psalm 6:1–4, 10:1; Habakkuk 1:2–3) and inviting believing friends to share in our trials (Galatians 6:2). God often encourages and strengthens us through their presence, their reassuring words and suggestions, and their prayers on our behalf (Romans 15:14; Philippians 1:19).

Psychiatrist Dr. Harry Tiebout once discovered from a female patient what was for him a new way to deal with stress. The woman was addicted to alcohol as a sedative for handling life's difficulties, but something happened to her that changed her life. She described it as something that gave her a good feeling and hope for a new life. The Bible talks about the possibility of a new life in 2 Corinthians 5:17: "This means that anyone who belongs to Christ has become a new person. The old life is gone; a new life has begun!" Tiebout saw a definite change and evidence of new life in this lady but had no explanation for what had happened to her. He noticed she had been unstable but now was at peace; she had formerly been tense and nervous but now was composed and felt safe; she had been afraid but now was relaxed; she had felt guilty but was now contented. How could this be? According to a paper Dr. Tiebout wrote, she could not even tell what happened to her until she discovered what it was that enabled her to experience such a change. At a church service, she heard the word *surrender* in a hymn.[43] It suddenly dawned on her that surrendering her life was what she did to experience this great spiritual transformation, thereby relieving her of a defeated life and the stressful feelings she could not handle.

To feel secure and experience His calming peace, I must be able to trust Him completely, knowing that no matter what happens, I am safe in His care. At times, I have said, *Even if I die, God will take care of me, and my loved ones who are left behind. All will be okay.* I think this is what Archbishop Bernardin meant when he used the words "putting Jesus first" to describe how peace and calm had entered his life. Continual frustration and debilitating fear are not from God; we must not allow our hearts to stay afraid. The way to do this is not to enter denial or withdraw into ourselves or drown our sorrows and woes with drugs or alcohol or anything else, but to face our situations by exercising faith in the presence and truths of our Lord. When I say that coming to possess a strong faith is often a process, I mean that God desires this for us and it may take many stressful situations for us to learn how to surrender our lives to our loving and all-powerful God. This world will always present challenges until God's kingdom comes in fullness. We must learn, in the midst of life's stressful times, to "Give all your worries and cares to God, for He cares about you" (1 Peter 5:7).

---

[43] Harry M. Tiebout, MD, "Surrender versus compliance in therapy with special reference to alcoholism," from Harry Tiebout papers collection *(www.thejaywalker.com/pages/tiebout).*

When King Ahaz and his people faced great stress, the Hebrew prophet Isaiah gave them a message from God to stop worrying and being fearful (Isaiah 7:4). That's encouraging, but how can we be calm under worrisome circumstances? The answer is that we must have faith to stand firm (Isaiah 7:9). By not being sure of God's presence and help, we will remain insecure. Faith is all about knowing and believing what God says and trusting Him to be with us and help us even though we have no answers or ways to fix things. Ahaz, however, did not trust God but looked to his own answers to relieve his anxious stress level. His answers did provide temporary relief but no lasting solution. It is tempting to look to ourselves when God does not seem to be helping.

Our American culture encourages us to be self-sufficient, to believe in our abilities to do things. How often do we hear, "You can become anything you want to be," "We believe in you," or "Take control of your life." It is good to have self-confidence and to exercise responsibly our abilities to the fullest, but in our human frailties and sinfulness, we often need power beyond ourselves. That power is the Spirit of God Jesus promised to send to those who followed Him (John 7:37–39). God's Spirit is a person who comes along side of us to be our helper. He comforts, guides, teaches, imparts peace too, and empowers us beyond our own strength, and guarantees a good future that will certainly come to pass (John 14:16–18, 16:13; Romans 8:14–15, 23, and 26). When we are stressed and feel weak, not in control, frustrated, or uncertain about what to do, it is God's Spirit who is able to give us what is needed (Zechariah 4:6). The key for us is to learn to step aside, humbly admit our needs, ask God to help us, and let Him work in His time to accomplish in us what we feel we cannot (Psalm 27:13–14; Proverbs 3:5–6).

It takes faith to know that God is interested in us as His truly beloved children. It takes a desire to want His will to be done in our lives and courage to surrender to whatever that might be. And it takes belief in Him that He can make happen what we cannot. In *Finding God*, Dr. Larry Crabb wrote, "When our strongest passion is to solve our problems, we look for a plan to follow rather than a person to trust."[44] In a corrupt world, our self-made plans or wants often fail at some point. We need a God we can trust to work things out in His time, and in ways

---

[44] Larry Crabb, *Finding God* (Grand Rapids: Zondervan, 1993), 172.

He knows are best for us. When we learn to surrender our lives to Jesus, trusting a trustworthy person, things can happen inside and outside of us that we ourselves could not make happen. So we first take care of trust, but we must also be responsible to do what God wants us to do. This is where wisdom becomes part of our God-given resources to deal with stress.

There are many in this world convinced we do not need Christ to help us deal with stress; they think we have all the help we need in our social, psychological, and medical sciences whose practitioners study human behaviors and conditions and have learned much about how to overcome stress. Books on the subject abound. These books do have some great suggestions for relieving stress, including questions we can ask ourselves to assess our situations. Do you have physical signs of stress such as headaches, muscle tension, fast heart rate, sleeplessness, or upset stomach? Are there emotional signs of stress like quick temper, frustration, anxiety, discouragement, or guilt? Does your mind race with preoccupations, worries, negative thoughts? Once you have seen how these symptoms affect you, you can ask what is causing the pressures and then look for ways to ease the stress. It may help to do physical exercise, reduce some of your tasks, get away for a while, or call someone to talk to.

Asking these kinds of questions and taking advice from these books is helpful. Some books recommend self-talk techniques. Do you need to change what you are saying to yourself? You can counter negative talk with statements such as, "Everything will be okay," "It's not as bad as you think," or "Calm down so you can think what to do." These suggestions work for many. As followers of Christ, we believe all truth is God's truth, no matter its source. God's wisdom can come not only from the Bible and from God's people but also from social and medical sciences, which have much to offer.

We should receive the helpful advice of books and medical practitioners, but if that is all we rely on for help, we can miss the wonderful work God wants to do in our lives. The stress relief that comes from what human knowledge alone can give does not go far enough to relieve certain stresses. This is because there is the stress that needs the knowledge of God in order to find true and lasting relief. For example, what do humans know about death and beyond and what it takes to calm those anxious fears? Jesus knows the truth about death:

"Everyone who lives in me and believes in me will never ever die" (John 11:26). What do humans know about future certainties that can calm many of our worries? Jesus reassures us of His help: "Seek the Kingdom of God above all else and live righteously, and He will give you everything you need" (Matthew 6:33).

What do humans know about helping people who feel stress because they are slaves to their own wrongdoing? Jesus said, "If the Son sets you free, you are truly free" (John 8:36). What power do humans have to change people from the inside out and give them a peacefulness they cannot find in this world? Jesus said, "I am leaving you with a gift—peace of mind and heart. And the peace I give is a gift the world cannot give. So don't be troubled or afraid" (John 14:27). Jesus' words make clear there is a divine help that surpasses human wisdom. Jesus was called "Wonderful Counselor" (Isaiah 9:6) who said, "Come to me, all who are weary and carry heavy burdens, and I will give you rest" (Matthew 11:28).

When we feel stress, we need faith in God to help us, hope in His promises, and the knowledge that He loves us and cares about us (Psalm 33:20–22). We also need His wisdom to tell us what we are to do; we should not wait for God to do everything. We too have responsibilities to perform. God wants us to consult Him in the midst of our trials (Isaiah 30:1–3, 8:19-20; Jeremiah 17:5–8; 2 Chronicles 16:12).

In a world like ours, we can never prevent stressful situations, but sincere Christ-followers know to turn to the God of lovingkindness for supernatural help (Isaiah 26:3–4; Psalm 13:5, 31:7, 69:16–17). Sometimes, God shows up and does something to help us unexpectedly, and that's one advantage of knowing God over human self-help methods.

God has a goal for us stated plainly in His word. We are to endure our stresses and pressures until they produce in us the completeness He desires. God wants us to feel secure that in Christ Jesus we lack nothing (Romans 5:3–5; James 1:2–4). But how do we get there in a satanic, corrupt world? When bad stuff happens, we can welcome our stress-filled trials, knowing that God wants to use them to grow us to be faith-filled, hope-filled, love-filled, and wisdom-filled. When life is stressful and is going from bad to worse we need to know, even if not at first, that God is interested in refining us further, testing our hearts to see if we will continue to believe in His loving presence and plans. God has confidence in us. Under stress, we may falter for a time as Peter did (Luke 22:31–34), but we will come back and be stronger.

Perseverance means to wait on God rather than to hurry out of a situation. When we see ourselves enduring our stress and its sufferings and still trusting God, we become confident that He will not disappoint us and will fulfill all He promised. And we are sure of this because, through our surrender, we experience how much He loves us. Ultimate faith is complete surrender to and trust in Jesus' goodness and wisdom with no questions. Such faith speaks volumes to those who live without hope. Our problems help us empathize with those who are hurting, and their observation of our God-enabled response gives us an opportunity to share with them the reason why we are at peace. It is our trusting and loving relationship with God (Psalm 27, 55:22; Romans 15:13). It is a matter of accepting our situation no matter what it is and asking God for what we need (James 1:5). He wants us to be faithful in doing what is right in the midst of our stress (Psalm 25:4–5).

A big contributor to our stress is the voices we let into our minds. The Bible says we are to think about things that are true, right, pure, of good repute, and so forth (Philippians 4:8), but we allow negative, corrupting thoughts to enter our minds. It is hard not to let thoughts in because our minds are bombarded almost every minute by other people's voices, books, media, our thoughts, God's words, and the Devil's tempting, destructive thoughts. Once we allow them in, we entertain them, and if we recognize they are wrong and bad for us, a battle begins that may result in believing them and giving in to them (James 1:14–15), arguing with ourselves, or trying to get rid of them. If we allow a fearful or worrisome thought to feed our minds, we feel stress. If we allow a lie such as, "You're no good" or "You should be ashamed of yourself" and we believe it when God would say otherwise, we can get down on ourselves and feel self-condemned or guilty.

The problem is that when we allow these thoughts in, it is often too late. We have given room for a potential inner battle to rage. The key is to recognize what kind of voice and thought it is, dismissing the thought before it settles in our minds, and quickly replace it with other thinking, especially something God would say to us. That is why it is good to know the Scriptures so that we have access to God's words when we need them. A prayer to say often is, "God, let your Spirit remind me of your truths at appropriate times throughout my day." We as God's

Spirit-filled people have the advantage of living and walking by the Spirit (Galatians 5:25). All who are being led by the Spirit are children of God (Romans 8:14). We are being led by God's Spirit when we allow His voice to speak His Word into our hearts at the right time. God speaks wisdom to us, and wisdom knows how to apply His words at the right time. The right time is before unwanted voices gain a foothold and increase our stress.

Some thoughts we need to let in, think about, and work through, but others are simply negative and destructive. For example, if I sense a feeling of false pride entering my mind, a voice that tells me, "Aren't you great! You're better than others," I dismiss the thought and refuse to let it linger in my mind. I am reminded of God's words of wisdom, which say, "Pride goes before a fall" and "Do not make judgments and think you are better than others". I learn to let godly thoughts control me, and I move on to good thoughts and other things that I am doing at the moment.

We can get good at recognizing damaging thoughts before they are even completed, and we can say no immediately before any stress comes up. This is one meaning of Ephesians 6, in which God told us to put on the armor of God to protect ourselves from Satan's darting thoughts being hurled at us. I do not practice this perfectly all the time, but I do it frequently, and it works.

We learn some practical ways to overcome stress by examining ways Jesus and His forefather, David, handled stress in their lives. It is no shame to falter under the weight of stress; Jesus was greatly distressed when He said, "My soul is crushed with grief to the point of death" (Matthew 26:38). What did Jesus do when He felt so overwhelmed by His situation? He spent time with God—He prayed. In Luke's gospel, it says that Jesus, being in agony, was praying very fervently (Luke 22:44). He also enlisted others to be with Him in His time of temptation. He realized that under pressure there is the temptation to give in and respond in wrong or immature ways such as running away, losing faith in God, or failing to endure and grow through the trial. Jesus got alone with God and spent time talking to His Father and listening for encouraging words. One result of His seeking God was that God sent an angel to strengthen Him.

We never know what God will do to help us, but we know by faith that God will be there to help us. A common temptation we all face is wanting things to turn out our way, but after time with His Father, Jesus was able to let go of what He wanted and accept whatever God's will was for His life. His time in prayer gave Him strength to think rightly as God would want and to persevere and go through the circumstances leading up to His death.

The Bible tells of some of the thoughts Jesus had, very possibly promises and thoughts from God's written Word that came to Him during His prayer time. For example, He knew that even though He would die, God would raise Him from the dead (Mark 8:31; Psalm 16:8–11). We who have faith in Jesus know this will be true for us as well (John 11:23–27). Jesus also felt joy surge in His soul, knowing His death would result in the salvation of many. God gave Him truths He could hold onto that helped Him endure execution. The joy of hope and seeing His offspring provided strength to endure (Hebrews 12:2; Isaiah 53:10). We can find the same strength by spending time with God and being reminded of truths in Scripture.

David, a shepherd who became king of Israel, also had experiences of great stress. When he and his friends returned from a trip, he discovered that enemies had burned their town and taken their wives and children captive. So great was their grief and loss, that David and the people cried until they had no more strength. To add to David's stress, the people were extremely angry, blamed him for this, and threatened to kill him. But "David found strength in the Lord his God" (1 Samuel 30:6).

I have often thought about this phrase and wondered how David found strength in the Lord. The account of this event tells us some of the things David did. First, allowing himself to feel the pain and to weep was a great stress reliever. He also inquired of the Lord to ask God for guidance in what he should do. He listened to what God told him, and he did it. When he stepped out in faith and obeyed God's Word, he found God was leading him along the way to help him accomplish what he had to.

It is important that in handling our stress, we see that we have a responsibility to act in certain ways. This requires wisdom from God, and it came to David as he spent time being strengthened in the presence of God. But exactly how did David strengthen himself in the Lord? That is something *we* need to learn how to do in times of stress. I think a big part of the answer to this question comes from reading the Psalms David authored. In his writings, we discover many things David thought and said in his times alone with God. Those thoughts can become our thoughts too. Believing that what we think has a powerful effect on how we live and handle life's stresses, Charles L. Allen, who wrote *God's Psychiatry*,[45] recommended that we read Psalm 23 in a certain way. Just as a doctor might prescribe the taking of medicine for physical problems, Dr. Allen prescribed Psalm 23 to people struggling with stress-filled problems. They were to get alone with God and read each verse slowly, meditatively, and prayerfully five times a day for seven days. They were to read it in the morning, after breakfast, after lunch, after supper, and at night before retiring to sleep. He said that many who practiced this time alone with God exactly as he prescribed it experienced a changed life.

David wrote this psalm, apparently, because these kinds of truths from and about God are truths he experienced when he trusted God. Such thoughts became a source of "strengthening himself in the Lord" to help him get through difficult days. We also can have faith in these words, trusting that what God says to us He will perform in our lives. As the prophet Isaiah said, "In quietness and confidence is your strength" (Isaiah 30:15).

We can cross the bridge from stress to peace by being with Jesus and applying the faith, hope, love, and wisdom He inspires and enables in us. When this happens, even in the midst of stressful situations, we will enjoy the calming presence of our faith.

---

[45] Charles Allen, *God's Psychiatry* (Grand Rapids: Fleming H. Revell, 1953).

## *Chapter 23*

# HEALING OUR GRIEF

---

I was with a group of men when one of them shared the news that the father of a family he was friends with had died in a car accident. When the victim's son learned his father had died, he was confused and asked if his dad was coming back. "No, your dad is not coming back." The son said he wanted God to send his dad back because he and his dad had made plans and they had not done them yet.

This triggered another man in the group to say that when he was six, his dad died. Two thoughts plagued him over the next twenty years before he was able to resolve them. Following his dad's death, his initial thought was it was somehow his fault that his dad had died because he should have been a better son. A second thought was that he would not let himself get too close to people because it would hurt too much if they died. He said he grew up feeling very insecure as if he weren't good enough. He felt sorry for himself that his dad had died, and he questioned God's love for him. Because he never allowed himself to get close to people, whenever he began a relationship with a girl, he sabotaged the relationship to make sure it would not work out. He grew to hate the way he was and kept busy so he would not have to think about it.

Later, when he developed somewhat of a faith in God, he believed that if he served God, God would help him overcome these personal problems. He eventually came to a place of telling God he could not live like this anymore, and by coming to see the truth from God's point of view, he is now doing well.

That man's story prompted yet another man in the group to divulge that his dad had died when he was a boy. About a year later, his mom remarried. He and his stepdad did not get along. He felt no one could replace his real dad, and he treated his stepdad poorly. One day, his stepdad died in an accident. He said he had a lot of guilt over the way he had treated his stepdad. He felt it was too late to experience his stepdad's forgiveness. Grief often leaves us with unfinished business.

A community organization that cares about people who have lost loved ones invited me to teach grief classes. I accepted the opportunity, and since then, I have taught many such classes. I learned to be very sensitive and sympathetic toward those suffering deep pain over loss. In addition to the examples above, another example of the kinds of grief people suffer is seen in this woman's story: "My seventeen-year-old daughter was killed in a plane crash. I am going through a time of deep loneliness and despair. I can hardly bear it sometimes. To find hope, I tried to find God and to find out why this happened. Actually, I hoped I would discover there was no God because it is hard for me to believe in God if I were to discover He had been there the night of my daughter's accident and chose to do nothing." These stories of grief may have brought back painful memories of your own, and I am sorry for your loss.

When something or someone we have loved and treasured leaves our lives, we experience grief. Grief can apply to every type of loss, whether divorce, job loss, or something else. Grief is often a painful, life-shattering feeling that adversely affects us physically, emotionally, spiritually, and mentally. We may experience loss of sleep and appetite, upset stomach, crying or sighing spells, withdrawal from people, fatigue, restlessness, and other stresses. Mentally and emotionally, we may experience a wide range of feelings and thoughts including shock, unbelief, sadness, sorrow, anger at self or others or God, regrets, guilt, fear, resentments, relief, anxiety or worry, loneliness, self-pity, depression, yearning and moping around, poor concentration, falsehoods we tell ourselves, and who knows what else. Grief can be a time of many mixed and confusing emotions and thoughts that need sorting out. That will take time and knowing things to do that can help you. Spiritually, grief can affect our relationship with God for good or ill. As some have said, grief presents us with an opportunity to choose to get better or get bitter.

Everyone grieves differently depending on many factors. How close or distant we were in a relationship with a person determines the depth of our grief. We all have a history of losses during our lifetimes, and from what people said to us at those times, we all have learned how we are supposed to grieve. We may have learned we should be strong and not cry, or that others do not want to hear about it so best keep it bottled up, or that we need to keep busy so we don't have time to think about it and be sad, or that it's okay to cry and talk about it. Whatever it is we have learned will influence how we grieve.

The age of the person we lost can make a difference in the depth of our grief, as can the kind of death it was. It will take us longer to get over sudden, unexpected deaths than it will to get over expected deaths. Other factors include differing personalities and differing faith levels. Some people know more about grief than others, so their grieving is helped because they know how to help themselves. The kind of relationship we had with a person may determine how we grieve. If our relationship was positive, the pain is different from what we experience at the death of someone with whom we had negative or few feelings. All these factors need taking into account when we seek healing for our grief.

Healing our grief does not mean we are ever totally over our loss. We will never fully forget the person who left us, nor should we. Memories are a part of our relationship, and some can surface many years later, surprising us with sadness and tears. Healing means that the deep heartache and painful feelings that first tore us apart when a loss occurred will gradually reduce in intensity until we return to living in a healthy way again. This is good news because when we first experience the hurtful feelings of grief, we may think the pain will never go away. Sometimes, we like to wallow in our grief because we want to keep the person we loved close to us, and feeling sad keeps them near. At some point, however, we realize we need to move on and live "normally" again. We still have a life to live and a love to give.

I have found two ways that are very helpful in getting over grief. One is to allow ourselves to feel the pain, not suppress it, ignore it, or fear it. No one likes to feel deep hurt, but like going to a dentist to have a tooth extracted, it may hurt, but we need to allow ourselves to hurt in order to get better. The other helpful thing in getting over grief is to talk about it. Find a person who does not mind listening to whatever you say, good or bad, without judging, even if you repeat yourself. The more you allow yourself to feel the pain and to talk about your feelings, the more quickly you will get back to productive living and happiness. At first, doing these things may not be what you can bring yourself to do. Each person will move forward at his or her own pace and in his or her own way. If you have a hard time talking to someone about your grief, writing your thoughts and feelings in a journal can help immensely.

People put off and delay their grief in many ways. At first, this may be the best way for them to handle their pain, and at that point, it is okay. But it is not okay to continue to shut down any feelings to minimize the pain, pretending you are doing fine. It is not okay to think the grief will go away, to avoid aspects of the grief process that are hard to face, to drown sadness and loneliness with alcohol, avoid others, or grieve to keep memories alive. At some point, those who are grieving need to make adjustments and get on with life.

Many people simply do not know how to help themselves. After a time, and it varies from person to person, failure to deal with grief can result in physical and psychological disorders. The experience of one of the men at the beginning of this chapter is an example of what can happen to those who do not know how to work through grief or fail to seek help to do so. Most people can get through grief with the help of a nonjudgmental friend who listens and supports them. Others may need counsel from someone who can help them get past more-serious blocks to returning to a healthy life. Certainly, the stories in this chapter teach us that children and families also need help with grief.

One of the problems I have had to overcome in my life was panic attacks. One time, I was quite sick and I thought I was going to die—that was a frightful time. My wife, in whom I would normally confide, was gone for a weekend retreat, so I was alone. My thoughts were driving me crazy, but since I knew how to help myself based on information in the classes I had taught, I thought about whom I could call. It is amazing how few friends come to mind who might be immediately available to help get through a felt crisis. I called a friend; he said I could come over. The first thing I did was to put him at ease by letting him know how he could help me. I said, "I need to talk about what is going on with me right now and I just need you to listen. I may cry, but really, I'm all right. You don't have to fix me or say anything to help me. Just listen and let me talk." I am glad the guy had a project to be working on because I talked for half a day. It helped me immensely, and I shall never forget his kindness and friendship. When I left, I said, "If I end up not dying soon, I think I will feel pretty foolish." But I did not feel foolish; it was something I needed at the time. Since then, and because of trials like that, my faith in God has grown and I am now much better equipped to handle my fears. Plus, I am much closer to my friend.

Many fine books offer various ways to work through grief.[46] Some do a good job of helping those stuck in grief. For example, they may not know how to say goodbye to primary or secondary losses. A primary loss would be the person you are grieving. A secondary loss might be the time you spent together gardening. Saying goodbye is an important step in overcoming grief, and the time it takes varies with everyone. Other books do a great job of helping people who had an incomplete relationship with someone who died. Even after someone has died, it is possible to complete a relationship with that person so you can feel better about it.

Spouses married for a long time sometimes lose their identities. They've lost their "we" and are now "I." They need help to create a new identity by redirecting their energy and love to other places or persons.

The Bible, unlike these other books, does not offer step-by-step ways to enable us to deal with grief, but it does offer support to grief sufferers. It can help us identify with other grief sufferers, help us find comfort, and bring us hope. Naturally, the Bible brings God into our lives and in this way offers a spiritual dimension that other books may miss.

Throughout the Bible are accounts of people who suffered losses. Grief is an unavoidable universal experience. These biblical accounts can help grief sufferers to identify with others going through the same pain they experience. Mothers who have lost infants may feel like the mothers in this biblical story: King Herod wanted to kill the infant Jesus, so he sent soldiers to Bethlehem to kill every baby two years old and younger. There was weeping and great mourning (Matthew 2:18). The mothers refused to be comforted; they cried out in unbelievable emotional pain. They may have been shouting cries of why but received no answer. They may have been extremely angry. They may have felt God had abandoned them. Words of comfort and hope are not helpful in such a time of grief. Like the abandonment these mothers must have felt, Jesus experienced abandonment on the cross: "Why have you

---

[46] Two helpful resources for those experiencing grief are Larry Yeagley, *Grief Recovery* (may be available on Amazon.com) and John W. James and Frank Cherry, *The Grief Recovery Handbook* (New York: Harper & Row, 1988).

abandoned me?" (Mark 15:34). We can panic when we hear loved ones express anger or unbelief in God during those times, but a person with true faith will not give up on God. Jesus felt forsaken, but He committed His Spirit into the hands of God. You may feel forsaken by God. Jesus went to visit the home of his friends whose brother had died and did the appropriate thing—He wept (John 11:35–36). It can be a help to know that if you are experiencing deep pain from your loss, Jesus knows your pain and weeps with you. The Bible tells us to weep with those who weep (Romans 12:15).

Job is an excellent example of what helps a person immediately after a deep heart-wrenching loss, and it is not words of comfort or hope. Job lost all his children in a storm, and then he lost his health. Three friends came to visit and for seven days sat in silence with him and wept with him; they saw his pain was too great for words (Job 2:12–13). They were doing well until they began to speak in a well-meant effort to "fix" Job. Job's comment was, "What miserable comforters you are!" (Job 16:2). Words of comfort and hope can be welcomed later, but the best thing to do at first is, simply be with people and express your sorrow and sympathy. Even though Job worshipped God and believed in His goodness, he still felt abandoned by God and wished he had never been born. At first, for many grief sufferers, it is difficult to be comforted and find hope.

Consider others in the Bible who suffered grief. Jeremiah expresses grief over the loss of his beloved city, people, and friends (Jeremiah 8:18–9:1). David agonized over his baby boy who died (2 Samuel 12:16–17). It helped him immensely to know that one day he would again see his child (2 Samuel 12:18–23). Joseph grieved the loss of life with his family when he pleaded with his brothers not to separate him from them by their wicked deed (Genesis 37:26–28, 42:21). God grieved the loss of the people He loved even though they were wicked and refused to acknowledge Him (Jeremiah 14:14–17). Perhaps you can identify with the many emotions Job expressed (Job 3:24–26, 7:1–16).

Even though we may not at first be able to receive words of comfort, there does come a time in our grieving when we can accept the words of others. God is the source of all comfort (2 Corinthians 1:3–4). Many scriptural passages, the words of God, can comfort us in our grief, including Isaiah 41:10, 13; Psalm 23, 34:18, 62:1–2; 2 Corinthians 4:8–9; Matthew 11:28–29; Lamentations 3:22–26; Proverbs 3:5–6;

Philippians 4:6–7; and 1 Peter 5:7. In Luke 24:13–35, Jesus asked two grieving men why they were sad and confused; He cared, and He listened to them. He took them to the Scriptures to show them how to think about their situation. He encouraged them to believe what God said and to rejoice in God's answers to their problem. His words touched their hearts and brought them comfort and hope, and His Word can revive us as well (Psalm 119:25, 28, 50, 105). Jesus stayed with them until they received the hope that God was present with them. Through His words and presence, he brought them back to life by giving them an excitement about future possibilities. Sticking with people throughout their grief can greatly help their recovery. What Jesus gave these men brings us to another blessed thing that the Bible offers us in our grief—hope.

Psalm 119:81–82 reads, "I am worn out waiting for your rescue, but I have put my hope in your word. My eyes are straining to see your promises come true. When will you comfort me?" Paul answered this question and brought comfort and hope to those who were grieving the deaths of their loved ones. Paul told the church at Thessalonica to encourage one another with words of hope (1 Thessalonians 4:18). Paul said he wanted these people to know something. It is good to be educated about grief so we can know how to help ourselves heal, though as long as death reigns, healing of grief will never be complete (1 Corinthians 15:26).

A friend told me he was struggling with a loss and was reading a book that was helping him. One of the assignments in the book was to write down his feelings about certain things and share them with another. I counted it a privilege that he trusted me to listen to him share very personal, in-depth feelings. He was acquiring knowledge of things he could do to help himself. The first thing Paul wrote in this portion of his letter is that it helps those suffering grief, to know things (1 Thessalonians 4:13). In their case, Paul wanted them to know what would happen to their deceased loved ones who were fellow believers in Christ Jesus. He did not want them to grieve like people who had no hope. He wanted them to know Jesus would return, that our loved ones who have died would be with Him and that we would be raised to new life and be reunited with those who died before us. We will live together and be with the Lord forever (1 Thessalonians 4:14–18).

Jesus gave us this same hope: "I am going to prepare a place for you. When everything is ready, I will come and get you, so that you will always be with me where I am" (John 14:1–3). As followers of Jesus, this is our blessed hope, and as we solidify our faith, we can anticipate a fantastic journey from this life to the next.

Other Bible words that promise hope and comfort include John 11:23–26; Romans 8:18-25; 1 Corinthians 15:50–57; 2 Corinthians 4:14; Philippians 3:20–21; and Revelation 21:3–7. Words of comfort and hope are wonderful companions to help us. Even with an aching heart, we can have joy (2 Corinthians 6:10). Remember that one of the reasons Jesus came was to comfort the brokenhearted and provide a restored and glorious future to all who know Him (Isaiah 61:1–3; Psalm 73:23–26).

Grief is difficult and painful. Most of us have probably suffered painful losses; if not, we will. Someone sent me an email in which he shared how his nineteen-year-old son had committed suicide and that the ache was still with him twelve years later. His sorrow increased two years after his son committed suicide when his twenty-four-year-old daughter died from a rare heart disease. Grief over one loss is devastating enough, but multiple losses compound grief and healing. Returning to a healthy way of living can take much longer.

I have often heard people say, "You must work through your grief." What does it mean to work through grief? I would give participants in grief classes a sheet of paper with a timeline. On the left edge was a sad-faced stick figure with the letter A, and on the right edge was a running, smiling stick figure with the letter B (stick figures are the best I can draw). A is the point at which the pain-filled and life-altering loss occurred, while B is the point at which a healthy life returns, that is, people are functioning more like normal and can talk about their loss and not feel the same pain they felt at first. They have refocused their energies from being absorbed in their loss to being able to give to others and other life pursuits. They have worked through most roadblocks between A and B. I would talk about the signs of grief and have them write on the timeline between points A and B the symptoms of their grief. These symptoms were the roadblocks they needed to overcome to become healthy again.

When we are grieving, we are filled with a confusing mixture of physical, mental, and emotional symptoms we need to work through to get back to a healthy life. Members of the class might write on their timeline that they can't eat or sleep, they sigh all the time, feel guilty, fearful, depressed, lonely, regretful, have nightmares, can't get motivated, don't want to meet people, are angry, resentful, preoccupied with thoughts of the loved one, can't say goodbye, have faltering family communications at home, and so forth. These symptoms of grief vary among individuals, but they are all normal experiences we need to work through for healing to occur. By learning to identify their many feelings and by learning how to work through their many grieving patterns, they can help themselves gradually return to a reasonably normal and healthy lifestyle.

Some like to know how long grieving lasts, but that depends on the many factors mentioned in this chapter. Six months to a year is a reasonable time for some kinds of death such as an expected death of a parent or grandparent or spouse. Two to five years is normal for other situations, such as a sudden death, murder, suicide, the death of a child, or compounded deaths. A timeline like the one used in classes is a practical way to help people visualize what they need to work on to get better.

Elisabeth Kubler-Ross (1926–2004) was a pioneer in the field of death and dying. She is known for her theory of the five stages of grief, which appeared in her book on death and dying.[47] In 1999, *Time* named Kubler-Ross as one of the "100 Most Important Thinkers" of the past century. She believed that life didn't end at death; that's when it started. She once said,

> Death is simply a shedding of the physical body like the butterfly shedding its cocoon. It is a transition to a higher state of consciousness where you continue to perceive, to understand, to laugh and to be able to grow.[48]

Her comments certainly agree with the truth of the Bible that this world is not our ultimate home. As we focus on the fact that Jesus saves us from the death and sadness that makes up so much of this world

---

[47] Elisabeth Kubler-Ross, *On Death and Dying* (New York: Scribner, 1969).
[48] Chaplain Paul G. Durbin, *Death, Dying and Grief: Tribute to Elisabeth Kubler-Ross (2004)*, Kubler-Ross quote taken from 4th article on Durbin website *(www.durbinhypnosis.com/deathdying.htm)*.

and promises us a home in the age to come, we can live each day with better objectives. Our experiences of grief serve as a constant reminder to give the best part of our daily living to the things that matter most.

## Chapter 24

## SORTING OUT THE GODS

A young college woman asked me, "There are so many religions in the world that I get confused. In finding a religion that is right for me, how do I know which one to choose?" Here was a person who had some knowledge of various religions, who was searching for truth or at least for the best way to live, and who wanted assistance in sorting out the gods.

In our pluralistic world, it is increasingly likely we may have Muslim, Buddhist, Hindu, Jewish, or Wiccan neighbors. Out of concern for tolerance and peace among religious groups, many culturally sensitive and pluralistic-minded persons would answer this young woman by saying that in spite of some differences, all religions worship the same god called by different names, that all religions share pretty much the same ethical or moral teachings, and that all religious paths lead to a similar desired destination. It does not much matter which religion you choose to live by, as long as you are sincere and it helps you. But the young woman's question deserves a better answer than "All religions are the same," if, in fact, they are not.

The word *god* means "to call" or "to invoke"; the idea is that God is a power-on whom we can call for help or blessing. The word is thought by many linguistic scholars to have its origin in German. When the German word was translated into English as "god," a capitalized *God* was used to show a distinction between a one and only monotheisti God and polytheistic gods. This English word *god* has become a standard term even though the names of each culture's God or gods may differ. How many gods are there? No one can say for sure, but according to the editors of the *World Christian Encyclopedia, A Comparative Survey of Churches and Religions*, there are 270 large faith groups and many smaller ones in nineteen major world religions. Other estimates say there are thousands, even millions of gods said to have existed. Literature throughout the centuries bears witness to the fact that each nation or tribe had a God or gods that differ from person to person, tribe to tribe, and nation to nation. Each people group had its own god, or gods, on whom they relied for power, protection, comfort, and various needs. Today's world has the same variety of gods. People relate to all sorts of gods in ways meaningful to them.

The facts are that religions and their gods vastly differ from each other and it does make a difference which one you follow because that will affect differently the way you live your daily life (Deuteronomy 12:31). For example, the god some follow leads them to a terrorist lifestyle, while the god others follow does not permit this. Or the god some follow leads to a life of love and security, while another god may lead to a life of fear, uncertainty, and constant concern about living right lest something bad happen. The god you follow may lead you to a destiny of losing your identity by becoming one with the cosmos or lead you to be a unique individual living on a new earth. An overwhelming number of options face those searching for what god is best to believe in. Even though some believe all religions are the same, studying and comparing them makes it clear that they are quite different and often contradictory in the way they view the world. If you accept the law of noncontradiction, understanding these differences helps a person realize that they cannot all be right and that some make more sense than others. How would you answer this college woman? I never saw her again, but I hope she did a comparative search and discovered what makes the Bible's God stand out from all other gods. My response was short and simple: "All religions are similar in that they have a God or gods to worship and they may promote similar moral teachings. But there is one God whose religion is substantially and uniquely different from all the others. If I were searching for a God or religion to follow, I would begin with religions whose founder did something none other did, rose bodily from the dead" (John 20:24–29; 1 Corinthians 15:12).

Consider what it means that the founder of Christianity arose bodily from the dead. Imagine that a friend of yours makes truth claims no one else has ever made, shares great moral teachings, performs miracles, demonstrates a life of perfect balance between love and justice, and dies. You go to the cemetery and witness his burial. A few days later, someone says your friend is alive again. You are skeptical, but he bodily appears to you, tells you what he wants you to do, then leaves the earth, promising to return someday. What kinds of thoughts would you wrestle with concerning that friend? You would certainly consider him unique and might puzzle over the meaning of it all, but others who you told about it would say, "You're crazy! You must be imagining it. That can't happen."

In our so-called modern world, some would have us believe that all religions are the same. In the name of tolerance, we are admonished to acknowledge all religions as equally valid. But are they the same? Do they have equal credibility especially since there are among them many irreconcilable differences and conflicting views of God? Judaism, Christianity, and Islam say there is only one eternal creator God, but their views of God differ. Hindus, *Shintos, and ancient cultures such as the Egyptians, Greeks, and Romans promoted the belief that there are many gods, some of whom possess characteristics of good and evil the same as humans, and some gods were human before becoming gods. Pantheists believe everything that exists is a part of God. New Age groups say we are divine and need to get in touch with the god within us. Some people's gods are the spirits of ancestors, the spirits of objects of nature, or demons. Buddhism has been called atheistic because to some it has no god as part of its religion but relies mainly on the teachings of Buddha for ultimate well-being. Has our society been so successful in generalizing the sameness of religions that it allows no distinctions in sorting out the gods? Are not some gods more worthy of worship than others?

A common criticism of religions, though not true of all, is that each claims its way is right and the others' ways are wrong. Is it legitimate to say no religion should claim to be the right one? But maybe there is nothing wrong with making such a claim. After all, nonreligious people also believe they are right and others wrong on some matters. Some insist that global warming is true and that those who do not accept that as fact are wrong, or that evolution is true and those who do not accept that as fact are wrong. What is wrong is the lack of respect and the nonacceptance of people who differ. Such intolerance often leads to conflicts and injustices. Christians violate their own teachings when they fail to heed the ethics of love taught by Jesus (Luke 6:27–28). The question is not whether religions ought to claim they are right and others wrong but if their claims are true. If something is true, which makes something else not true, why is that wrong to say? It is okay to be open to other points of view and judge whether they have valid or invalid points.

A person who wants to sort out the gods of various religions should focus on what each says about four basic issues. First, what does each religion declare about the nature and abilities of their God, gods, or goddesses? What is their god-like, what can their god do, and what has he or she done? Second, what does their god say about the nature of human beings? What is the human problem, condition, or situation? Third, what solution do the gods offer for overcoming humanity's problem or dilemma? Fourth, what is the future hope offered by God or gods? How are evil and suffering dealt with? What is their answer to death? What is the ultimate destination of their followers?

Once you have searched out these matters, you can make an intelligent, informed decision on what God or gods you believe are worthy of your commitment and worship. You will be better able to answer why you have decided to trust your life to that God, or those gods or goddesses, and their teachings or why you choose to believe in no God. In Joshua 24:15, why do you think Joshua chose his God over others?

What makes the God of the Judeo-Christian Bible supremely different from all others? Psalm 86:8 gives the answer: "No pagan god is like you, O Lord. None can do what you do" (Deuteronomy 3:24). The supernatural acts done by this God in human history are insurmountable. For example, the God of the Bible demonstrated He was the God above all gods when He sent Moses to Egypt as His spokesman to help free an enslaved people. When Aaron threw his staff down, it turned into a serpent. Egypt's religious leaders did the same when they threw down their staffs, but Aaron's serpent ate their serpents (Exodus 7:8–12). Elijah was a prophet of God who challenged people one day to a test to see whose god was real. He had altars built with a sacrifice put on each to see which god would send fire to consume the sacrifice. Four hundred and fifty prophets earnestly called on their gods, but nothing happened. Elijah called on his God, and fire immediately came from heaven and consumed the sacrifice (1 Kings 18:20–24, 36–39).

Another act of God occurred in the sight of the Babylonian king Nebuchadnezzar. Three men were thrown into a fire but were not burned (Daniel 3:14–29). Later, Nebuchadnezzar had other experiences with God that convinced him He was the God to worship (Daniel 4:34–37). In the days of Darius the Mede, Daniel was thrown into a lion's den but was not hurt. The king eventually realized there was no god like Daniel's God and said so to his people (Daniel 6:25–27).

The Hebrew and Christian Scriptures are full of miraculous works of God, demonstrating that He alone was God. No other religion shows such works by their gods, and no other spokespersons from other religions have done miracles like these in their gods' names. "Only myths," say some, but if these are historical events, such supernatural works are distinctive to the God of the Bible and set Him apart from all other gods. And if such a God exists as is presented in the Bible, why would such acts in history be far-fetched? If the Bible is reliable historically as evidenced by archaeological finds, why not believe the accounts of God's actions?

Jesus once said to the people in His day that they needed to believe in Him if not because of His words, because of the supernatural works He performed such as instantly healing the sick, blind, or lame and raising the dead to life (John 10:25, 37–38; Matthew 11:2–6; John 11:38–48). Those who had differing religious beliefs refused to honestly consider His claims, but since they could not deny His supernatural works, they said His works were not of God but of an evil devil.

Some say the early church made up the stories. We, humans, are good at turning a blind eye to what we do not want to see or admit. The Christian Bible offers explanations for our blindness that undoubtedly would be unacceptable to most. One is that we do not want to believe because we do not want to expose our lives to the truth (John 3:19–20). Another is that there is a god of this world who has blinded our eyes (2 Corinthians 4:3–4). Of course, in our modern world, all must have a natural rather than a supernatural explanation. But I ask why could not these events have actually happened? And if Jesus did in fact go about doing miraculous good deeds, and die, and come back to life again, why would we not believe it and worship such a one who exhibits powers none other has ever duplicated? Why does it seem incredible to us that there is a powerful God who raises the dead (Acts 26:8)? Are the biblical reports mythical events that did not happen, but only stories to create faith and to teach moral truths we are to practice (2 Timothy 4:3–4) or is there a difference between the mythical language and kinds of stories told in other religions and the language and kinds of events reported in the Bible? Some who study mythology say there is a clear difference; this might be a subject for interested persons and true seekers to check out. People deny miracles occurred because scientific or humanistic-minded people say they could not have happened. Why assume that? Why live in a closed universe? Why cannot the universe be open to other possibilities such as the existence of a miracle-working God?

Why and how did people come to believe in God or gods? Christians believe that God created all things and spoke to His human creatures, thus making Himself known to them (Genesis 1:27–30). But after they acquired a knowledge of evil, (Genesis 3:22), people separated themselves from God, and that opened the door for all manner of beliefs about Him. God continued to make Himself known to a few people whose responsibility it was to make Him known to others. But as most continued to reject the God who created them (Romans 1:25), they formed gods of their own to serve as sources of help for their fears, problems, and needs. God warned them through His spokespersons that this was wrong because what they worshipped were not real gods that could lead them to their desired ends (Exodus 20:3; Isaiah 45:5–6). The apostle Paul gave the same warning to god-worshippers of his day, although he respected the fact that their religious needs and longings were valid (Acts 17:22–31).

Evolutionists and many anthropologists have developed the theory that early man evolved into self-conscious beings, developed a sense of moral responsibility and in the face of many uncontrollable happenings realized their limitations and mortality and invented their gods and religions to help with their anxieties, fears, and needs. In *The Future of an Illusion*,[49] Sigmund Freud, father of modern psychoanalysis, promoted this view when he wrote that people invented gods in their minds. People want there to be gods because they feel the need for protection against things they fear or a future justice that they perceive to be lacking in this world. Like Freud, many believe that knowledge of a reality outside themselves comes only through science and that even though it would be nice to believe in a benevolent Creator who promises an afterlife, such belief is only wishful thinking. Actually, there is truth to the evolutionist, anthropologist, and Freudian theories; according to the

---

[49] Sigmund Freud, *The Future of an Illusion* (London: Hogarth Press, 1928).

Bible, people did worship gods who were figments of their imagination, who were actually no gods at all (1 Chronicles 16:26; Jeremiah 5:7, 16:20–21; 1 Corinthians 8:4–6; Galatians 4:8). Such false ideas of god are to be put away (Joshua 24:23; Matthew 4:9–10).

Why give up belief in other gods to worship and serve the Judeo-Christian God? To do so only makes sense if you are convinced that this God can do and offer what no other god can. The Bible contains many accounts of those who left their gods because they saw the supernatural works of the God of Christ Jesus. Examples include the Israelites who witnessed God's powers in Egypt (Exodus 14:31) and those who witnessed the resurrected body of Jesus (Acts 2:22–24, 32). Saul, a staunch Jew, left his former religion because of a supernatural experience with Jesus (Acts 9:3–18; 26:12–18). Many other people also left their gods because they believed what they heard about the supernatural works of God. Examples include Rahab, who joined the Israelites because she heard about what God had done in Egypt (Joshua 2:8–13), and certain Athenians because they heard Paul's report of the resurrection of Jesus and the call for faith in this God (Acts 17:29–34). The disciple Thomas said he would not believe unless he saw the risen Christ. Jesus showed himself alive to Thomas, who was convinced by this supernatural act. Jesus responded that those who had not seen and yet believe are blessed (John 20:24–31).

We sort out the gods to arrive at whether there is a God above all gods who is worthy of our worship. If all religions are not the same, are there good reasons to consider the God of Jesus Christ? It is true that all religions offer to make you a better person. All religions produce good people who live by their religion's moral guidelines. All religions seem to answer the big questions of life and claim to have a way to help their adherents solve daily problems. All religions have admirable people who are sincere and willing to live and die for their God. All religions offer promises of some form of eternal existence to all who do what they say. What is different about the God of Jesus is not that He makes you nicer, solves your problems, gives you the courage to face martyrdom, or gives you eternal life, for all religions can claim the same. A valid reason to consider the God of Jesus and the Bible is because He performed powerful supernatural acts in history, and you see He can do things that other gods cannot. He is a God who can actually fulfill all the promises that other religions make. You worship Him when you are convinced that He is the real God above all other gods. The Bible is a record of the acts of God in history (Psalm 86:8). People who do not see God's acts but hear about them believe that this God is real, and if they believe He is real, they know He can and will fulfill His promises (Hebrews 11:6).

But other than seeing or hearing about His supernatural acts, there is a greater reason to believe God is the one and only Savior God, His love. God demonstrated His love for us by becoming a human being (John 1:1–3, 14; Philippians 2:6–8), who without sin (2 Corinthians 5:21), paid for our sins by voluntarily dying on a Roman cross (Romans 5:8). He satisfied the need for justice so God could forgive and save all who came to Him (1 John 2:2, 4:10). God's love is unparalleled. What other god humbles himself to become a man and gives up his life to save us from a world of evil, from our guilt, from judgment, and from death (Philippians 2:5–8)? The God of the Bible cares about the well-being of all people everywhere. We are suffering, hungering for love and relief, and dying. Like the suffering people ministered to by Mother Teresa, God comes for us (Luke 19:10). Humans crave and need supreme love. Paul Copan put it this way: "This act of divine service to humans is utterly unique in human history." Copan quoted the late German scholar Martin Hengal, who wrote, "The pre-existent divine figure who becomes man and humbles himself to a slave's death is, as far as I can see, without analogy in the ancient world." [50] Who would not want to follow the God who became one of us and gave His life to save us? This God is love (1 John 4:9–10). This God puts divine love in believers' hearts by giving them His Holy Spirit (Romans 5:5). We experience His love because He first loved us (1 John 4:19).

For anyone confused by many options and who is seeking a God to follow, why not consider Jesus? He is remarkably different from all other religious figures. He said, "I am the way, the truth, and the life" (John 14:6). Was He wrong to say this, or does He have credentials that put His claims well above those of the acclaimed prophets of other religions (Deuteronomy 18:18–22)? Which of the many religions' prophets said they came down from God and accepted the designation of being God's Son (John 8:42; John 1:14; Matthew 16:13-17), or did the kinds of miracles He did (Mark 1:40–42; John 11:38–44), or said they could

---

[50] Paul Copan, *Is God a Moral Monster?* 33.

forgive sin (Mark 2:5–7) or claimed all must believe in Him for His gift of life eternal (John 10:28-30; 11:25–26)? What other religious leader has eyewitnesses who saw Him alive after He had died (Luke 24:36–43; Acts 2:32)? I respect people who have religious longings; I wish they would consider Jesus enough to seek the answer to Jesus' question, "Who do you say that I am?" (Matthew 16:13–15). Why do you think His disciples answered as they did?

If Jesus truly was God (John 1:1) and came from God (Philippians 2:6-8), would He not be the most valuable source of information for sorting out the gods? The Judeo-Christian God and Father of Jesus is not like other religions' gods with only words, scriptures, teachings, and promises. He is a God who acts in history, including demonstrating an amazing love in the person of God the Son (Deuteronomy 18:15–22; 1 John 1:1–3, 4:9–10). Many people say they don't see God, but do they really look (Jeremiah 29:13)?

## Chapter 25

## THE PROBLEM WITH BEING A GOOD PERSON

If you are a good person, good for you; doing good is how God defeats the evils of the world. The Bible says, "Don't let evil conquer you, but conquer evil by doing good" (Romans 12:21). But to do that better and more efficiently, we need to get to another level of goodness. Unfortunately, and as strange as it may seem, our goodness might be what keeps us from getting there. Jesus loves good people and tries to help them reach the next level. One day, a good man who kept God's Commandments approached Jesus with a question. "Looking at the man, Jesus felt genuine love for him" (Mark 10:21). But the man walked away from Jesus, unwilling to take that step to reach the next level of goodness. By the end of this chapter, I trust you will understand something about the next level of goodness.

How would we describe a good person? I suppose that by reading the title of this chapter, some might think, "Okay, the problem with good people is that they are always helping others and don't have time for lives of their own." Some definitely are very kindhearted and have a problem saying no, so people do take advantage of them. But I will be discussing a different kind of problem with being a good person. A popular belief is that all people are basically good, and there are valid reasons for this belief. People have goodness within them and show it in many ways. Good people help their neighbors and friends when needs arise. When my neighbor had surgery, I mowed his lawn until he recovered. He did the same for me. Good people are honest, law-abiding citizens who give to charities, care for their families, love their kids, say please and thank you, show tender hearts and express sympathy when others suffer, volunteer for community organizations, work hard at their jobs to serve the needs of others, perform random acts of kindness, attend religious groups, and so on. A group in our area banded together to send reading material and other goods to our military troops overseas. Good people perform acts of heroism during emergencies or crises. Good people are sometimes activists for good causes that promote the betterment of humankind. People who do these good things include Christians and non-Christians, religious and non-religious alike. Even bad people are good to their own kind. Good people like the feeling they get when they do things for others, and this adds to their view of themselves as good people.

We do have a good side to us. Where does our goodness come from? The Bible declares that God is good and that God created us in His image (Psalm 34:8, 100:5, 119:68; Genesis 1:27; 5:1–2). Jesus declared that God is good (Mark 10:18). Some naturalists, materialists, or Darwinian evolutionists might say that through natural evolutionary processes and environmental factors and through our life experiences, we have learned how to choose and determine our own purposes, meaning, and morality. I would say that while there is some truth to experience and environmental causes, our basic propensity for goodness comes from the fact that we are the creation of a good God who made us to be like Himself. This would certainly explain why we possess inherent goodness.

Those who believe all humans are basically good must find a reason to explain why, if we are basically good, there is evil, badness, or wickedness in and around us. Their explanation of why people are bad may go something like this: "The only reason people are evil and bad is because they were raised in poor environments, or lacked education, or had bad experiences that turned them in negative directions. We are all coming out of an evolutionary process that has yet to eliminate evil from our human experience. If we improve people's environments, help educate them, get them counseling, and provide opportunities for better lives or learn to control their DNA makeup, we could eliminate a lot of evils and build a better society."

There are also those who are not bad people but they do not see themselves as good. They may not act like themselves because of alcoholism, other life-dominating habits, poor self-image, failures, shame for their actions, or abuses done to them. Though they may be victims of evil, the same assessment and rehabilitative help, apply to them as to wicked people. There is a lot of truth in the need for changing environments and for better education and counseling and other kinds of assistance; it is good to help people overcome their situations and their character defects so they can be better. In fact, the Bible agrees when it says, "So let's not get tired of doing what is good... We should do good to everyone" (Galatians 6:9–10). God wants us to be good people and doers of good, but unhappily, evil often hinders our good intentions.

Though some believe that evil in people is due to conditions outside themselves and if we can eliminate those conditions, our basic goodness will rise to the top, I think of the saying, "You can dress a man in a new suit, but it won't change the man." Those who believe in Christ rather than in naturalism or Darwinian evolution believe evil entered the world and human hearts because of our choice to allow it (Genesis 3; Romans 5:12). By choosing to let evil in, we corrupted our former perfect selves and the world (Romans 8:19–23). But no one has to believe in this explanation of the origin and existence of evil for us to see we and our world are full of evil tendencies and actions. Experience shows us that human nature is a mixture of good and evil; we easily excuse ourselves with reasons why it's okay to break laws. I find that when I break the law, I look to make sure no one sees me so I can get away with it, but I am not being a law-abiding citizen. It is because of the evils within us that our relationship with the God of perfect goodness has been affected. We have lost our relationship with God (Psalm 14:1–3). When I break the speeding law, I lose my relationship with the police, who no longer see me as law-abiding. To a degree, I lose my relationship with my wife when she has to say, "How fast are you going? You should be going the speed limit." We may be good in our own eyes or the eyes of our peers, but we have lost our ability to be good in the eyes of God (Mark 10:18; Romans 3:9–12). "For everyone has sinned; we all fall short of God's glorious standard" (Romans 3:23). Because of "missing the mark" with God, we are not at peace with Him. We become separated from a holy God and become subject to His loving judgment; there is a penalty to pay for not being in good standing with God (Genesis 2:15–17; Romans 6:23; John 8:21–24, 12:47–48).

Of course, we who see ourselves as good people do not feel this way about our relationship with God; most feel all is okay. It's like the man whose marriage is falling apart because his wife is unhappy with him, but he doesn't know it until she leaves. To him, everything was great;

she may have tried to reveal the problem to him all along, but he would not listen or believe it.

What specifically is the problem with being a good person? First, good people often fail to honestly deal with their evil nature, their "dark side." They easily ignore or excuse it and do not let it get to them. They prefer not to look at it and admit the truth about themselves. Most people see me, a minister of God, as a good person, but I see and know my sinful nature. I see how self-centered I am and how falsehoods and lying to others and myself have been a part of my life. Years ago, it was very painful for me to admit that the only reason I did good for people was so that I would look good. I have had to admit I really don't love people as God defines love. It's not that I never do anything well, but I have come to see myself as the apostle Paul saw himself: "I know that nothing good lives in me, that is, in my sinful nature… I want to do what is right, but I can't. I want to do what is good, but I don't. I don't want to do what is wrong, but I do it anyway" (Romans 7:15–21). This is a remarkable statement by Paul, for he at one time saw himself as a very righteous person who took great care to practice the teachings of God.

Jesus confirmed that many evils come out of our hearts (Mark 7:21–23). He gave the basic reason why people would not be honest and allow their evil selves to come into the light. He said that people love the darkness rather than the light because they do not want their evils to be seen (John 3:19–20). The problem with being a good person is the tendency to overlook one's evil nature and not deal with it, and this hinders us from reaching what I call the next level of goodness.

Another problem with being good is, those good people put too high a value on their goodness. We are deceived in thinking we are better than we are (Jeremiah 17:9). An honest person would agree with the apostle Paul that we cannot measure up to God's character of goodness. An example of valuing our goodness too highly is seen in a story Jesus told about two men praying in a temple. Jesus told us that a very religious man looked down on another when he compared his life to the other's life. He saw that his own lifestyle was good compared to the man next to him, and so he believed he was better than the other man (Luke 18:9–14). When good people compare themselves to others who appear less good, it confirms and elevates their own goodness. At times, I have asked people who say they believe in God a question popularized by James Kennedy:[51] "If you were to die today and go to the gates of heaven and someone asked you, 'Why should I let you into heaven?', what would you say?" The answer that I get most frequently is, "I am not perfect, nobody is, but I am basically a good person and did not hurt other people. I did not do things bad people do." On that basis, they believe God will accept them into heaven.

It's so easy to see ourselves as good when we compare ourselves to others. I used to play racquetball as a daily exercise and would win a lot, so I had the idea I was a good player. One day, I played a professional baseball player and thought, "What does a baseball player know about racquetball?" I never scored a point against his superior athleticism. More humiliating than that was that my wife played him and scored four points. I clearly had too high a value of how good I was. The Bible plainly says, "Don't think you are better than you really are. Be honest in the evaluation of yourselves" (Romans 12:3). When we value our goodness too highly, we deceive ourselves about our true condition. The problem with being a good person is that such a high view of one's own goodness leads us to think that we don't need God in our life or that God accepts us because of our goodness.

Good people assume that God grades on a curve. I liked it in school when the teacher graded on a curve, which meant I did not have to meet a certain standard to get a good grade. Jesus said, "Only God is truly good" (Mark 10:18). Jesus set the standard for us when He said, "You are to be perfect, even as your Father in heaven is perfect" (Matthew 5:48). The Lord said, "You must be holy because I, the Lord your God, am holy" (Leviticus 19:2; 1 Peter 1:14–16). Impossible, you say. Exactly. That's why it's a problem being good. A good person who believes God grades on a curve does not repent and turn to God's solution for becoming acceptable to Him.

Is God an ogre for requiring people to be perfect when He knows they cannot be? No, it is God's nature not to have any evil in His own being or His kingdom of righteousness. But God is good in that He provides a way for us to be accepted and enter once again into His holiness and righteousness. The apostle Paul was a good person. Pharisees were good at obeying God's laws, better by far than most. But Paul came to see he was not good enough for acceptance by a holy God

---

[51] D. James Kennedy, *Evangelism Explosion* (Carol Stream: Tyndale, 19

(Philippians 3:4–11). By God's merciful and gracious help, Paul came to see he needed more than his own goodness to be acceptable to God and enter His kingdom.

Although I may see myself as a good person, I find no exception to the charge that I am a sinner in need of saving. The good news is that we can be restored to goodness in God's eyes and to the practice of goodness that is no longer corrupted by impurities in our nature (1 John 3:4–9; Ephesians 2:1–10). That is the next level of goodness. The statement "God accepts you just as you are" is true and not true, but I do not want to get into explaining it as I have done that elsewhere, only to say that God accepts us as we are not because we are acceptable but because of something Jesus did.

Another problem with being a good person is that good people reject Jesus. What I mean is that they do not want Christ Jesus on His terms. "I don't reject Jesus" you might protest, and good people think they do not reject Jesus, but when confronted with their need to surrender their lives to Him or when told they are to love Him by doing His will, they reject Him. Most good people have little idea of what Christ Jesus requires of them and would have no intention of doing it even if they knew. They do good things if those things conveniently pertain to their own comfort zones and choices of what they want to do, but they have little to do with the good deeds and works Jesus wants them to do. Jesus said to a group, "In fact, you are trying to kill me." The crowd responded, "Who's trying to kill you?" They acted innocent as if he were crazy to think such a thing (John 7:19–20). But some were planning on how to get rid of Him, and later, many became responsible for His death. Jesus said, "Some of you are trying to kill me because there is no room in your heart for my message" (John 8:37). We do not want Jesus to tell us the truth about ourselves or what we need to do to live lives pleasing to Him. One day, a wealthy man approached Jesus to ask how he could have eternal life. Jesus loved him and said, "You know the commandments." The man claimed he kept all the Commandments. The man wanted to know what else he needed to do. Jesus said, "Go and sell all of your possessions and give the money to the poor, and you will have treasure in heaven. Then come, follow me." The man rejected Jesus because he did not want to accept Jesus' word to him. He went away, unwilling to do as Jesus said (Mark 10:17–22).

Jesus could give every one of us an assignment that would determine whether we would accept Him. Bono, famous for his singing with the rock band U2, is reported to have said, "It's very annoying, following this person of Christ around." Apparently, he was implying how it was seemingly hopeless trying to keep up with Jesus' demands on one's life.[52] I am not saying Bono rejects Jesus, only that he admits it is difficult to do what Jesus says. Some consider themselves to be good but think Jesus requires too much and are unwilling to follow Him (John 6:66–69). Most people do not want to surrender their lives to Jesus Christ. When most are asked if they want to receive Jesus, they will say, "I'm not ready for that yet" or "I'm not interested" or "I don't see why I need to." Many will have some excuse as to why they cannot follow Him. Good people, when asked to do what Jesus wants them to do, reject Jesus and His terms and continue to go their own ways. The problem with good people is that their will and what they want are more important than God's will and what He wants.

Other problems with being a good person come to mind. I will give a couple of examples and then move on. One problem is that many think the purpose of goodness is to make the world a better place. It's certainly far better to do good than evil, and it does make the world better. But does doing good and making the world a better place lead to anything of lasting value? Is not our earthly goodness futile if it does not lead to anything of eternal value or significance? Your goodness may lead to a satisfying life for yourself and the people around you, but there is no guarantee you will have left the world a better place, which is one of the arguments for being good. Evil will likely continue, and there is no guarantee that what good you have done will carry on. Your good can very well be undone after you are gone. There must be a greater reason for doing good.

One other problem is that many good people, especially those who believe in God, assume they will get to heaven. With this assumption, they focus almost exclusively on this world and what it offers, thinking, *My eternal issue is settled because I'm a good person.* Thus they find it easy to focus on fun and good times, seeking to enjoy a self-chosen materialistic lifestyle without worrying about what happens to them when they die. Because of thinking their eternity issues are settled,

---

[52] Bono, in an interview by Jim Daly with *Focus on the Family*, quoted in *Christianity Today* (September 2013), 13.

many good people tend to forget about God unless He is needed; they keep God on the periphery of their lives so He does not interfere with their worldly pursuits. Jesus was definitely careful to caution people about their future life. He said things like, "And what do you benefit if you gain the whole world but lose your own soul?" (Mark 8:36). The problem with being a good person is that we can easily miss God's eternal kingdom (Matthew 7:13–14).

Good people who are not Christ-followers may believe they are just as good as Christians are. If they believe in an afterlife, they believe they have just as much right to it as believers do, because they are just as good as or better than believers are. I have no quarrel about that; some unbelievers live greater moral lives than some Christians do. But being a good person with good morals is not what will earn them a place in God's future kingdom. So what if I am the best person in the world and enjoy life to its utmost? Good people can live a great life on earth, but that doesn't lead to eternal life. I die the same as everyone else, so what then? Jesus offers us the opportunity to enter His eternal realm (John 17:3, 3:16). We should not assume we will enter Christ's new heaven and earth simply because we have lived the right way to the best of our ability.

In review, here are five reasons mentioned above as to why there is a problem with being a good person. Good people often fail to honestly deal with their evil nature, their "dark side." Good people put too high a value on their goodness. Good people assume God grades on a curve. Good people reject Jesus; they do not want Him on His terms. And good people assume their eternity question is already settled and so they focus almost exclusively on living for what this world can give them. Of course, these problems do not apply to all good people, for some recognize their limited condition and can move on to another level of goodness.

Dallas Willard, a philosopher at the University of Southern California for nearly fifty years, wrote a number of books that have helped many to develop a deeper spiritual life. I came across a statement of something he said that intrigued me: "The four great questions humans must answer are: What is reality? What is the good life? Who is a good person? And, how do you become a good person?"[53] Since these questions relate directly to the subject of this chapter, I will share a few thoughts in response to them, nothing in great depth, but thoughts I believe are from God's perspective that makes sense to me at this juncture in my life.

What is reality? Reality is whatever exists, both visible and invisible (Colossians 1:15–16). The God of the Bible has no beginning and no end and is the only eternally existing entity, the ultimate reality. Whatever God creates is real; He created the material universe, so it is real (Genesis 1:1). God created humans and other life forms, so they are real. God's nature or character is real. For example, God is good, so good is real. God is love, so love is real. Whatever God thinks or reveals to other minds is real. Also, reality is what potentially could exist. God created us and the universe with the potential we need to discover and use. When that takes place, products of human industry become real.

Another potential reality is evil. When God created the world, He knew evil was a potential reality. We may not know the exact origin of evil, but evidently, it had potentiality outside of God and came into being. But God is not evil, nor is He the source of evil (James 1:13). Some quote Isaiah 45:7 to prove God created evil, but the Hebrew expression there is too general to say that God created evil; rather, it implies that God can use evil or bad things to come on people as a judgment or testing. Other passages give that sense as well, including Isaiah 31:2, 47:10-11; Amos 3:6; and Job 2:10. All potential realities are worth pursuing except for evil; God gave a clear warning against it because it will destroy one's life (Genesis 2:16–17). Evil is something we must contend with among the other realities of life.

What is the good life? In a world in which evil exists, the good life can be difficult to define because humans can easily be deceived. God's Word says we can actually get to the place where we say that evil is good and good is evil (Isaiah 5:20). The recognition or determination of what the good life is, depends on what defines it. Am I the determiner of what is good? Something in us enables us to recognize what is good, but an evil form of self-centeredness within so easily mars our character and perceptions. The good life for me can be what I want or have that will

---

[53] Dallas Willard, a tribute given to him by John Ortberg in *Christian Today* (July/August 2013), 64–68.

give me pleasure and happiness. But so often, we discover that what we think is good for us betrays us in the end and we find out we are not the best source for defining good.

Is society or culture the determiner of what is good? Just because the majority of people say something is good doesn't mean it is. Does government define and determine what is good? How can anything, government or citizens, corrupted by evil be a trustworthy source? A God of pure goodness and no evil would be the best determiner of what is good. The best source of what is good is a perfectly good God. Originally, everything God made was good (Genesis 1–2). Does that mean I can enjoy and take pleasure in the material things of this world? Absolutely! Does that mean I can feel good about the work I do and take pride in my skills and achievements? Absolutely! Does that mean I can appreciate the beauty in this world? Absolutely! Does that mean I should exhibit the moral character of God in my everyday living? Absolutely! Does that mean I can enjoy relationships with family and friends? Absolutely!

The only thing God forbids is participation in evil because it destroys what is good. Of course, variety and diversity, being a result of the genius and wisdom of God, mean that we will experience these good aspects of life in differing ways that reflect our God-given uniqueness. It seems that whenever I ask people what they want in life, the most common answer is "to be happy." For many people, gaining happiness depends on doing what they want and having what they want—but I agree with those who think that happiness ought not to be the primary goal of our lives, that happiness is a by-product of seeking what is good. Recognizing the good and doing the good God intends is what results in ultimate happiness.

Is not knowing God and continually improving on that relationship the greatest good? Parents know their kids will have a better chance to develop into good kids if they hang around with others who are good instead of those who would be a bad influence. This principle is taught in the Bible where we are reminded that friends sharpen friends (Proverbs 27:17) and bad company corrupts good character (1 Corinthians 15:33). The same is true concerning our relationship with God. We become good by hanging around someone who is good. If we hang around with God, we will learn to recognize and practice the good.

Only God's intended goodwill brings us true happiness in an evil world. Good includes whatever becomes necessary in the fight to overcome evil (Romans 12:21). The good life is to know God and experience whatever life comes from God, including whatever life He prescribes for us (Deuteronomy 6:18).

Who is a good person? As defined at the beginning of this chapter, because we are made in the image of a good God, we possess general goodness and the good things we do definitely make for a better world (Romans 5:7; Ephesians 4:28; 1 Peter 2:18; Proverbs 13:22). But God defines a good person differently than we do; He defines a good person as one on the next level of goodness. Those on this "next level" are not better than others, for all are of equal worth to God. Those on this next level do good things with a different motivation.

You will not find most good people doing the good works God asks them to do. A good person in God's eyes is one who possesses a right standing with God. People who are good in God's eyes are people who accept God's messages and live by faith in God's truths rather than suppress His truth (Romans 1:17–18). People who are good in God's eyes are connected to Him in such a way that they want to live as God wants them to live and make every effort to do so.

In the movie *Evan Almighty*, Evan was told by God, he was to build an ark to save the people of his neighborhood from a coming flood. God also used Evan to stop corruption in government. The people thought Evan was crazy and they mocked him for building his huge boat in the middle of their neighborhood. The media reported on his activities and made fun of him. A reporter asked Evan, "What makes you think God has called you to do this?" Evan quickly responded, "God has called all of us."[54] Evan was involved in what I call the next level of goodness; he was doing the work God wanted him to do. The good people around him had no clue what God was up to and they were not involved in cooperating with God.

The Bible makes it plain that Christ-followers are co-workers with God (1 Corinthians 3:5–9). "He [God] has created us anew in Christ Jesus, so we can do the good things He planned for us long ago" (Ephesians 2:10). Before Jesus ascended to His Father, He said His followers would do greater things than He had done (John 14:12). Jesus

---

[54] *Evan Almighty*, Universal Studios, 2007.

said, "Let your good deeds shine out for all to see, so that everyone will praise your heavenly Father" (Matthew 5:16).

God calls us to do the same kinds of good deeds done by many people of the world (Galatians 6:10; Titus 3:1, 8, 14; Matthew 25:34–40; Luke 10:25–37). But there are other works of God that people who get to the next level of goodness are to do; they are to work toward complete personal holiness (2 Corinthians 7:1). Other works include telling others about Jesus' good news (2 Corinthians 5:17–20; Philippians 1:3–5; Proverbs 13:17) and helping other believers grow in faith (Hebrews 10:24–25; Colossians 3:16). Those works are things that most "good" people are not motivated or willing to do. Even many of us Christians have not yet reached some of the good works involved in the next level of goodness.

How do we become good persons? We may already be good people in the sense that we do good because God created us in His image. To get to the next level of goodness means seeking God and connecting with Him. When we connect with God, true goodness comes out of our relationship with Him. Jesus said that a good tree produces good fruit and a bad tree produces bad fruit (Matthew 7:17–18). In this sense, we must be good before we can do good. We become good in the most completed sense when we repent of living without Christ and when we put our trust in the gospel of Christ (Mark 1:14–15; Acts 2:37–40). God then declares us to be right with Him (Philippians 3:7–9). We can tell if we have become righteous and good in God's eyes when we find within ourselves a desire to be doers of God's Word (James 1:21–22).

In this world, we find the essence of the good life in the exhilarating and satisfying but tiring work of giving our lives away for the good of others. A life that does that, if you are fortunate enough to witness it, is beautiful to behold. No one took Jesus' life; rather, He gave His life for everyone else. That is rare among us humans. It is what Jesus must have meant when He said, "If you give up your life for my sake, you will save it" (Matthew 16:25). He also said, "You must turn from your selfish ways, take up your cross daily, and follow me" (Luke 9:23).

So few of us consistently do that, but when it happens, it is the ultimate level of good Jesus leads us to. Who is willing and able to give and give and give until others are drawn to the ultimate reason for why they do it? When that happens, we can accomplish a greater good—others will want to live like that. The reward for those who receive that life and give their lives for is peace, joy, love, wonder, and adventure not only in this lifetime but also in the world to come. When we come out of darkness and into God's wonderful light (Colossians 1:13), we have the potential to show others the goodness of God (1 Peter 2:9). The greatest problem with being a good person is that we think it is enough, and we miss the greater good.

## Chapter 26

## HUMILITY—THE VIRTUE THAT MAKES US GREAT

Most people, if not all, have an inner desire to be recognized, to be important, to be noticed. Some want to be in power, in charge, popular, or famous so others will notice them. We tend to think of great people as those who have positions of authority or who have achieved fame or recognition due to respected achievements. Many of us want to be great at something, but if that requires humility, most would balk at that. To be great seems to require having to market yourself and push yourself into prominence. How can we be great by being humble? At first thought, it seems a humble person would be considered weak and insignificant, a person to be walked on; wouldn't humility leave us unnoticed? This very well could be true since a person with humility is unlikely to seek public recognition. How then is humility the virtue that makes us great?

Jesus is most qualified to define greatness and how to achieve it. On one occasion, His followers were discussing who would be the greatest among them, thinking that the greatest would be the one with the highest position of honor and authority. Jesus reminded them that great people are normally thought to be those who have authority over others such as a king or the boss of a business. However, Jesus taught that the greatest were those who put themselves last and were servants of all (Luke 22:24–26; Mark 9:34–35). He asked, "Who is more important, the one who sits at the table or the one who serves?" The obvious answer would be the one sitting at the table and being waited on. But, Jesus continued, "I am among you as one who serves" (Luke 22:27).

On another occasion, the mother of two of Jesus' disciples came to ask Him if her sons could sit at His right and left hand when He came into His kingdom. Jesus reiterated that the greatest shall be servants

(Matthew 20:25–28). He was teaching that greatness is in the eyes of God, not humanity, and greatness requires humility. That God esteems the humble person is clear: "And all of you, serve each other in humility, for God opposes the proud but favors the humble. So humble yourselves under the mighty power of God, and at the right time He will lift you up in honor" (1 Peter 5:5–6).

Jesus is the supreme example of a great person in God's eyes. He provides for us a good role model because He practiced the humility He taught. Without a doubt, in all the history of humankind, an unsurpassable act of humility was performed when God the Son took the role of a servant and gave up His position of power and authority as Creator and Sustainer of the universe to become a human being like us (John 1:1, 14; Colossians 1:16–17; Philippians 2:6–8). He further humbled himself by becoming obedient to death on a cross (Isaiah 53). In this act of dying on a Roman cross, He allowed Himself to suffer extreme humiliation, rejection, and derision. He was rejected, made fun of, laughed at, lied about, and accused of wrongs he never did. He experienced an unfair trial and was beaten and tortured. He allowed himself to be publicly stripped of His outer clothing and shamefully displayed in the eyes of the people as a common criminal deserving of death. But He was completely innocent, absolutely right in all He did, and totally undeserving of such treatment.

Jesus suffered this for people who needed forgiveness and reconciliation with God; He had our interests in mind and regarded us as more important than Himself. His was a most unselfish act because he gave up, for a time, all that it meant for him to be God, in order to serve our need for a savior. For this, God exalted Him at the proper time by raising Him from the dead and declaring Him to be Lord of all (Acts 5:30–31, 2:36). Jesus was made great through His humility.

From Jesus, we learn humility means serving others (Philippians 2:3–8). Jesus considered the interests of others as more important than His own and had a lifestyle of giving to meet the needs of fellow human beings by loving them even to the point of sacrificing His own comfort, safety, and well-being for their good. "Impossible for us," you say. "Our self-centeredness and personal desire for comfort is too ingrained within us." This is true if we remain in our natural state (1 Corinthians 2:14;

Romans 8:7–8). But if converted (Matthew 18:3–4; John 1:12–13), we no longer need to be controlled by our natural state (Romans 6:5–18).

Jesus did not say we should never be concerned about ourselves; He said, "Love your neighbor as yourself" (Matthew 22:39). Given the fact we need to mature to be more like Jesus in serving others, Jesus has given us His divine Spirit that enables us to be transformed into the likeness of our Maker (2 Corinthians 3:18; Romans 12:2).

Jesus gave us a further lesson in humility by showing us how He related to His Father in heaven. To accomplish what God wanted Him to accomplish, He relied totally on God the Father rather than on Himself. This is evident by His prayer life and by statements He made, such as, "I can do nothing on my own… For I have come down from heaven to do the will of God who sent me, not to do my own will" (John 5:30, 6:38, 12:50). Jesus understands the importance of relying on others for help. He understands the weaknesses we have as humans that hinder us from living a lifestyle of serving. He overcame weakness because He relied on God for strength and chose to do nothing on His own. Jesus said this could also be true of us as we abide in Him to produce such a divine lifestyle (John 15:5).

Humility recognizes personal weaknesses, believes that God can help, surrenders to His power, and exercises the kind of praying that enables His will to be done. Truly humble people rely on God because they know there is no greater source of guidance, comfort, strength, and well-being. Rejecting God and His help is the height of arrogance and makes true humility difficult (2 Chronicles 12:1–7; Daniel 5:20–23). An apostle of Jesus named Paul was not afraid to admit his own weaknesses. In fact, he said, "I am glad to boast about my weaknesses, so that the power of Christ can work through me… For when I am weak, then I am strong" (2 Corinthians 12:9–10). He meant that his awareness of his weakness was good because that made him rely on what God can do to help him.

Humility requires honesty about who we are, but being honest about ourselves is difficult since our nature is one of self-deception (Jeremiah 17:9). We easily see ourselves to be something we are not or not something we are. A friend of mine said, "Humility is not thinking too highly of ourselves, which leads to pride and boasting; nor is it thinking too low of ourselves, which leads to being falsely humble. A humble person is one who lives each day by being who he or she really is."

Knowing and being ourselves is not easy. There can be many reasons for not knowing or being who we are. A dysfunctional upbringing may have caused us to live in a way to protect ourselves from being hurt. Perhaps we developed a lifestyle of lying to avoid trouble, running away from problems, withdrawing into our own world to escape painful feelings, finding negative ways to get attention, or developing an angry and bitter personality. As a result of these and other protective life patterns, we can end up with an improper view of ourselves and a faulty view of our world. Having an inability to be honest, which Jesus clearly pointed out (Revelation 3:17–18), results in being negatively tainted, thus hindering the virtue of humility. Without honesty, evils take over (Micah 7:1–3).

It takes courage to be honest, but it is necessary for true humility to rise within us (Romans 12:3; Proverbs 19:1, 28:6). What can help us become genuinely humble people? I have witnessed people being able to come to an honest view of who they are through my connection with a treatment center for alcoholics and addicted drug users. A most helpful assignment was for them to write down the good and bad character qualities in their lives—for example, "I am a person who helps others" or "I am a person who is kind." On their bad side, they might write, "I am a liar" or "I am a person who is always critical of others." This list was to be as long as they could make it within the time frame of the program. And the list was not to be general statements. The key to self-discovery required them to write down three specific times in their lives when they helped someone, or showed kindness to someone, or lied, or had a critical thought or word. Seeing their lives lived out in these specific, concrete ways helped them see clearly, who they really were.

Most had a long list of bad traits and could not think of much in their lives that was good, so the assignment helped them get in touch with the goodness buried within. Getting honest was truly humbling, especially when they shared their self-assessments with others. But the result, when coupled with the acceptance and love of others, was very liberating; they were able to see who they were and where they needed to be heading. They became strong through their humiliating experience; they lost their false sense of grandiosity and gained humility. They lost being despised by family and friends and gained new family and friends who thought they were people of great worth. Humility demands a certain degree of honesty with one another about who we are (Roman 12:16).

We need humility to be real rather than phony or hypocritical. Humility allows us to have the courage to be vulnerable. When other people need our help to overcome personal problems, they need to know that they are not alone, that others are also very much like them and have been through similar experiences. It is difficult to help people who are going through distressing problems when we are unable or unwilling to share our own weaknesses, mistakes, sins, and feelings in a way that helps them know that others have gone through similar things. Humility is not prideful arrogance and boasting or putting up a front to portray ourselves as better than we are. Neither is humility self-put-downs. To have the attitude "I'm no good. I can't do anything. Nobody likes me. Poor me" can be a false humility and a form of pride that tries to get others to feel sorry for us so they will tell us how wonderful we are.

Of course, due to unfortunate humiliating life circumstances or shame-based relationships, it is possible that a person actually does feel they are no good. It's difficult for those without a proper sense of self-worth or self-respect to exercise true humility. People must come to know they are loved and accepted for humility to become a genuine virtue. And how can a healthy self-image grow in us? Jesus gives us a healthy self-image when we see ourselves as He sees us.

How can humility become more of a virtue in my life? The following biblical statements give us ideas on what God would have us think or do to develop genuine humility.

1. We have already discussed Paul's instruction, "Be humble, thinking of others as better than yourselves. Don't look out only for your own interests, but take an interest in others too" (Philippians 2:3–4). Such a mindset and practice will help us become more humble as we find ourselves giving more attention to others. We can learn to become more aware of others and help them when we see an opportunity. It helps us develop this mindset when we can see or hear each other's stories about various times we have helped others in little ways. I once was riding a bus in Seattle and was sitting close to the front. I witnessed a

person on crutches needing to get on the bus; someone got up and helped the person onto the bus.

2. Another mind-set to adopt is that of John the Baptist's relationship to Jesus: "He must become greater and greater, and I must become less and less" (John 3:30). How would you understand becoming less and less? Your answer is sure to contribute toward increasing humility.

3. Jesus said, "Apart from me you can do nothing" (John 15:5). He was not being egotistical; He was speaking the truth. He was not saying we were weak, incompetent, stupid, or insignificant, but that we needed to develop a mindset of relying on Him to work in and through us in everything we do. Such reliance is important if we want to affect others in a way that accomplishes the results God wants. Perhaps a daily prayer that goes something like this will bring Jesus into the mix: "Lord, show me today someone I can help and let me have the wisdom and ability to do it, amen."

4. "Be thankful in all circumstances" (1 Thessalonians 5:18). The more we develop a spirit of gratitude and express appreciation and thanks to others for who they are or what they do, the more we become genuinely humble.

5. "Let someone else praise you, not your own mouth" (Proverbs 27:2). To go about our work and do the best we can in all we do will be noticed by others without forcing self-recognition or promotion, and in time, they might elevate us. Of course, we need to figure out a humble response to people who praise us; maybe something like, "Very kind of you to say, thank you." Knowing the truth about ourselves and our true source of strength will prevent other's compliments from corrupting us. Humility cannot exist where pride rules. I am not talking about the healthy pride we feel from a good deed or job well done; I am talking about the pride of elevating ourselves above those who contribute to our personhood and accomplishments.

6. In Proverbs 31:28, we find a husband praising his wife. It is good to praise others; it builds their confidence and sense of significance. Of course, our expressions of praise must be

sincere, based on fact, and not flattery that produces false self-images in them, which can be damaging later on.

7. "God opposes the proud, but favors the humble" (1 Peter 5:5). Knowing that God hates pride can help us recognize and want to resist any feeling of pride and thus dismiss it immediately as soon as it wells up within us. When I sense a "look at me" kind of pride in myself, I think, *Nope, not going there.* I appreciate God's grace in reminding me and helping me to resist.

8. "What do you have that God hasn't given you? And if everything you have is from God, why boast as though it were not a gift?" (1 Corinthians 4:7). Becoming more humble can come from the recognition that we are interdependent creatures and nothing we have is totally from our own doing.

9. Circumstances often overcome us. "In fact, we expected to die. But as a result, we stopped relying on ourselves and learned to rely only on God" (2 Corinthians 1:8–9). When things happen beyond our control and we don't know what to do, it forces us to humble ourselves and seek help from God. Humility comes from realizing we are not in control and giving control to someone else. Praise be to God when such adverse events happen to us that produce life-lasting changes in us. Humility accepts adversity without resentment or bitterness or blaming God; it believes God is with us and is helping us grow from the experience (Job 2:9–10; Psalm 119:67, 71).

10. Humility graciously accepts correction and rebuke from others (Proverbs 17:10, 19:20, 25, 20:30). Such a person remains open to comments from others. The Bible says those who listen to rebuke and counsel become wiser, but those who reject them are foolish or stupid (Proverbs 12:1, 15, 13:1, 27:5–6). Humility comes from brokenness. We are humbled by truth if we are willing and strong enough to listen to it. Jesus reproves those He loves (Revelation 3:19).

11. "As iron sharpens iron, so a friend sharpens a friend" (Proverbs 27:17). It encourages us when we can be around others of like faith who are denying themselves and sacrificially meeting the needs of others. I have often been inspired by fellow believers

who set an example of self-giving without any regard for repayment, self-glory, or safety of one's own life. We cannot be perfect as Jesus was, but we can become better servants. Being in community with others of like faith, helps us achieve growth as God wants. A humble person relies on communion with other believers to enable personal growth in the practice of learning to meet needs (Hebrews 3:12–13; 1 Thessalonians 5:11, 14).

Here are other ways humility is demonstrated. Humility gives credit where credit is due. Rather than boasting of our accomplishments, humility recognizes our reliance on God and others who have enabled us in some way to accomplish what we did. Humility credits them and is grateful to them for their part. Another way humility can be part of our daily lives is when it enables us to treat everyone with respect and love, as persons of equal worth, no matter what their race, gender, or lifestyle. We are truly one race, the race of humanity. Christ-followers are from every tribe, tongue, people, and nation, neither Jew nor Greek, slave nor free, male nor female (Revelation 5:9–10; Galatians 3:28). Humility eliminates racial, social status, and gender prejudice. Humility allows us to admit our wrongs to God and others. People admire those who are honest rather than those who refuse to accept responsibility. And as stated above, we do not need to fear being honest because Jesus made a way for our wrongs to be forgiven and for our relationships to be reconciled. Humility enables us to ask forgiveness of those we wrong. Humility also makes us givers instead of takers. We often think that taking is what gets us ahead and giving is losing, but Jesus said, "It is more blessed to give than to receive" (Acts 20:35).

Truly humble people are great in God's eyes and will one day receive great rewards (Matthew 23:12; Luke 22:28–30; Mark 9:41). One of God's rewards is that God may make you great in the eyes of your fellow man. Humility does not mean you can never achieve greatness in the eyes of the world; God for good reason may want it. Humility means such greatness will not destroy us or those around us. But for any greatness to happen, we need to discover our God-given abilities and passion and use them fully. Wanting to be popular or great is not our role; being who God made us to be is our role. We must discover what that ability and passion entails. We should pay attention to what we are good at and things other people also notice to be our abilities. We discern our passion by paying attention to what we care most about. It may take living life a while to discover these things, but when we do, that is where we must put particular emphasis.

So, discover your God-given abilities and passion; it may be in science, math, the arts, philosophy, psychology, or truck driving, or whatever, but when you discover it, give most of your attention to it, seek to improve your skills, and in whatever you do, seek to please God (Colossians 3:23–24). Achieve your potential but never forget that humility is the virtue that makes us great, not fame, or power, or riches, but it is humility that makes us great. Humility is saying to yourself with all sincerity and resolve, *I want to be great in God's eyes rather than seeking greatness in my own eyes or in the eyes of my fellow man.*

# DISCUSSION GUIDE

You may already have an idea of how you would like to use these chapters in a discussion group. Have at it. The following provides suggestions if you need some ideas of where to begin. The format can be used for every chapter. The leader can prepare by studying the material and Bible verses and personally answering some of the discussion and application questions to get a better idea of how others might answer. Planning ahead will also help the leader to make personal input as a way to get a discussion started and so others might be more open.

In addition to learning more about the Bible, an important purpose of a group is to get to know one another and build deeper friendships and loving support. If we are followers of Jesus, our relationships need to become more than just information sharing.

You can discuss a chapter a week or stretch it out longer to allow your discussion to take its natural course. You can also skip around in the book and talk about subjects of interest.

## A Format for Discussion for All the Chapters

1. Consider the title of the chapter. Why would you be interested or not about the topic?

2. Read the opening paragraph and share whatever thoughts or personal experiences come to mind.

3. Read each paragraph (or a larger part of the chapter), including the Scripture references. Stop before going to the next paragraph or section and choose any of the following questions to discuss. As a leader, you may have some of your own. The leader might want to determine the places to stop for discussion. If you have a lively group, they may not need to use many questions.

    - What is your response to what we just read?
    - What point do you think is being made?
    - What is God saying in the Bible verse or verses?
    - How does the verse or verses support or not the point?
    - Where do you agree or disagree and why? Is it based on opinion or fact?

- Do you have anything to add to the topic that could benefit the group?
- What questions come to mind?
- Can you share any personal stories that came to mind as you read the paragraph or Bible verses?
- What have you heard others or the media say about the subject?

4. Application questions. Choose whatever ones work for your group.

- What did you learn?
- How does this information benefit your life?
- What would you like to do with this information?
- Is there any way you can use this information to benefit others?
- How and when would be the right time to pass on some of these concepts to your kids?
- Is anyone struggling with anything involving this topic?
- What is the darkness discussed in this chapter, what does it mean to come into the light, and how does one come into the light?
- How would your life be different if you lived out these words and ideas?

# ABOUT THE AUTHOR

Jay and his wife grew up in Ohio. He is a Master of Divinity graduate from Trinity Evangelical Divinity School in Deerfield, Illinois. Jay pastored and taught forty-four years in a steadily growing church in the rural town of Glasgow, Montana. He worked for twenty years as a fifth-step counselor and lecturer in an alcoholic-drug treatment center getting to know the hearts of people struggling to get well. He also taught grief classes at a hospital. In Montana, he enjoyed reading, racquetball, golf, hunting, fishing, and traveling the Big Sky State. He and his wife of over fifty-six years retired to Michigan to be near family, including their two married children and seven grandchildren.

## OTHER BOOKS BY THE AUTHOR

Building a Life with God: A Study for Individuals and Groups (ISBN:978-1-7331399-2-2 pbk; ISBN: 978-1-7331399-3-9 eBooks)

Building a Life with God Workbook: A Study for Individuals and Groups (ISBN 978-1-7331399-9-1) pbk

UPLOAD YOUR FAITH SERIES

Book 1 – The Power of Life-Giving Hope in Troublesome Times
(ISBN 978-1-61314-412-1) pbk

Book 2 – FAITH
(ISBN 978-1-61314-487-9) pbk

Book 3 – LOVE: The Only Power that can Transform Our Life and World (ISBN: 978-1-61314-676-7) pbk

www.ingramcontent.com/pod-product-compliance
Lightning Source LLC
Chambersburg PA
CBHW021056080526
44587CB00010B/267